THE COMPLETE IDIOT'S GUIDE® TO

Fast and Fresh Meals

by Ellen Brown

ALPHA

A member of Penguin Group (USA) Inc.

This book is dedicated to the memory of my father, who introduced me to the tantalizing world of foods with childhood trips to Chinatown.

ALPHA BOOKS

Published by the Penguin Group

Penguin Group (USA) Inc., 375 Hudson Street, New York, New York 10014, U.S.A.

Penguin Group (Canada), 10 Alcorn Avenue, Toronto, Ontario, Canada M4V 3B2 (a division of Pearson Penguin Canada Inc.)

Penguin Books Ltd, 80 Strand, London WC2R 0RL, England

Penguin Ireland, 25 St Stephen's Green, Dublin 2, Ireland (a division of Penguin Books Ltd)

Penguin Group (Australia), 250 Camberwell Road, Camberwell, Victoria 3124, Australia (a division of Pearson Australia Group Pty Ltd)

Penguin Books India Pvt Ltd, 11 Community Centre, Panchsheel Park, New Delhi—10 017, India

Penguin Group (NZ), cnr Airborne and Rosedale Roads, Albany, Auckland 1310, New Zealand (a division of Pearson New Zealand Ltd)

Penguin Books (South Africa) (Pty) Ltd, 24 Sturdee Avenue, Rosebank, Johannesburg 2196, South Africa

Penguin Books Ltd, Registered Offices: 80 Strand, London WC2R 0RL, England

Copyright © 2007 by Ellen Brown

THE COMPLETE IDIOT'S GUIDE TO and Design are registered trademarks of Penguin Group (USA) Inc.

International Standard Book Number: 978-1-59257-632-6
Library of Congress Catalog Card Number: 2006938599

09 08 07   8 7 6 5 4 3 2 1

Interpretation of the printing code: The rightmost number of the first series of numbers is the year of the book's printing; the rightmost number of the second series of numbers is the number of the book's printing. For example, a printing code of 07-1 shows that the first printing occurred in 2007.

Printed in the United States of America

Note: This publication contains the opinions and ideas of its author. It is intended to provide helpful and informative material on the subject matter covered. It is sold with the understanding that the author and publisher are not engaged in rendering professional services in the book. If the reader requires personal assistance or advice, a competent professional should be consulted.

The author and publisher specifically disclaim any responsibility for any liability, loss, or risk, personal or otherwise, which is incurred as a consequence, directly or indirectly, of the use and application of any of the contents of this book.

Publisher: *Marie Butler-Knight*
Editorial Director: *Mike Sanders*
Managing Editor: *Billy Fields*
Acquisitions Editor: *Michele Wells*
Production Editor: *Megan Douglass*
Copy Editor: *Ross Patty*

Cartoonist: *Shannon Wheeler*
Cover Designer: *Bill Thomas*
Book Designer: *Trina Wurst*
Indexer: *Angie Bess*
Layout: *Ayanna Lacey*
Proofreader: *Aaron Black, Mary Hunt*

Contents at a Glance

Part 1: **Fundamentals of Fast Food** 1

1 Kitchen Efficiency 3
Find out what equipment is really necessary, and learn about shopping and food safety.

2 Skill Builds 13
Gain new confidence in the kitchen by learning how to use knives better and how to handle specific fruits and vegetables.

Part 2: **Beginning Hors d'Oeuvres and Appetizers** 27

3 Dippity-Do 29
Dazzle guests with the contents of your dip bowl with these tasty hot and cold options.

4 Nibbles and Noshes: Hors d'Oeuvres for All Occasions 43
Entertain with style, serving this array of finger foods to launch special evenings.

5 Appealing Appetizers 55
Shine from the start of the meal when serving these innovative vegetable and seafood dishes.

6 The Bountiful Bowl: Soups 67
Savor these soups for all seasons made with healthful vegetables, luscious legumes, and more.

Part 3: **Casual Cuisine** 79

7 Sunny Starts: Breakfast 81
Celebrate mornings with this enticing array of breakfast and brunch dishes.

8 Convertible Cooking: Casual Meals for Brunch or Supper 93
Discover how you can serve the same dish at different times of the day by varying the accompaniments.

9 Crusty Creations: Hot Sandwiches and Quiches 107
Renew your ideas about sandwiches with these quesadillas, paninis, and more.

10 A Potpourri of Pasta and Pizza   119
*Expand your repertoire with quick-cooking sauces and gour-
met pizzas.*

Part 4:   Salad Daze   131

11 On the Side: Small Vegetable Salads   133
*Make the sidekick the star of the show with this panoply of
side salads.*

12 Cold Carb Salads   149
*Garner kudos when serving these pasta, rice, and potato
salads with international flavors.*

13 The Main Event: Entrée Salads   161
*Keep cool while munching one of these refreshing salads com-
bining protein and a cornucopia of vegetables and fruits.*

Part 5:   Redefining Fast Food   175

14 Sensational Seafood   177
*Net compliments when serving these dishes made with an
ocean-full of aquatic species.*

15 Poultry Pals   193
*Celebrate the diversity of chicken cooked with flavorful sauces
from around the world.*

16 Grazing Greats   205
*Focus your spotlight on beef, along with pork, lamb, and
veal.*

Part 6:   Great Grills   215

17 Ready, Set, Grill!   217
*Utilize easy toppings and sauces to create quick-cooking
masterpieces from your grill.*

18 Burger Bonanza   233
Explore the possibilities of burgers beyond traditional beef.

19 Flavor Without Fuss: Marinated Dishes   245
*Plan ahead to use the grill and give food time to gain flavor
from quickly prepared marinades.*

Part 7: **Desserts on a Deadline** 257

20 Fruity Favorites 259
Treat yourself to a range of sweet treats glorifying fruits and other popular flavors.

21 The Best Baked Goods 271
Imagine luscious baked goods on the table in less time than it takes to eat the meal they follow!

22 Chocolate Cravings 283
Indulge in a variety of decadent but easy desserts starring this "food of the gods."

Appendixes

A Glossary 295

B Metric Conversion Tables 307

C Yields of Common Ingredients 311

Index 313

Contents

What the recipe symbols mean:
▲ Fast
● Healthy
■ Make-Ahead
+ Vegan

Part 1: Fundamentals of Fast Food   1

1 Kitchen Efficiency   3
A Panoply of Pans 3
The Pots' Pals.. 5
The Cutting Edge 6
The Electric Aisle.. 7
Divine Disposables 8
Shopping Savvy 8
    Other Produce Department Options 9
    I Love Farmers' Markets! 9
Safety First... 9
    Safe Shopping and Transport 10
    Banishing Bacteria...................................... 10
    Avoiding Cross-Contamination 11

2 Skill Builds   13
Careful Cutting 13
Sizing the Situation 14
Help for Handling... 16
    Apples.. 16
    Asparagus... 16
    Bell Peppers 17
    Cabbage... 17
    Carrots... 18
    Celery.. 18
    Cucumbers... 18
    Eggplants 19
    Garlic.. 19
    Ginger.. 20
    Mangoes... 21
    Mushrooms... 21

Onions..22

Peaches...23

Tomatoes...24

Part 2:   Beginning Hors d'Oeuvres and Appetizers   27

3   Dippity-Do   29

Dip Diversification...30

+   *Tuscan White Bean Dip*..31

▲   *Sun-Dried Tomato Dip*...32

+   *Guacamole*..33

▲   *Mexican Black Bean Dip*..34

▲   *Spinach Dip with Feta and Dill*..................................35

▲   *Classic Cheese Fondue*...36

▲   *Brie, Stilton, and Wild Mushroom Dip*......................37

▲   *Smoked Trout Dip*...38

▲   *Two-Salmon Dip*..39

▲   *Crab Rangoon Dip*..40

■   *Mexican Beef and Chili Dip (Chili con Queso)*..........41

■   *Sausage Pizza Dip*...42

4   Nibbles and Noshes: Hors d'Oeuvres for All Occasions   43

Assembly Line Logic...44

+   *Fresh Tomato Bruschetta*...45

●   *Herbed Goat Cheese and Roasted Pepper Spirals*........46

▲   *Cheddar Crackers*..47

▲   *Southwest Smoked Salmon Pinwheels*.........................48

●   *Salmon Tartare on Cucumber Slices*............................49

▲   *Southwest Miniature Crab Cakes*................................50

●   *Baked Shrimp Toast Rolls*...51

▲   *Asparagus Wrapped in Herbed Cheese and Prosciutto*.....52

■   *Vietnamese Spring Rolls (Cha Gio)*.............................53

5   Appealing Appetizers   55

Mad for Mollusks...56

Mussel-ing In...56

■   *Black Bean Cakes*..57

■   *Deviled Leeks*..58

■   *Baked Clams Casino*...59

▲   *Garlic-Steamed Clams*..60

■ *Oysters with Green Chili Cilantro Pesto* *61*

▲ *Creole Marinated Shrimp* *62*

■ *Bourbon Shrimp* *63*

▲ *Crab Cakes with Mustard Sauce* *64*

▲ *Chicken in Lettuce Cups* *65*

6 The Bountiful Bowl: Soups   **67**

Taking Stock 67

■ *Quick Chicken Stock* *69*

+ *Gazpacho* *70*

● *Dilled Cream of Cucumber Soup* *71*

■ *Leek and Potato Soup (Vichyssoise)* *72*

■ *Cream of Celery Soup with Tarragon* *73*

■ *Grilled Corn Chowder* *74*

■ *Nantucket Clam Chowder* *75*

■ *Dilled Corn and Oyster Bisque* *76*

▲ *Greek Lemon Egg Soup with Chicken and Orzo (Avgolemono)* *77*

■ *Tuscan White Bean Soup with Sausage* *78*

Part 3: Casual Cuisine   **79**

7 Sunny Starts: Breakfast   **81**

Pancake Pointers 81

The Fine Points of Frittatas 82

Cutting Cholesterol 82

▲ *Oven-Baked Apple Pancakes* *83*

▲ *Gingerbread Pancakes* *84*

▲ *Whole-Wheat Blueberry Pancakes* *85*

▲ *Banana Pancakes with Banana Syrup* *86*

▲ *Raspberry French Toast with Raspberry Sauce* *87*

▲ *Potato, Onion, and Bacon Frittata* *88*

▲ *Western Frittata* *89*

■ *Vegetable Frittata with Pasta* *90*

▲ *Baked Eggs with Herbed Cheese* *91*

8 Convertible Cooking: Casual Meals for Brunch or Supper   **93**

Brunch Bonuses 94

Sides for Supper 94

▲ *Southwest Sweet Potato Pancakes with Salsa Cream* *95*

■ *Summertime Baked Eggs* *96*

▲ *Smoked Salmon Hash with Poached Eggs* 97

■ *Grilled Chicken Hash* 98

▲ *Welsh Rarebit with Tomatoes and Bacon* 99

▲ *Baked Macaroni and Cheese with Ham* 100

■ *Sausage and Pepper Hash* 101

■ *Stuffed Peppers* 102

▲ *Bacon, Egg, and Arugula Salad* 104

■ *Corned Beef Hash with Baked Eggs* 105

9 Crusty Creations: Hot Sandwiches and Quiches 107

Great Grill! 107

Sophisticated Sandwiches 108

Quiche Quickie 108

▲ *Eggplant and Red Pepper Panini* 109

▲ *Grilled Chicken, Sun-Dried Tomato, and Mozzarella Panini* 110

▲ *Cuban Quesadillas* 111

■ *Springtime Quesadillas* 112

▲ *Tuna Melt with Olives* 113

▲ *Kentucky Hot Brown Sandwich* 114

▲ *Grilled Reuben Sandwich* 115

■ *Crab Quiche* 116

■ *Herbed Sausage and Tomato Quiche* 117

■ *Classic Quiche Lorraine* 118

10 A Potpourri of Pasta and Pizza 119

Pasta Power 120

Perfect Pasta Tips 120

Fresh from the Refrigerator Case 121

▲ *Spaghetti with Escarole, Pine Nuts, and Raisins* 122

▲ *Pasta with Garlic and Oil (Pasta Aglio e Olio)* 123

● *Fusilli with Porcini Puttanesca Sauce* 124

■ *Linguine with White Clam Sauce* 125

▲ *Spaghetti with Egg and Bacon (Pasta Carbonara)* 126

■ *Basic Pizza Dough* 127

▲ *Pizza Margherita* 128

▲ *Smoked Salmon Pizza* 129

▲ *Prosciutto Pizza* 130

Part 4:   Salad Daze   131

11 On the Side: Small Vegetable Salads   133

  Olive Oil Savvy...134
+ *Warm Vegetable Salad*..135
■ *Stir-Fried Vegetable Salad*...136
● *Green Bean and Tomato Salad*......................................137
+ *Asian Eggplant Salad*...138
▲ *Tomato and Mozzarella Salad with Oregano*.................139
▲ *Fennel Salad*...140
+ *Three-Pepper Gazpacho Salad*......................................141
+ *Black Bean and Papaya Salad*..142
+ *Gingered Asian Red Cabbage Slaw*................................143
+ *Dilled Cucumbers*..144
■ *Thai Cucumber Salad*..145
+ *Pear Dressing*..146
+ *Balsamic Vinaigrette*...147
+ *Sesame Ginger Dressing*..147
+ *Celery Seed Dressing*..148

12 Cold Carb Salads   149

  Rice Size Specifics..149
  Potato Pointers...150
▲ *Sesame Noodles with Asian Vegetables*........................151
▲ *Rigatoni with Vegetables and Mozzarella*.....................152
▲ *Gemelli with White Beans, Tomatoes, and Sage*............153
● *Coconut Rice and Vegetable Salad*...............................154
■ *Thai Rice Salad*...155
▲ *Spicy Asian Brown Rice Salad*......................................156
● *Tabbouleh with Feta*...157
■ *Janet's Potato Salad*..158
■ *Garlicky Potato Salad*..159
■ *Sweet Potato Salad with Mustard Dressing*..................160

13 The Main Event: Entrée Salads   161

  Savvy Greens Subbing..162
▲ *Thai Shrimp Salad*...163
● *Scallop and Asparagus Salad*..164
● *Salmon and Cucumber Salad*..165
● *Gazpacho Chicken Salad*...166

● *Stir-Fried Chicken and Papaya Salad*...................................167
▲ *Smoked Turkey Salad*...168
▲ *Asian Chicken Salad* 169
■ *Jambalaya Salad*...170
■ *Pork, Peach, and Orange Salad*...171
▲ *Vietnamese Beef Salad* 172
▲ *Warm Lamb Salad* 173

Part 5:   Redefining Fast Food   175

14 Sensational Seafood   177
Choosing the Choicest..177
Fish Families..178
Shrimp: Sizing Up the Situation 179
● *Asian Shrimp and Stir-Fried Vegetables*...............................180
▲ *Prawns in Garlic Sauce with Fettuccine*..............................181
▲ *Scallops with Pine Nuts*...182
▲ *Pan-Fried Flounder with Black Walnut Butter* 183
● *Scrod with Red Onion Marmalade* 184
● *Roast Monkfish in Plum Wine Sauce* 185
● *Fish Steamed in Napa Cabbage with Red Pepper Sauce* 186
▲ *Creole Swordfish* 188
▲ *Salmon with Basil Cream Sauce*..189
● *Halibut in White Wine with Pearl Onions and Oranges* 190
● *Tuna Steaks with Tomato Relish*..191

15 Poultry Pals   193
Stir-Fry Strategy..194
▲ *Mock Mu Shu Chicken* 195
▲ *Chicken with Plum Sauce*...196
▲ *Chicken Fajitas*..197
▲ *Chicken with Garlic and Parsley* 198
▲ *Poached Chicken with Balsamic Vinegar*.............................199
▲ *Tarragon Chicken with Spring Vegetables*............................200
▲ *Chicken Marsala with Mushrooms and Sage* 201
▲ *Italian Chicken with Lemon and Capers (Pollo Piccata)*..............202
■ *Turkey Chili* 203
■ *Turkey Meatloaf* 204

16 Grazing Greats **205**

Sauté Savvy 205
Subbing with Success 206
▲ *Pork Scaloppine*..207
▲ *Pork with Prosciutto, Mozzarella, and Sage* (Porchetta
    Saltimbocca) 208
▲ *Herb-Crusted Pork Tenderloin* 209
▲ *Japanese Sautéed Beef with Scallions* (Negimaki) 210
▲ *Pan-Seared Filet Mignon with Red Wine Sauce*...........211
▲ *Beef Stroganoff* 212
▲ *Mustard-Crusted Rack of Lamb* 213
▲ *Veal Scaloppine with Fresh Shiitake Mushrooms*............214

Part 6: Great Grills **215**

17 Ready, Set, Grill! **217**

Gas vs. Charcoal..217
Where There's Smoke 218
Taking Your Grill's Temperature 218
Play It Safe..219
● *Salmon with Tomatillo Sauce* 220
▲ *Tuna with Ginger Vinaigrette*.........................221
■ *Sea Scallops with Mango Salsa and Chili Vinaigrette* 222
■ *Swordfish with Smoked Cheddar Sauce* 224
▲ *Ham and Cheese–Stuffed Chicken* 225
▲ *Mexican Chicken with Mole Sauce* 226
▲ *Sweet and Hot Chicken Skewers*.....................227
● *Chicken with Three-Tomato Salsa* 228
▲ *Caribbean Pork Chops*..................................229
▲ *Steak with Shiitake Cognac Sauce* 230
■ *Steak with Southwest Corn Sauce*....................231
■ *Butterflied Leg of Lamb with Garlic, Rosemary, and Lemon*..........232

18 Burger Bonanza **233**

Between the Bread..233
Classy Condiments...234
+ *Middle Eastern Lentil Burgers* 235
▲ *Creole Shrimp Burgers* 236
■ *Dilled Salmon Burgers* 237
▲ *Italian Turkey Burgers*.................................238

▲ *New England Turkey Burgers* 239
▲ *Mexican Burgers* 240
▲ *Caribbean Burgers* 241
▲ *Chinese Pork Burgers* 242
▲ *Bombay Lamb Burgers* 243

19 Flavor Without Fuss: Marinated Grilled Dishes   **245**

The Soaking Solutions 246
Combination Cooking 246
● *Salmon Provençale* 247
▲ *Aegean Swordfish* 248
● *Caribbean Shrimp* 249
■ *Middle Eastern Chicken* 250
▲ *Chicken Satay with Spicy Peanut Sauce* 251
■ *Cranberry-Maple Spareribs* 252
■ *Stuffed Flank Steak* 253
▲ *Mexican Steaks with Chipotle Mayonnaise* 254
▲ *Korean Steak* 255
■ *Rosemary Lamb Chops* 256

Part 7: Desserts on a Deadline   **257**

20 Fruity Favorites   **259**

The Fruit Family 259
▲ *Fig and Raspberry Gratin* 261
● *Blueberry Shortbread Gratin* 262
● *Mixed Berry Compote* 263
● *Dumpling-Topped Berry Grunt* 264
■ *Fresh Berries with Lemon Mousse* 265
● *Peach Skillet Cake* 266
■ *Easy Berry Trifle* 267
▲ *Lemon Curd Mascarpone Fondue* 268
▲ *Bananas Foster Fondue* 269
▲ *Piña Colada Fondue* 270

21 The Best Baked Goods   **271**

Procedural Matters 271
Careful Creaming 272
▲ *Caramel Apple Quesadillas* 273
▲ *Cherry Clafouti* 274

■ *Blueberry Crème Fraîche Tart*..*275*
▲ *Gingered Pear Crisp* *276*
▲ *Strawberry-Rhubarb Cobbler* *277*
▲ *Strawberry Shortcake*..*278*
▲ *Oatmeal Cranberry Cookies* *279*
▲ *Chocolate Malted Cookies* *280*
▲ *Carrot Cookie Sandwiches*..*281*
■ *Fudgy Brownies* *282*

22 Chocolate Cravings   283

Chocolate 101..283
Handle with Care 284
▲ *Classic Chocolate Fondue* *285*
▲ *Bittersweet Chocolate Coconut Cream Fondue* *286*
▲ *White Chocolate Cranberry Orange Fondue* *287*
▲ *Candy Bar Quesadillas*...*288*
▲ *Mini-Molten Chocolate Tortes* *289*
▲ *White Chocolate Strawberry Sundaes* *290*
▲ *Quick Mocha Soufflé* *291*
▲ *Chocolate Pudding*...*292*
▲ *Chocolate Peanut Butter Turnovers* *293*
■ *Chocolate Bread Pudding with Easy Bourbon Caramel Sauce* *294*

Appendixes

A Glossary   295

B Metric Conversion Tables   307

C Common Ingredient Yields   311

Index   313

Introduction

We seem to have gotten away from the idea of eating fresh food. At one time, though, that's all there was. People ate whatever crops the land around them yielded. And everything available—from eggs and chickens to vegetables to fish—was organic. (Of course, this was before twentieth-century pesticides, herbicides, and other dangerous chemicals were invented.) At that time, the definition of *convenience food* could be found in the cupboards: jars of jams, jellies, and pickles that were "put up" during the summer for later enjoyment.

But during the last century, "progress" was viewed as getting as far away from fresh food as possible. After World War II, the country's dependence on canned food was supplemented by the ever-growing options of frozen food. The size of refrigerators shrank as appliance manufacturers lured customers by promising enough freezer space so the average household would only have to shop once every few weeks. The food groups seemed to evolve into take-out, eat-out, frozen, and canned.

But today that seems to be changing for the better. In this century, we're taking pleasure in turning back the clock by eating food in season and reveling in the joys of fresh foods. In the past 10 years, the trend toward the expansion of space given to frozen foods in supermarkets has been halted. The section now gaining space the most rapidly is the produce section. And that's the way it should be.

The dishes in this book are "real food." They're not made with tons of convenience products that list more chemicals on their labels than words recognizable as foods; you won't find a can of cream-of-something soup anywhere. They're made with healthful vegetables and vivid fresh fruits—the foods we should be eating to fulfill the 5 to 9 servings a day recommended for our overall good health.

There are times that using minimally processed ingredients can save time, and not diminish the quality of the completed dish. I do give such foods as canned tomatoes and preroasted red bell peppers as alternatives to starting from scratch with many recipes, and the beans in all recipes are canned to save the long amount of time it takes to begin a dish with dried beans. In the same way if you don't have a fresh herb on hand, there's no reason to eliminate a recipe; just use a dried version.

But there's another need in today's fast-paced life, and these recipes acknowledge it. We want fresh food, but we want it fast. Time is our most precious commodity, even though commodities take time to prepare. And as you'll see when cooking the recipes in this book, fresh and fast can be joined, and joined deliciously.

You'll notice that there's no time frame given as part of this book's title. I'm not promising that you can have dinner on the table in less time than it takes to watch the evening news. But I do promise you that the recipes are straightforward so your actual involvement with cooking is less than 30 minutes in all cases.

What underpins this book is my 30 years as a food writer, knowing what foods cook fast. There aren't any recipes for beets, although they're one of my favorite vegetables. They take too long to cook properly. Nor are there any slowly braised stews.

What you will find is a wide range of cooking methods, all of which are fast because they utilize high heat. There are sautées, stir-fries, and grilled dishes. But there are not any fried foods, although that's another high-heat cooking method. While there are high-fat foods in the book that use cheese or cream, the goal is to trim fat when possible.

If you're one of the vast majority of Americans who want to eat a more healthful diet, this book is for you!

How This Book Is Organized

The book is divided into seven parts:

In **Part 1, "Fundamentals of Fast Food,"** I give you information on equipment as well as cooking skills to make you a more efficient cook. I offer tips for choosing equipment to make life in the kitchen easier and knife skills and ways to speed up the chopping and dicing that are part and parcel of fresh cooking.

Part 2, "Beginning Hors d'Oeuvres and Appetizers," contains a kaleidoscope of small dishes that give any meal a delicious start. There are chapters on dips and hors d'oeuvres, many of which start out as big batches to minimize labor. Also featured are recipes for small appetizers and soups for all seasons.

Part 3, "Casual Cuisine," includes recipes to make everyday meals special at all times of day. You'll find recipes for breakfast and brunch dishes, many of which would also work as a supper. Also in Part 3 is a chapter on hot sandwiches and quiches, and one on pastas and pizzas.

Part 4, "Salad Daze," encompasses everything cold and crunchy. There's a chapter on small side salads and some distinctive dressings to elevate the basic tossed green salad to new levels of elegance. You'll also find ways to satisfy a carb craving with the small pasta, rice, and potato salads in Chapter 12. Part 4 ends main dish salads, often featuring cooked protein with raw vegetables and some fruits, too.

Part 5, "Redefining Fast Food," gives you ways to have a great dinner on the table fast. The chapters include recipes for seafood, poultry, and meats, prepared with the herbs and spices of Asia, the Mediterranean, and most of the remainder of the world.

Part 6, **"Great Grills,"** is simply that. Here you'll find recipes for foods that are quickly seasoned and then topped with delicious relishes and sauces. You'll also find marinated dishes, and burgers made with everything from lentils to lamb.

Part 7, **"Desserts on a Deadline,"** is full of quick and easy recipes to end meals with a sweet finale and flourish, whether you crave fresh fruits, anything chocolate, or baked goods like homey cobblers and creative cookies.

In the appendixes, you'll find a glossary to expand your knowledge of food words. That's followed by an appendix of charts to help you convert measurements to or from the metric system, and one giving weights and measures of ingredients to ease your shopping.

Extras

In every chapter you'll find boxes that give you extra bits of information:

Fast Talk _____

Cooking has a language all its own. Look to these boxes for quick definitions.

Fresh Ways _____

Look here to find tips about specific recipes or to boost your general cooking knowledge.

Speedy Solutions _____

Check these boxes for time-saving tips on shopping, food prep, cooking, or kitchen cleanup.

Stale Stuff _____

Be sure to check out these warning boxes to be alerted to potential problems in advance.

A Note on "Active Time" and "Start to Finish"

You'll notice that the times given with each recipe are broken into two segments. Cooking is like sports; there are participants and spectators, and these two time measurements are similar.

The first is the "active time." That's the time you actually have to be in the kitchen chopping, sautéing, or stirring. In all cases, this time 30 minutes or less. You're not going to be spinning swans from sugar or boning tiny quail. When you're the cook, this is the measurement you need to factor into your day.

The second measurement is simple enough to understand—"start to finish" means just that. It's the combination of the active time with the cooking time and then any additional time that's needed for marinating before cooking or chilling after cooking. But during most of this time you can be reading a book in the living room. The start to finish time is so you know when to begin a dish so you can have it ready by a particular time.

Acknowledgments

Writing a book is a solitary endeavor, but its publication is always a team effort. My thanks go to …

Michele Wells of Alpha Books and Ed Claflin, my agent, for proposing this project.

Christy Wagner, Megan Douglass, and Ross Patty for their eagle-eyed editing.

Karen Konopelski for her nutritional analysis and culinary insights.

Grace Skinger Lefrancois for her editorial assistance.

Tigger and Patches, my furry companions, who personally approved all seafood recipes.

Special Thanks to the Technical Reviewer

The Complete Idiot's Guide to Fast and Fresh Meals was reviewed by an expert who double-checked the accuracy of what you'll learn here, to help us ensure that this book gives you everything you need to know about creating dishes chock full of fresh foods—fast! Special thanks are extended to Karen Konopelski.

Trademarks

All terms mentioned in this book that are known to be or are suspected of being trademarks or service marks have been appropriately capitalized. Alpha Books and Penguin Group (USA) Inc. cannot attest to the accuracy of this information. Use of a term in this book should not be regarded as affecting the validity of any trademark or service mark.

Part 1

Fundamentals of Fast Food

The chapters in Part 1 set the scene for the recipes in the rest of the book. In this case the scene is your kitchen, and you learn how to equip it and become more efficient when you're cooking in it.

In the first chapter, you learn the rules for food safety and how to streamline your trips to the supermarket, because time saved. The second chapter is your lesson in fast and fresh cooking. It begins by helping you use knives more efficiently and then gives you pointers on cutting and selecting fresh produce.

Kitchen Efficiency

In This Chapter

◆ Necessary kitchen equipment

◆ Tips on organizing your kitchen

◆ Savvy food shopping

◆ Understanding and practicing good food safety

Efficiency is as important in cooking as it is in any other aspect of your life—maybe even more so when you and your family are hungry and waiting on dinner! In this chapter, I give you several pointers on saving time, even before you start cooking. You learn the equipment you need to cook not just the recipes in this book, but in all books. Plus, I give you tricks for arranging your kitchen to enhance your efficiency and ways to make trips to the supermarket less stressful.

Food safety is a cornerstone to every aspect of eating, so this chapter ends with guidelines to keep your food healthful and healthy at all times.

A Panoply of Pans

Many cooks often make the mistake of just grabbing any size pan, but using the correct size pot or pan listed in a recipe is important to the success of the dish. It's easy to know if a pot is too small: the food won't fit in it! But don't over-compensate and use the largest pan you have, either. If you're sautéing one shallot in a 12-inch skillet, you can't control the food well and keep it stirring. A 6-inch skillet works better for this.

When it comes to selecting pots and pans, consider the thickness and kind of metal used. I prefer enameled iron, but stainless-steel and anodized cast aluminum are other good choices. One thing to keep in mind when selecting pots and pans is whether or not you plan to wash them in the dishwasher. Such upscale brands as Calphalon should not be washed in the dishwasher. You also shouldn't wash pots with wooden handles in the dishwasher because the handles will eventually rot and break off.

Here's the list of pots I think you need, along with some suggestions for what you'll do with them:

Skillets   Ideally, you should have a 6- or 7-inch skillet for sautéing small amounts of vegetables, a 10-inch skillet for browning food, and a 12-inch skillet with a tight-fitting cover and sloping sides to cook all the recipes referred to as "skillet meals." Skillets now come with nonstick coatings, and should you choose one of these, it's important to use only plastic utensils. Metal utensils can scratch off the nonstick coating.

Dutch oven   These heavy, squat pots usually hold between 6 and 8 quarts. Because they have a large surface area that sits on the burner, you can use Dutch ovens for frying and sautéing as well as for simmering. It's important that the Dutch oven be sturdy and that the cover fits tightly.

Saucepans   You'll need a small, 1-quart pan for making white sauces, a 2-quart for general boiling, and a 4-quart for soups and pasta. As with the other pots detailed in this section, a key to performance is a tight-fitting lid, especially when cooking foods such as rice. When it comes to nonstick coating, the same cautions apply as with skillets.

Stockpot   A good stockpot should be at least 12 quarts and have a lid in case you're cooking lobsters or boiling a lot of corned beef. However, it can be made of thinner metal and less expensive than other pots.

Stale Stuff

When it comes to pots and pans, being penny-wise is being pound-foolish. You only buy them a few times in a lifetime, and while the quality of your can opener doesn't matter so much, the quality of your pots does. Flimsy pans have "hot spots" that can cause food to stick and burn.

Roasting pans   You need a 9×13-inch glass or metal baking pan for roasting meats and vegetables as well as baking, and a 10×14-inch pan for larger cuts of meat and whole chickens. You also need a ½-size sheet pan with 1-inch sides for toasting nuts and general baking.

Metal colanders   You need a hand-held colander for small jobs and one with feet that sits firmly in the sink for draining pasta.

Mixing bowls   No kitchen is complete without a set of stainless-steel or glass mixing bowls in graduated sizes from 2 cups to 2 quarts. Stainless steel is more durable, but glass can go into the micro-wave for reheating.

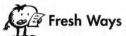 **Fresh Ways**

If you frequent yard sales and thrift shops, you might uncover treasure troves of inexpensive kitchen items. I don't trust used electrical equipment, as it could lead to fires, but a mixing bowl is a mixing bowl.

The Pots' Pals

Pots and pans don't exist in a vacuum, and any cook who has had to improvise a soup ladle from a mug or try to do without a slotted spoon knows it's the inexpensive equipment that makes cooking efficient.

Here's a list of miscellaneous odds and ends to complete your kitchen list:

- Measuring spoons, graduated from ¼ teaspoon to 1 tablespoon
- Dry measuring cups, graduated from ¼ cup to 1 cup
- 2-cup liquid glass measuring cup
- A few plastic cutting boards
- Glass and stainless-steel mixing bowls
- Some long-handled cooking spoons
- Heatproof rubber spatula
- 8-inch tongs
- 12-inch tongs
- Slotted spatula

◆ Offset spatula

◆ Slotted spoon

◆ Sturdy meat fork

◆ Large and small balloon whisks

◆ Flat-bottom whisk

◆ Soup ladle

◆ Garlic press

◆ Vegetable peeler

◆ Instant-read meat thermometer

◆ Wire mesh strainer (can double as a sifter)

◆ Four-sided box grater

◆ Puncture bottle opener (for opening cans of liquid)

◆ Manual can opener

◆ Corkscrew

Fresh Ways

A corkscrew comes in handy even if you don't drink wine. They're great for opening bottles of vinegar and fancy olive oils, too. And an instant-read thermometer should be mandatory in every kitchen. Just stick it in the thickest part of food and leave it in for 20 seconds.

The Cutting Edge

Knives are so important to cooking that some chefs travel with their own sets. It's important that the knife is made from carbon steel and that the blade goes the entire way to the end of the handle. That's called full tang, and it makes knives sturdier.

You don't have to go nuts and buy a huge knife set with a wooden block to take up counter space. Here's a list of the basic cutlery you need:

◆ At least one paring knife with a 4-inch blade for peeling, slicing, and dicing small foods

◆ A chef's knife with an 8- to 12-inch blade for chopping, mincing, dicing, etc.

◆ A serrated knife with a 12- to 14-inch blade for slicing bread, tomatoes, and meats

◆ A sharpening steel to keep the knives razor-sharp

Be sure you've got some way of keeping knives sharp. People cut themselves with poorly sharpened knives much more often than with a sharp knives, and dull knives make cutting harder and can detract from the appearance of the food. A steel rod or sharpening stone is much less expensive than the electric knife-sharpening gizmos and serves the same function with the aid of a little elbow grease. (In Chapter 2, you learn tricks on how to best use your knives.)

Stale Stuff

Don't skimp on knives; they're a once-in-a-lifetime purchase, but they are dear. A set of three knives from Sabatier, Wüsthof, or Henckels—the three market leaders—cost in the $200 and up range.

The Electric Aisle

You also need a few small appliances in the kitchen. The most important is a food processor. The food processor's on-and-off action has revolutionized formerly laborious cutting and chopping tasks. When testing these recipes, I do the chopping by hand to calculate the active time, and I'm always amazed at how long it takes without a food processor! Even if you're shopping off the salad bar, chances are you might have to do additional dicing, mincing, and fine chopping.

Speedy Solutions

Don't bother spending money on a toaster; you can toast anything your heart desires underneath the oven broiler. The same is true for a blender. While they might make smoothies better than a food processor, they can't chop and dice for you, so if you're only going to buy one appliance, make it a food processor.

My food processor has a permanent spot in the dishwasher because I use it every day. I start by chopping foods that leave a residue that's easy to rinse out such as parsley or nuts. Then I finish with foods like garlic or onions, after which the work bowl really needs soap and water.

Here are some other good additions to your electric arsenal:

Immersion blender with whisk attachment   If you like puréed soups, you've got to get one of these. Just place it into the pot, and there's no need to take the time to transfer the solids to the food processor (or risk the spills!). The whisk is excellent for beating egg whites or cream, too, and for small quantities of batter that would get lost in the beaters of an electric mixer.

Handheld electric mixer   Unless you're a serious baker who makes large cakes or needs a dough hook to knead bread dough, this is the only mixer you'll need. Such mixers are inexpensive and easy to store.

Hinged-top grill   These are the new kids on the block, the most prominent of which is the George Foreman Grill. These grills are great for making pressed sandwiches and for indoor grilling, and they come in a variety of sizes to fit your household.

Divine Disposables

Next to the food processor, the roll of heavy-duty aluminum foil is my best kitchen friend. Any time you can cover a baking sheet or line a roasting pan with foil, you save clean-up time. The only time you can't use foil for baking and roasting is when food might have a tendency to stick. You don't want bits of foil on your crusty chicken!

The heavy resealable plastic bag is one of the most useful items in a kitchen. This bag revolutionized marinating, and there's no dish or bowl to wash, either!

Shopping Savvy

Supermarkets charge a premium price for items in those chilled bins in the salad bar, but the amount of time you can save by letting the supermarket to do your prepping makes shopping the salad bar an appealing alternative. The salad bar has done all the vegetable prep work for you, which means you can substantially decrease the active time you spend chopping, slicing, etc. Carrots? Already peeled and sliced! Onions? Prechopped—and tear free! Spinach? Already rinsed and stemmed!

But the salad bar isn't limited to produce. Want to make egg salad? You'll find hard-cooked eggs already peeled. Want just a few beans rather than a 15-ounce can? Most salad bars offer garbanzo beans, sometimes kidney beans, and frequently other bean-y options as well.

> **Stale Stuff**
>
> One fear of shopping from—and eating from—salad bars is that the produce might have been sprayed with chemicals to prevent discoloration and wilting. Question the supermarket about this practice.

Other Produce Department Options

For quantities larger than what you can get at the salad bar, shop in the preprepped vegetables section of the produce department. This section is constantly growing, and now includes everything from preshredded cabbage for coleslaw to preshredded carrots and prechopped onions.

All the stir-fried recipes in this book call for individual vegetables, but remember that recipes are guidelines and not laws. If you see an appealing mix of vegetables preprepped for you, it's likely the right volume for these recipes.

I Love Farmers' Markets!

The hints thus far in this chapter have been geared to supermarket shopping. But there's an alternative at least during the summer months, even in large cities—the farmers' market. I'm addicted to farmers' markets. Here you can find an incredible variety of the freshest possible ingredients. You won't find plastic-wrapped bunches of carrots; you get lovely individual carrots sold by the pound!

In many larger cities, especially in downtown areas, you can shop at the farmers' markets' first cousins: sidewalk vendors. One great advantage to buying fruit from sidewalk vendors is that their fruit is always ripe and ready to eat or cook.

 **Fresh Ways**

Since 1994, the U.S. Department of Agriculture (USDA) has published the National Directory of Farmers' Markets. In 1994, the number was less than 2,000; today it's double that! To find a farmers' market near you, go to www.ams.usda.gov/farmersmarkets.

Safety First

Speaking of safe, the first—and most important—requirement for good cooking is knowing the basic rules of food safety. This begins with trips to the supermarket and ends after leftovers are refrigerated or frozen at the end of a meal. The sections that follow might seem like common sense, but after many decades as a food writer who has heard horror stories about very sick people, please believe me, they're not.

Safe Shopping and Transport

I mentioned earlier in the chapter that you should hit the seafood and meat counters last before the checkout. Here are some other food safety tips:

- Never buy meat or poultry in a package that's torn and leaking.

- Place all meats and poultry in the disposable plastic bags available in the produce department to keep them from contaminating other foods in your basket.

- Check the "sell by" and "use by" dates, and never purchase food that exceeds them.

- For the trip home, carry an insulated cooler in the back of your car if it's hot outside or if the perishable items will be out of refrigeration for more than 1 hour.

- In really hot weather, ask your seafood department or meat counter for some crushed ice in a separate bag to keep your fish and meat cool.

Banishing Bacteria

All fruits and vegetables should be rinsed before eating or cooking them unless they're peeled such as apples or potatoes. Even salad greens that proclaim they're prewashed should still be rinsed again for the sake of safety.

Fruits and vegetables can contain some bacteria, but it's far more likely that the culprits will grow on meat, poultry, and seafood. Store these foods on the bottom shelves of your refrigerator so their juices cannot accidentally drip on other foods. And keep these foods refrigerated until just before they go into the dish.

Bacteria multiply at room temperature, in a so-called "danger zone" between 40° and 140°F. As food cooks, it's important for it to pass through this zone as quickly as possible.

If you want to get a jump-start on dinner by browning meats or poultry or cutting up vegetables in advance, that's fine. Just refrigerate all foods separately until it's time to combine them and cook the

Fresh Ways

If you have questions about food safety, the USDA—specifically the Food Safety and Inspection Service—is the place to go for answers. The website, www.fsis.usda.gov, provides a wealth of information in a very user-friendly format.

finished dish. Like all rules, this one has exceptions: raw eggs—you can make batters in advance and refrigerate them.

Avoiding Cross-Contamination

Cleanliness is not only next to godliness, it's also the key to food safety. Wash your hands often while you're cooking, and never touch cooked food if you haven't washed your hands after handling raw food. The "cooked food and raw food shall never meet" precept extends beyond the cook's hands. Clean cutting boards, knives, and kitchen counters often. If you have the space, section off your countertops for raw foods and cooked foods, as many restaurant kitchens do. Don't place cooked foods or raw foods that will remain uncooked (such as salad) on cutting boards that have been used to cut raw meat, poultry, or fish. Bacteria from raw animal proteins can contaminate the other foods.

 **Fresh Ways**

A good way to prevent food-borne illness is by selecting the right cutting board. Wooden boards might be attractive, but you can never get them as clean as plastic boards that can be run through the dishwasher. Even with plastic boards, it's best to use one for only cooked food and foods such as vegetables that are not prone to contain bacteria, and another one devoted to raw meats, poultry, and fish.

The Least You Need to Know

◆ It's important to use high-quality pots and pans to avoid burning food.

◆ The best knives are made from carbon steel and have blades that go all the way to the end of the handle.

◆ Buying precut vegetables from supermarket salad bars is more expensive but can save considerable time and you're not left with leftovers.

◆ The same utensils, serving dishes, cutting boards, etc. should not be used for raw foods and then cooked food without being thoroughly washed first.

Chapter 2

Skill Builds

In This Chapter

- ◆ Tips for safe and efficient knife handling
- ◆ A mini-glossary of cutting terms
- ◆ Perfect produce pointers

Cooking fresh food fast requires some culinary skills—none of which are difficult to master. In this chapter, I give you tips to make you more efficient in the kitchen. When you're more efficient, you're also speedier! You learn in this chapter the difference between *dice, mince, and slice*, along with knife-holding tips that will have you dicing, mincing, and slicing like a pro. I end the chapter with some tips on how to select, store, and cut popular produce.

Careful Cutting

Learning how to hold a knife is a little like learning to hold a tennis racket or a golf club. Once you've mastered it, you're good for life. You want to be sure you're holding a knife for comfort, control, and safety, all with minimum stress on your hand.

To do this, grip the knife by its bolster. The bolster is your knife's balance point, and it serves as a finger guard. Only your last three fingers should rest on the handle. Your thumb and index finger should be on opposite sides of the blade. When you hold a knife at its balance point, it becomes an extension of your hand.

Regardless of what you're cutting, the hand not holding the knife serves a vital role. It stabilizes the food you're cutting and guides the knife to determine the size of your cuts. Be sure your fingers are curled inward with your thumb tucked underneath the palm of your hand. The side of the knife—and *never* the blade—should rest against your knuckles.

Fresh Ways

The best way to cut food is with a forward cutting motion. If you cut back to front, the knife is doing the work. If you cut up and down, your arm is doing the work.

Stale Stuff

Take it slow at first, and don't try to imitate a TV chef with great speed or bravado. Your speed increases naturally as you become more confident and sure about your knife skills.

For slicing, begin by initiating the cut with the tip of the knife and pushing the knife forward across the food until you reach the knife's heel. If you find you have to push down with the knife, your knife probably needs sharpening. If you reach the heel and haven't finished your cut, bring the knife back to the tip and repeat the motion.

For large items that sit high on the cutting board like potatoes or carrots, start with the tip of the blade on the food. For smaller foods like celery or herbs, start with the tip on the cutting board.

For fine mincing and chopping, you use your knife in a different way. When food is cut into small pieces, and you want to make the pieces yet smaller, your guiding hand should be placed on top of the blade. This hand helps the one holding the knife pivot repeatedly along its curved edge in a rocking motion. You never lift your knife off the cutting board except to scrape the food you're cutting into a pile.

Sizing the Situation

There are many traditional ways of cutting food, many of which can be done quickly in the food processor, using the steel blade for chopping and using special discs for shredding and cutting. The use of one cut rather than another is determined by how the ingredient functions in a recipe. If the food must cook quickly in a sauté or stir-fry, the pieces have to be smaller than if they're going into a stew that will simmer for hours. And if a food is intended as a garnish, chances are it'll be cut in a manner to make it attractive.

One constant for all cutting methods is to make the pieces uniform; this is important for both cooking and appearance. Here is a list of cutting methods used frequently in recipes:

Coarse chopping   Coarse chopping is usually used for foods such as vegetables added to stews or foods such as cooked potatoes or chicken that form the basis for cold salads.

Speedy Solutions

Many supermarkets stock packages of prechopped onion or trimmed broccoli or cauliflower florets. The time saved might be worth the additional money to buy these convenience foods.

Mincing   This is an even, very fine cut that's especially appropriate for herbs, garlic, and shallots. Gather herbs or roughly chopped garlic or shallots in a pile on a cutting board and position the knife above the pile. Keeping the tip of the blade against the cutting board, lower the knife firmly and rapidly, repeatedly chopping through the herbs or vegetables. Continue chopping until the desired fineness is attained.

Julienne and batonnets   These are long, rectangular cuts used for vegetables and for any ingredient that's to be finely cut, like the julienne of prosciutto used to top a pizza. For hard vegetables like carrots or potatoes, trim them so the sides are straight, which makes it easier to create even cuts. Slice the vegetable length-wise, using parallel cuts of the proper thickness. Stack the slices, aligning the edges, and make parallel cuts of the same thickness through the stack. Batonnet cuts should be thick. To make a fine julienne, the cuts should be very thin. For soft foods like cooked meats, it's easier to slice it thinly, trim the slices into a neat shape, and then make the thin cuts.

Stale Stuff

Meats should be cut into a julienne *with* the grain because they'll fall apart if cut *against* it.

Dice   The results of dicing are cube-shaped pieces, and a recipe usually specifies the size of the dice (¼-inch dice, etc.). Everything from vegetables to meats, cheeses to chocolate are diced.

To dice, trim and cut the food as for julienne or batonnet. Gather the julienne or batonnets, and cut through them cross-wise at evenly spaced intervals.

Help for Handling

Cooking is at best an inexact science because every piece of food has a unique composition. Perhaps "a rose is a rose is a rose," but a swordfish steak was cut from a fish of a certain size that was caught on a specific date and cut to a certain thickness. There is no such thing as two chickens that are exactly alike, nor are carrots grown in the soil of California identical in flavor to those grown in New Jersey. And even different brands of all-purpose flour contain differing amounts of protein so they perform differently when used in baking.

The following sections help you select and handle produce and give you other tips for storing or efficient handling.

Apples

Look for large apples that have good color, are free of bruises, and are firm to the touch. The bruised cells of apples release an enzyme, polyphenoloxidase, that hastens the oxidation or decay of the flesh. Overripe apples feel soft, and the flesh feels mushy. To check apples in a plastic bag, turn it upside down and examine the apples on the bottom.

While traditional slicing methods call for first quartering and coring apples, these steps are unnecessary. After you peel the apple, start shaving off slices from the outside with a paring knife, turning the apple in quarter turns. Continue slicing until you reach the core and then discard the core.

> **Fresh Ways**
>
> If you do need to core an apple to make fanned slices for an apple tart, a melon baller is the best instrument to use. Cut the apple in half, and use the large side of the instrument to remove the core and seeds, leaving an even, circular hole.

Asparagus

Look for asparagus with rich green color; firm and straight stalks; and closed, compact tips. Its appearance should be crisp and firm, not limp or wrinkled. For ease of cooking, it's best to select same-diameter stalks.

Rinse all stalks under cold water. Then break or cut the spears at the point where the stem turns woody. This will be easy to determine because it's where the stem naturally snaps. For thick stalks, use a small paring knife or a vegetable peeler to peel almost up to the base of the tip. Wrap peeled asparagus in a damp towel and refrigerate until ready to cook, but don't peel them more than a few hours in advance of cooking.

Bell Peppers

The best bell peppers are plump; have a vibrant color; and have long, fresh-looking green stems. Peppers should look crisp and be firm when purchased. Flimsy stems, cracks, and bruises or soft spots are signs of an old pepper.

Most recipes with bell peppers specify "seeds and ribs removed." Here's a quick way to do this: cut a slice off the bottom of the pepper so it stands firmly on the cutting board. You can see the ribs indenting the contour of the pepper. Holding the cap with your free hand, slice down the natural curve of the pepper in sections. You're left with all the pepper and none of the seeds and ribs. You can then chop the flesh, or cut as indicated in the recipe.

Achieving perfect roasted peppers is a two-part process: you have to heat them and then cool them to separate the skin from the flesh. For all peppers, cut a small slit near the stem end with the tip of a paring knife to insure they won't explode. For a large number of peppers, and to retain the most texture, lower them gently into 375°F oil and fry until the skin blisters. Turn them with tongs when one side is blistered, because they'll float on the surface of the oil. You could also place the peppers 6 inches from the broiler element or grill, turning them with tongs until all surfaces are charred. The fastest way to cool peppers is to plunge them into ice water. This stops the cooking action immediately and cools them enough to peel them within a minute.

> **⏱ Speedy Solutions**
>
> Like canned tomatoes for cooking, jarred already-roasted and peeled peppers can provide great time savings. Try to buy an imported brand in a glass jar, and look to see if bits of charred skin are attached. That means they were really roasted and not just heated and peeled.

Cabbage

A head of cabbage should be heavy for its size, free of brown spots or streaks, and have crisp leaves. In green cabbage, look for cabbage with dark green leaves still attached; many markets pull these off because they're the first to turn yellow. Black edges in red cabbage is a sign of age.

To clean cabbage, discard outer leaves or any leaves that are discolored or wilted. Halve the head, and cut out the tough core with a knife. For shredded cabbage or leaves, remove the entire core; for wedges to be boiled, leave some of the core in place to keep the wedges from falling apart. To shred cabbage, put it cut side down on a board and cut crosswise in very fine slices. (For best appearance on the plate, cut or shred cabbage just before cooking or serving.)

Carrots

It's best to buy carrots that still have the green tops attached. Look for firm, bright orange-yellow carrots with fresh, crisp, green tops. Trim off the green tops before you store carrots, because the leafy tops will wilt and rot long before the sturdy root.

Rather than time-consuming peeling, you can preserve better color if you cover the carrots with boiling water for 5 minutes and then place them in ice water. The skins will then slip right off. Cross-slices of carrots are always appropriate, but they look more decorative if they're cut on the bias. Hold the knife at a 20-degree angle to the carrot and slice, beginning with the small end.

Celery

Select a medium-size stalk that has a solid, rigid feel and a glossy surface of light to medium green. The leaves should be green and fresh, and the ribs should be crisp.

Rinse the ribs, and trim off the bottom; save these pieces for making stock later. Cut the ribs lengthwise into the size pieces you want. Then pile the thin strips and slice across them. If using ribs whole, slice them with the curved side up so they'll sit firmly on the cutting board.

> **Fresh Ways**
>
> If celery is wilted, soak the ribs in ice water for 2 to 3 hours. Or wash the celery and stand it vertically for 2 hours in a pitcher of cold water plus 1 teaspoon salt in the refrigerator.

Cucumbers

Select smaller cucumbers because they tend to have fewer seeds. Look for cucumbers that have a clean break at the stem end. An uneven stem means the cucumber was harvested from the vine before it was ready.

While no organic cucumbers are waxed, many conventional ones are coated with a shiny wax to prevent dehydration during transport, and all waxed cucumbers should be peeled. That's why English cucumbers are wrapped in plastic as an alternative to waxing. Use a vegetable peeler or paring knife to remove the dark, waxy coating.

To seed cucumbers, halve them lengthwise and spoon out the seedy centers with a melon baller, or use the tip of a teaspoon or measuring spoon.

Eggplants

The freshest eggplants are plump, have shiny skins and a bright green cap, and should not weigh more than 1 pound or they might be old and bitter. Eggplants should be firm and heavy for their size. Avoid damaged, bruised, or soft eggplants, because even slightly soft eggplants are bitter. Eggplants turn brown easily, so slice them just prior to cooking.

About two-thirds of an eggplant's weight is water, and the flesh is also porous, which is why eggplants seem to drink up oil when fried. For these reasons, most eggplants should be salted and pressed before cooking to compact the flesh so it won't absorb as much fat. This also works to extract the bitter juices in some types of eggplants.

Although you can avoid this step when dealing with most Asian or tiny Italian eggplants, salting is needed to extract the bitter juices found in mature eggplants. Slice or dice the eggplant as specified in the recipe, and sprinkle the pieces liberally with salt. Place the salted eggplant in a colander in the sink or in a mixing bowl. Place a plate on top the salted eggplant, and top the plate with some cans. Drain for 30 minutes and then rinse the pieces thoroughly to remove the salt and bitter juices. Dry well on paper towels, especially if the eggplant is to be sautéed, to remove excess water.

Garlic

Look for whole heads with no cloves broken off, tightly packed large cloves, and no sign of green sprouts at the tips. The clove skin should be tight and snug, because loose cloves indicate deterioration. When the cloves are pressed, they should feel firm and solid. Papery skin or skin that's pulling away from the cloves is a sign of old garlic. Keep garlic in a cool, dark, dry space with fresh, circulating air. Fresh garlic should keep from 3 to 6 months if properly stored.

 **Fresh Ways**

Raw garlic is always stronger than cooked garlic, and the finer garlic is processed, the stronger it is. Adding raw garlic during a dish's cooking process results in a stronger flavor than if you sautée the garlic in oil prior to adding other ingredients.

Separate the cloves from the head as needed. For a few cloves, you can easily pry off the outer cloves with your thumb. To quickly separate the entire head, hit the base firmly onto a counter or cutting board; the cloves will easily pull apart.

To peel a clove, place the side of a heavy knife over the clove and bring your fist down hard on the blade (be careful not to cut yourself!). This is the easiest method and is best to use if the clove is to be pounded or minced. You can easily pull off the skin with your fingers. For several cloves, it's easier to drop the cloves into boiling water for 10 to 20 seconds. Refresh them under cold water and then use your fingers to slip off the skins.

To mince garlic, cut the peeled clove lengthwise with a very sharp knife. Keeping the garlic together, make a quarter turn and slice again. Continue to chop the garlic, using a rocking motion with your knife. Hold the tip end of the knife with your other hand, and use quick, small strokes. As the garlic spreads out, use the knife to push it back to the center. Keep chopping until the garlic is very fine.

Ginger

You can find ginger in pieces from a few inches to a foot long. The freshest ginger is plump and very firm, and the skin should be tan, shiny, smooth, and unwrinkled. Try to buy the largest knobs possible without many small bumps; you'll have to remove those, and they're virtually useless for cooking. Store ginger refrigerated for up to 2 weeks, wrapped in paper towels to absorb moisture, inside a plastic bag or store in a paper bag. After the ginger has been peeled, you can cover it in dry sherry and refrigerate it for up to 3 months.

If the ginger is to be used to flavor a marinade or dish and then discarded, there's no need to peel it. Scrub it with a vegetable brush under cold running water and then slice or dice it as specified. In most cases, however, ginger should be peeled not only for aesthetic reasons, but because the peel never softens.

Using a sharp paring knife, trim the small stubs off the knobs. Then peel with the curve of the knobs, along the grain rather than across it. Cut the ginger into slices, and crush them with the flat side of a large knife; the crushing separates the fibers, which makes it easier to chop or slice further. To grate ginger, use the tiny-hole side of a box grater, or drop cubes through the feed tube of a food processor with the motor running.

Mangoes

Look for mangoes that yield slightly to finger pressure but are not mushy. Smell the stem end; the aroma should be faintly sweet and floral. Because the soft, pulpy, juicy flesh clings so tightly to the flat stone, mangoes are one of the most difficult fruits to cut neatly. Cut away the mango peel with a vegetable peeler or sharp paring knife. Slice the mango flesh until you reach the central stone. Continue slicing on the other side of the stone and then cut away, in chunks, any flesh that remains on the stone.

 **Fresh Ways**

Place unripe mangoes in a paper bag and keep them in a dark, warm place until they ripen. If you have too many ripe mangoes becoming ripe at once, peel and purée the flesh. It can be frozen for up to 6 months.

Mushrooms

White mushrooms grow from a stem and have a cap and a veil (a membrane between the stem and the cap). Fresh mushrooms are firm, smooth, plump, and have a consistent color that ranges from creamy white to light brown. The caps should be spongy and tightly closed, hiding the gills. In small, delicate mushrooms, look for mushrooms with the veil still attached to the mushroom cap. Mushrooms should be slightly moist, but with no damp patches. Avoid slimy mushrooms or those with some yellow underneath.

Store mushrooms in their unopened packages in the refrigerator until ready to use (they're packaged with ventilation holes for air). Once the package is opened or if you purchase loose mushrooms, refrigerate them where they can get good air circulation in a paper bag poked with a few holes. You could also cover them with wax paper, a damp cloth, or a damp paper towel to help them retain moisture.Mushrooms bruise easily, so handle them gently. If mushrooms are pristine, simply rub them gently with a damp paper towel and trim the stem. Never soak mushrooms because they absorb water.

Slice mushrooms just before cooking, as oxidation causes the mushrooms to turn an unattractive purplish brown. If the recipe calls for mushroom caps without the stem, loosen the stem with the tip of a knife or teaspoon, or twist until loosened, and then remove. Cultivated mushrooms never need peeling due to their soft, thin skin.

To slice: Cut a mushroom in half, and place the cut side on the cutting board. Slice with a sharp paring knife, using a front-to-back motion. Do not press straight down, or you can bruise the mushroom.

To dice: Slice the stem so it's level with the mushroom cap. Cut the mushroom horizontally into medium to thick slices. Arrange the slices, or stack them on top of each other, and cut into medium-size sticks. Gather the mushroom slices together, and cut across.

Wild mushrooms should be firm with a wholesome odor. Brown, shiny, or slimy spots or a strange smell is an indication of decay. Check mushrooms for worm holes or gills that are fragmenting. Store as you would white mushrooms.

Clean wild mushrooms about 30 minutes before you plan to use them to allow them to dry. Use as little water as possible, and never soak mushrooms in water. If they don't appear dirty, it's best to just wipe them with a damp cloth. Unless necessary, do not wet underneath the caps of fresh wild mushrooms.

Onions

Choose onions that are firm and nicely shaped. The skins should appear tight and healthy. Sprouting is a sign of age, and sprouting onions should be avoided. Also avoid onions with soft spots, a dried appearance, or black or powdery spots, all of which are signs of internal decay. For green onions and leeks, look for perky green stems with no signs of wilt, limpness, marks, or bruises on the bulb.

If you store onions in a cool, dry area with good air circulation, they should keep for 3 or 4 weeks. At cooler temperatures (55° to 60°F), they could keep for several months. Refrigerate onions only after they've been cut, wrapped tightly in plastic wrap to avoid the odor affecting other foods. If you only need part of an onion for a recipe, slice off only that much, leaving the remainder of the onion in its skin.

To peel onions: Take a small slice off the top and root ends using a stainless-steel paring knife (iron can cause the onion to discolor). Pull away the papery skin with the blade of the paring knife or with your fingers if possible.

To slice and dice onions: Place the onion on a chopping board, and slice it in half lengthwise. Cut down at regular intervals, holding the onion by its root end with the hand not holding the knife. To dice it, place the onion cut side down, and slice lengthwise at intervals from ¼ to ½ inch, depending on the size pieces you need. Slice to—but not through—the root end. Next, hold the knife horizontal, and slice at the same intervals from bottom to top. Then slice down vertically, and the onion will be diced. To chop more finely, use a chef's knife to chop the onion into smaller pieces by rolling the blade back and forth over the diced onion.

Stale Stuff _____

While both onions and potatoes should be stored at cool room temperature, they shouldn't be stored together. Potatoes give off moisture and produce a gas that causes onions to deteriorate more quickly.

Peaches

Look for peaches that have a consistent creamy or golden color all over. (The blush is an indication of variety, not of ripeness.) Avoid wrinkled peaches, or peaches with any trace of green, blemishes, or brown spots. Because peaches ripen so easily at home, it's best to buy peaches that are still a bit firm. The fruit's ripe when it's slightly soft. Store firm peaches at room temperature; to speed ripening, place them in a brown paper bag. Keep the soft fruit in the refrigerator, and use it within a few days.

To peel peaches: You can peel firm peaches using a vegetable peeler just as you'd peel a potato. Or you can place ripe peaches in boiling water for 30 seconds and then the skins will slip right off. You can also microwave a peach on high for 10 seconds and then let it stand for 5 minutes before peeling.

Fresh Ways _____

Rub cut peaches with a cut lemon or toss with lemon juice to prevent discoloration.

Tomatoes

Tomatoes should be smooth and heavy for their size with firm flesh. Avoid any that appear watery. Avoid bruised tomatoes, as many times damaged tomatoes are rotten inside. Mold growing around the stem is a bad sign, and the mold may be toxic or poisonous. Vine-ripened varieties often have the green stems attached. Press these tomatoes gently between your palms; they should give slightly.

Never refrigerate unripe tomatoes; they won't ripen in the refrigerator. Store unripe tomatoes in a cool spot, out of direct sunlight, which could encourage tomatoes to turn to mush and may also destroy vitamins A and C. Store them between 60° and 75°F. For quicker ripening, place unripe tomatoes in a closed paper bag. Refrigerate only fully ripe tomatoes, and use them within 3 to 5 days after ripening.

> **Speedy Solutions**
>
> If using canned tomatoes, which are already partially cooked, subtract about 5 minutes from the cooking time listed in a recipe. If canned tomatoes taste acidic, add 1 teaspoon sugar to the recipe.

To peel tomatoes: Cut out the core from the stem end, and with a knife, lightly cross-hatch over the bottom of the tomato. Plunge tomatoes in boiling water and boil for exactly 10 seconds. Remove with slotted spoon to a bowl of cold water. This change in temperature damages the layer of cells just below the skin, allowing the skin to easily slip off.

To remove the seeds: Slice the tomato in half through the middle. Squeeze gently over a bowl and the seeds should loosen and drop. Remove any clinging seeds with the tip of a paring knife or your finger.

To dice a tomato: Cut the tomato in half, slice it into strips, and cut the strips crosswise into a dice.

Once you've become familiar with how to handle produce, your cooking will become faster when you enter the kitchen. But do keep in mind that no two pieces of food are identical, so there will always be some variation as to color, flavor, and texture.

The Least You Need to Know

◆ The goals for holding a knife are comfort, control, and safety.

◆ Knowing what various cutting instructions mean can save you precious time in the kitchen.

◆ By following proper selection, storage, and preparation steps, you can cook confidently with fresh fruits, vegetables, and other foods.

Part

Beginning Hors d'Oeuvres and Appetizers

Because the recipes in this book are so quick to make, they're ideal to consult when you're entertaining. That's where the chapters in Part 2 fit in.

Whether it's a small dinner party or a large cocktail party, you'll probably want to start off the evening with hors d'oeuvres. Two chapters are devoted to finger foods, one for hot and cold dips and the other for individual nibbles.

The next two chapters are for small dishes to start your meal. Some are light and luscious vegetable and fish appetizers and some are soups, including chilled soups to cool you in the summer and hot soups to warm you in the winter.

Dippity-Do

In This Chapter

- ◆ Easy bean dips
- ◆ Gooey cheese dips
- ◆ Hearty meat and seafood dips

Dips are part and parcel of nearly every party. They're easy on hosts, they require no last-minute hors d'oeuvres assembly, and there's no need to pass anything during the party. After the party is over, there's no mountain of small plates stacked up like the Leaning Tower of Pisa awaiting washing in the kitchen.

And dips are easy on guests. Your friends and family can eat dips with one hand, eliminating the need for a juggling lesson to learn how to simultaneously handle glasses, forks, and plates. Dips encourage people to talk and mingle because they're a gathering point of a party.

In this chapter, you'll find recipes for a wide range of dips, both hot and cold, inspired by cuisines as varied as Chinese and Mexican. Most are vegetarian, some are vegan, and a few contain seafood or meat.

Dip Diversification

Sure, you know what to do with a dip. You stick something crunchy—a tortilla chip or a carrot stick maybe—into it and then chomp down on dip and dipper. But that's not the only way many of these dips can be served.

Thick cold dips can be transformed into *canapés* (that's a fancy French word for "nibble"). Place the dip in a pastry bag fitted with a large fluted tip, and pipe a rosette onto anything from a slice of cucumber to a piece of melba toast.

Thick cold dips can also be served as spreads for breads. Many chic Italian and French restaurants serve small ramekins of savory spreads along with butter and bread. These dips are far lower in fat than butter, plus they add more flavor to the bread.

Both hot and cold dips can be used as toppings for grilled or broiled foods. Spread thin dips over the food, and place a dollop of thick dips off to the side. A bite of chicken breast or steak can be just as good for dipping as a celery stick!

Tuscan White Bean Dip

Flecks of roasted red pepper and parsley enliven this garlicky dip that also makes a great bread spread.

2 red bell peppers

2 (15-oz.) cans white cannellini beans, drained and rinsed

⅓ cup extra-virgin olive oil

¼ cup freshly squeezed lemon juice

3 garlic cloves, peeled

½ cup chopped fresh parsley

1 TB. fresh thyme or 1 tsp. dried

Salt and freshly ground black pepper to taste

Serves: 10
Active time: 20 minutes
Start to finish: 20 minutes
Each serving contains:
173 calories
70 calories from fat
8 g fat
1 g saturated fat
6.5 g protein
21 g carbohydrates

1. Preheat the oven broiler. Place red peppers on the rack of a broiler pan and broil 4 inches from the broiler element until skin is charred and black. Turn peppers with tongs to char all sides.

2. Plunge peppers into ice water, and when cool enough to handle, remove and discard the cap, skin, and seeds. Cut peppers into 1-inch dice and set aside.

3. Combine beans, olive oil, lemon juice, and garlic in a food processor fitted with a steel blade. Purée until smooth.

4. Add parsley, thyme, and red peppers. Chop finely, using on-and-off pulsing. Season to taste with salt and pepper.

5. Serve immediately, or refrigerate for up to 2 days, tightly covered.

Speedy Solutions

If you opt for jarred roasted red peppers rather than roasting them yourself, you can reduce the active time this recipe takes to 5 minutes.

Sun-Dried Tomato Dip

This intensely flavored dip is a wonderful topping for grilled foods, too.

Serves: 10

Active time: 10 minutes

Start to finish: 10 minutes

Each serving contains:

196 calories

176 calories from fat

19.5 g fat

8 g saturated fat

2.5 g protein

3 g carbohydrates

1 (8-oz.) pkg. cream cheese, softened

½ cup mayonnaise

½ cup sour cream

3 garlic cloves, peeled

2 tsp. *Herbes de Provence*

½ cup sun-dried tomatoes packed in oil, drained

4 scallions, rinsed, trimmed, and cut into 1-inch sections

Salt and freshly ground black pepper to taste

1. Combine cream cheese, mayonnaise, sour cream, garlic, and Herbes de Provence in a food processor fitted with a steel blade. Purée until smooth.

2. Add sun-dried tomatoes and scallions, and chop finely by using on-and-off pulsing. Season to taste with salt and pepper.

3. Serve immediately, or refrigerate for up to 2 days, tightly covered.

Fast Talk

Herbes de Provence, found in the spice section of many supermarkets and gourmet stores, is a dried blend of many herbs associated with the sunny cuisine of that part of France, including basil, thyme, fennel, rosemary, sage, and marjoram.

Guacamole

This classic version of Mexican avocado dip is a perennial favorite.

4 ripe avocados

1 small red onion, peeled and finely diced

1 jalapeño chili, seeds and ribs removed and finely diced

½ cup chopped fresh cilantro

1 tsp. ground cumin

2 TB. freshly squeezed lime juice

Salt and freshly ground black pepper to taste

Serves: 10

Active time: 10 minutes

Start to finish: 10 minutes

Each serving contains:

121 calories

95 calories from fat

10.5 g fat

1 g saturated fat

2 g protein

8 g carbohydrates

1. Place avocados, red onion, and jalapeño in a medium mixing bowl. Use a table fork to mash mixture together, leaving some avocado in chunks.

2. Add cilantro, cumin, and lime juice, and season to taste with salt and pepper. Mix well, and serve immediately. (You can make this dip up to 8 hours in advance. Push a piece of plastic wrap directly into the surface to prevent discoloration, and then refrigerate.)

Fresh Ways

An easy and efficient way to remove the flesh from avocadoes is to run a rubber spatula under the skin after the avocado is cut in half and the pit has been discarded. You can then pop out the flesh without scraping the skin.

Mexican Black Bean Dip

This hearty dip can be served in place of refried beans with any Mexican meal.

Serves: 10
Active time: 15 minutes
Start to finish: 15 minutes
Each serving contains:
155 calories
85 calories from fat
9.5 g fat
2 g saturated fat
4.5 g protein
14 g carbohydrates

⅓ **cup olive oil**

1 **small red onion, peeled and chopped**

4 **garlic cloves, peeled and minced**

2 **(15-oz.) cans black beans, drained and rinsed**

½ **cup crème fraîche**

¼ **cup freshly squeezed lime juice**

1 **tsp. ground coriander**

1 **tsp. ground cumin**

1 **TB. chopped fresh oregano or 1 tsp. dried**

Hot red pepper sauce to taste

½ **cup chopped pimiento**

¼ **cup chopped fresh cilantro**

Salt and freshly ground black pepper to taste

1. Heat olive oil in a large skillet over medium heat. Add onion and garlic, and cook, stirring constantly, for 3 minutes or until onion is translucent. Scrape mixture into a mixing bowl and set aside.

2. Combine beans, crème fraîche, lime juice, coriander, cumin, oregano, and red pepper sauce in a food processor fitted with a steel blade. *Purée* until smooth, and scrape mixture into the mixing bowl. Stir in pimiento and cilantro, and season to taste with salt and pepper.

3. Serve immediately or refrigerate for up to 2 days, tightly covered.

Fast Talk

Purée means to turn foods to a thick, creamy texture resembling thick baby food. The most efficient way to do this is with a food processor. Unless there's a lot of liquid, a blender isn't really up to the job.

Spinach Dip with Feta and Dill

This dip is right out of the Greek islands with flavors of tangy cheese, aromatic dill, and lemon.

1 lb. fresh baby spinach

2 TB. unsalted butter

1 medium onion, peeled and chopped

1 garlic clove, peeled and minced

2 cups crumbled *feta cheese*

1 (3-oz.) pkg. cream cheese, softened

¼ cup chopped fresh dill or 3 TB. dried

2 TB. chopped fresh oregano or 2 tsp. dried

3 TB. freshly squeezed lemon juice

Salt and freshly ground black pepper to taste

> Serves: 10
> **Active time:** 15 minutes
> **Start to finish:** 20 minutes
> **Each serving contains:**
> 145 calories
> 108 calories from fat
> 12 g fat
> 8 g saturated fat
> 7 g protein
> 4 g carbohydrates

1. Place spinach in a large bowl of cold water. Rinse spinach in water and then remove it from the top of the water and place it in a colander to drain. Remove stems, if large.

2. Place a large skillet over high heat. Add spinach by the handfuls, and toss until spinach wilts, adding additional spinach until all is wilted. Drain spinach in a colander, and chop coarsely.

3. Heat butter in the skillet over medium-high heat. Add onion and garlic, and cook, stirring frequently, for 3 minutes or until onion is translucent.

4. Stir spinach, feta cheese, cream cheese, dill, oregano, and lemon juice into the skillet. Reduce heat to low, and cook, stirring frequently, until mixture comes to a boil. Simmer for 3 minutes, stirring occasionally. Season to taste with salt and pepper.

5. Transfer dip to a fondue pot or other heated serving dish, and serve immediately.

 Fast Talk

Feta cheese is a classic Greek cheese traditionally made from sheep's or goat's milk, although today it's often made with cow's milk. White, crumbly, and rindless, feta is usually pressed into square cakes. It has a rich, tangy flavor and can range in texture from soft to semidry.

Classic Cheese Fondue

This Swiss favorite doubles as a dinner for 4. Serve it with a tossed salad.

Serves: 10

Active time: 15 minutes

Start to finish: 15 minutes

Each serving contains:

250 calories

143 calories from fat

16 g fat

10 g saturated fat

15 g protein

3 g carbohydrates

1 garlic clove, peeled and halved crosswise

1½ cups dry white wine

2 cups Emmenthal cheese, coarsely grated

2 cups Gruyère cheese, coarsely grated

2 TB. *kirsch*

1 TB. cornstarch

1. Rub the inside of a heavy 2-quart saucepan with the cut sides of garlic. Discard garlic. Add wine to the pot and bring to a simmer over medium heat.

2. Add Emmenthal and Gruyère cheeses to wine by ½ cup measures, stirring constantly with a whisk in a figure-eight pattern. Add additional cheese only after the previous addition is melted.

3. Combine kirsch and cornstarch in a small bowl, and stir to dissolve cornstarch. Add cornstarch mixture to fondue, and bring to a simmer, stirring constantly. Cook over low heat for 1 or 2 minutes or until fondue has thickened.

4. Transfer fondue to a fondue pot or other pot with a heat source, and serve immediately.

Fast Talk

Kirsch, also labeled *kirschwasser,* is a clear, tart cherry brandy distilled from cherry juice and cherry pits. In addition to the characteristic flavor in cheese fondue, kirsch is what's used to flame cherries jubilee.

Brie, Stilton, and Wild Mushroom Dip

This hearty dip is a great sauce for grilled or broiled meats or poultry.

1 garlic clove, peeled and halved crosswise

2 TB. dried porcini mushrooms, finely chopped

2 tsp. fresh thyme or ¾ tsp. dried

1½ cups dry white wine

¼ lb. fresh shiitake mushrooms

2 TB. unsalted butter

2 TB. olive oil

2 cups Brie cheese, at room temperature

1 cup coarsely grated Stilton cheese

1 TB. cold water

1 TB. cornstarch

Salt and freshly ground black pepper to taste

Serves: 10
Active time: 15 minutes
Start to finish: 25 minutes
Each serving contains:
244 calories
163 calories from fat
18 g fat
10 g saturated fat
10 g protein
4 g carbohydrates

1. Rub the inside of a heavy 2-quart saucepan with cut sides of garlic. Discard garlic. Add porcini mushrooms, thyme, and wine to the pan, and bring to a simmer over medium heat. Reduce heat to low, and simmer for 1 minute. Turn off heat and allow mixture to *steep* for 10 minutes.

2. While mixture is steeping, wipe mushrooms with a damp paper towel. Discard stems, and chop mushrooms finely.

3. Heat butter and olive oil in a medium skillet over medium-high heat. When butter foam begins to subside, add chopped shiitake mushrooms. Cook, stirring constantly, for 3 minutes or until mushrooms are soft and browned. Add cooked mushrooms to the pan with wine.

4. Scrape the top rind off Brie, and scoop out interior cheese using a spoon. Discard bottom and side rinds.

5. Bring wine back to a simmer over medium heat. Add Brie and Stilton cheeses to wine by ½ cup measures, stirring constantly with a whisk in a figure-eight pattern. Add additional cheese only after the previous addition is melted.

6. Combine water and cornstarch in a small bowl, and stir to dissolve cornstarch. Add to fondue, and bring to a simmer, stirring constantly. Cook over low heat for 1 or 2 minutes or until fondue has thickened. Season to taste with salt and pepper.

 **Fast Talk**

To **steep** means to soak dry ingredients such as dried mushrooms, tea leaves, and dried herbs and spices in hot liquid until the food's flavor is transferred into the liquid.

7. Transfer fondue to a fondue pot or other pot with a heat source, and serve immediately.

Variation: You can substitute Camembert or Explorateur cheese for the Brie, and Gorgonzola or blue cheese can be used in place of the Stilton.

Smoked Trout Dip

Bits of sweet pickle balance the saltiness of the fish in this creamy dip.

Serves: 10

Active time: 10 minutes

Start to finish: 30 minutes, including 20 minutes for chilling

Each serving contains:

172 calories

102 calories from fat

11 g fat

3 g saturated fat

11 g protein

6 g carbohydrates

1 cup sweet pickle slices, drained

1 lb. smoked trout fillets, skinned and broken into 1-inch pieces

⅓ cup mayonnaise

¼ cup heavy cream

¼ cup freshly squeezed lemon juice

½ tsp. cayenne or to taste

1. Place pickle slices in a food processor fitted with a steel blade. Chop finely, using on-and-off pulsing. Scrape chopped pickles into a mixing bowl and set aside.

2. Place smoked trout, mayonnaise, cream, lemon juice, and cayenne in the work bowl of the food processor and purée until smooth. Scrape trout mixture into the mixing bowl, and stir well to combine. Refrigerate until well chilled.

Variation: Substitute smoked salmon, smoked whitefish, or smoked bluefish for the trout.

 **Fresh Ways**

A pretty way to serve this dip—or any very thick dip—is to line a small bowl or mold with plastic wrap and pack the dip into the plastic-wrapped bowl. To serve, invert the mold onto a platter, discard the plastic wrap, and decorate with herbs.

Two-Salmon Dip

Delicate fresh salmon is joined with bits of succulent smoked salmon in this colorful dip.

1 (½-lb.) salmon fillet

1 tsp. *Old Bay* **seasoning**

2 (8-oz.) pkg. cream cheese, softened

3 TB. freshly squeezed lemon juice

2 TB. white horseradish

¼ lb. smoked salmon, finely chopped

3 scallions, rinsed, trimmed, and chopped

3 TB. chopped fresh dill or 2 tsp. dried

Freshly ground black pepper to taste

Serves: 10

Active time: 15 minutes

Start to finish: 1 hour, including 45 minutes for chilling

Each serving contains:

218 calories

169 calories from fat

19 g fat

11 g saturated fat

10 g protein

2.5 g carbohydrates

1. Sprinkle salmon fillet with Old Bay seasoning and place it in a microwave-safe dish. Cover the dish with plastic wrap, and microwave salmon fillet on high (100 percent) for 3 minutes or until cooked through. Refrigerate salmon until cold. Remove and discard skin, and break salmon into 1-inch chunks.

2. Place salmon, cream cheese, lemon juice, and horseradish in a food processor fitted with a steel blade, and purée until smooth. Scrape mixture into a mixing bowl, and stir in chopped smoked salmon, scallions, and dill. Season with pepper, and refrigerate for at least 45 minutes or until chilled. (You can make this dip up to 2 days in advance and refrigerate, tightly covered.)

Fast Talk

Old Bay is a seasoning mix developed for Chesapeake Bay's prized steamed crabs. It contains celery salt, mustard, cayenne, bay leaves, cloves, allspice, ginger, and paprika.

Crab Rangoon Dip

Hints of ginger, garlic, and other Asian flavors enliven this creamy hot dip.

Serves: 10

Active time: 15 minutes

Start to finish: 20 minutes

Each serving contains:

133 calories

100 calories from fat

11 g fat

8 g saturated fat

6.5 g protein

3 g carbohydrates

♨ Speedy Solutions

A fast way to soften cream cheese is to cut it into cubes, place it on a microwave-safe dish, and microwave for 10 seconds. Repeat, if necessary.

½ lb. crabmeat

3 scallions

1 (8-oz.) pkg. cream cheese, softened

½ cup coconut milk

2 garlic cloves, peeled and minced

2 TB. soy sauce

2 TB. grated fresh ginger

1 TB. Worcestershire sauce

2 TB. chopped fresh cilantro

Salt and freshly ground black pepper to taste

1. Place crabmeat on a dark-colored plate. Rub it gently with your fingertips, and discard any bits of shell or cartilage you uncover. Set crabmeat aside.

2. Rinse and trim scallions. Discard all but 2 inches of green tops, and chop scallions.

3. Combine scallions, cream cheese, coconut milk, garlic, soy sauce, ginger, and Worcestershire sauce in a heavy 2-quart saucepan. Cook over medium-low heat, stirring frequently, for 5 minutes or until mixture is hot and bubbly. Stir in crabmeat and cilantro, and season to taste with salt and pepper.

4. Transfer dip to a fondue pot or other heated serving dish, and serve immediately.

Variation: Substitute chopped shrimp or finely chopped cooked chicken for the crabmeat.

Mexican Beef and Chili Dip
(Chili con Queso)

This hearty dish is like nacho topping just awaiting the dipping.

8 ripe plum tomatoes or
1 (14.5-oz.) can petite diced
tomatoes, drained

2 TB. olive oil

1 onion, peeled and diced

3 garlic cloves, peeled and
minced

1 lb. lean ground beef

1 (4-oz.) can chopped mild
green chilies, drained

½ cup heavy cream

2 cups Monterey Jack cheese,
coarsely grated

2 cups mild cheddar cheese,
coarsely grated

1 TB. cold water

1 TB. cornstarch

Salt and freshly ground black
pepper to taste

Serves: 10
Active time: 15 minutes
Start to finish: 30 minutes
Each serving contains:
321 calories
215 calories from fat
24 g fat
13 g saturated fat
22 g protein
5 g carbohydrates

1. Rinse, core, and seed tomatoes. Chop tomatoes finely, and set aside.

2. Heat olive oil in a large heavy skillet over medium-high heat. Add onion, garlic, and ground beef. Cook, breaking up lumps with a fork, for 3 to 5 minutes or until beef is brown and no pink remains. Add tomatoes and green chilies, and cook for an additional 3 minutes. Remove contents of the skillet with a slotted spoon, and discard grease from the skillet.

3. Return contents to the skillet, and add cream and Monterey Jack and cheddar cheeses. Cook over medium heat, stirring frequently, for 3 minutes or until cheese is melted and bubbly.

4. Combine water and cornstarch in a small bowl, and stir to dissolve cornstarch. Add cornstarch mixture to dip, and bring to a simmer, stirring constantly. Cook over low heat for 1 or 2 minutes or until dip has thickened. Season to taste with salt and pepper. (This can be done up to 4 hours ahead. Reheat over medium heat until boiling.)

5. Transfer dip to a fondue pot or other heated serving dish, and serve immediately.

Variation: Use Mexican chorizo sausage instead of ground beef, and for a spicier dish, try jalapeño Jack cheese instead of the Monterey Jack.

Speedy Solutions

Petite cut tomatoes, a relative newcomer to the market, are great for dips. Regular diced tomatoes should really be cut into smaller pieces or someone's dip into the bowl could yield nothing but tomato. The petite cut ones are preferable and save time.

Sausage Pizza Dip

If your favorite part of a pizza is the gooey topping, here's all the flavors you love in a dip.

Serves: 10

Active time: 15 minutes

Start to finish: 25 minutes

Each serving contains:

209 calories

129 calories from fat

14 g fat

7 g saturated fat

16 g protein

4 g carbohydrates

1 TB. olive oil

¾ lb. mild or hot Italian bulk sausage

1 cup spaghetti sauce

1 TB. chopped fresh oregano or 1 tsp. dried

1 TB. chopped fresh basil or 1 tsp. dried

2 tsp. fresh thyme or ½ tsp. dried

4 cups whole milk mozzarella cheese, coarsely grated

Salt and freshly ground black pepper to taste

1. Heat olive oil in a large skillet over medium-high heat. Add sausage and cook, breaking up lumps with a fork, for 3 to 5 minutes or until sausage is no longer pink. Remove sausage from the skillet with a slotted spoon, and discard grease from the pan.

2. Return sausage to the pan and add spaghetti sauce, oregano, basil, and thyme. Bring to a boil, reduce heat to low, and simmer 10 minutes or until slightly thickened. Stir in mozzarella and cook until cheese is melted. Season to taste with salt and pepper. (This can be done up to 4 hours ahead. Reheat over medium heat until boiling.)

3. Transfer dip to a fondue pot or other heated serving dish, and serve immediately.

Variation: Personalize this recipe using your favorite pizza toppings. Try ground beef or diced pepperoni in place of the sausage, or make this a vegetarian dip by removing sausage and adding sautéed onion, green pepper, or mushrooms.

Fresh Ways

If you can't find bulk sausage for recipes, add a few minutes to the prep time for removing the sausage meat from its casings (the casing turns into nasty rubber bands when cooked). Just push on one end like a tube of toothpaste.

4

Nibbles and Noshes:
Hors d'Oeuvres for
All Occasions

In This Chapter

- ◆ Fun finger foods
- ◆ Roll-ups and wraps
- ◆ Seafood starters

Maybe your standard hors d'oeuvres are a bowl of sesame sticks or a handful of cherry tomatoes while you're cooking dinner (or waiting for dinner to be cooked for you!). But chances are, when you're entertaining, you want to enjoy foods a bit more elegant with your predinner beverage. That's when the recipes in this chapter come in handy.

Hors d'oeuvres should be simple to make and simple to eat, and all the dishes here qualify as both. In these pages, you'll find recipes that produce crunchy textures; those are the sort of dressed-up chips of one type or another. And you'll also find some elegant seafood nibbles and various types of wraps that are quick to make and easy to slice into individual portions.

Assembly Line Logic

I'm not one for ditsy hors d'oeuvres. And I pride myself on telling you that I've never stuffed a snow pea. All the individual hors d'oeuvres in this chapter start out as a big batch of something. You do the individual portioning of the hors d'oeuvre either before or after baking, but it's basically an assembly line process. When you're reading through the recipes here, note how far in advance dishes can be prepared up to a certain point. Then start a countdown from the time your party starts.

Fresh Tomato Bruschetta

Luscious rosy tomatoes flavored with herbs and garlic make a great toast topper.

1 French baguette, cut into ½-inch-thick slices

4 TB. olive oil

6 ripe plum tomatoes, rinsed, cored, seeded, and finely chopped

4 garlic cloves, peeled and minced

¼ cup chopped fresh basil

2 TB. chopped fresh parsley

2 TB. balsamic vinegar

Salt and freshly ground black pepper to taste

> Yield: 24 toasts
> **Active time:** 20 minutes
> **Start to finish:** 20 minutes
> **Each serving contains:**
> 78 calories
> 26 calories from fat
> 3 g fat
> 1 g saturated fat
> 2 g protein
> 11 g carbohydrates

1. Preheat the oven broiler and cover a baking sheet with aluminum foil. Brush both sides of bread slices very lightly with 3 tablespoons olive oil. Broil bread 6 inches from the broiler element for 1 minute per side or until browned. Remove and set aside.

2. Combine tomatoes, garlic, basil, parsley, and vinegar in a mixing bowl. Add remaining 1 tablespoon olive oil. Season to taste with salt and pepper, and stir well.

3. To serve, place 1 tablespoon tomato mixture on each toast slice, and serve immediately. (The toasts can be made up to 1 day in advance and kept at room temperature, tightly covered. The tomato mixture can be made up to 2 hours in advance and kept at room temperature. Do not top toasts until just before serving.)

Variation: Reduce the number of tomatoes to 4 and add ½ cup canned white beans, drained and rinsed, and ¼ cup chopped pitted kalamata olives.

Fast Talk

Bruschetta (pronounced *broo-SKEH-tah*) comes from the Italian word *brus-care*, meaning "to cook over the coals." Or it's the fancy Italian word for toast. While traditional bruschetta is grilled, broiling in the oven is just fine.

Herbed Goat Cheese and Roasted Pepper Spirals

Tart cheese is a perfect foil for sweet peppers in these colorful spirals.

Yield: 36 spirals

Active time: 15 minutes

Start to finish: 15 minutes

Each serving contains:

29 calories

20 calories from fat

2 g fat

1.5 g saturated fat

1.5 g protein

1 g carbohydrates

3 red bell peppers, or 3 jarred roasted red peppers

½ lb. (1 cup) mild goat cheese, softened

2 TB. heavy cream

2 garlic cloves, peeled

8 sprigs parsley, rinsed and stemmed

2 tsp. Herbes de Provence

Salt and freshly ground black pepper to taste

1. Preheat the oven broiler. Place red peppers on the rack of a broiler pan and broil 4 inches from the broiler element until skin is charred and black. Turn peppers with tongs to char all sides. Plunge peppers into ice water, and when cool enough to handle, remove and discard cap, skin, and seeds. Cut peppers in half and set aside.

2. Combine goat cheese, cream, garlic, parsley, and Herbes de Provence in a food processor fitted with a steel blade. Purée until smooth and then scrape mixture into a mixing bowl. Season to taste with salt and pepper.

3. Spread herbed cheese onto pepper halves, and roll peppers lengthwise into cylinders. Refrigerate peppers for 3 hours, tightly wrapped with plastic wrap. To serve, slice each roll into 6 slices. (Peppers can be stuffed 1 day in advance and refrigerated, tightly covered. Slice rolls just before serving.)

 **Stale Stuff**

You'll see precrumbled goat cheese next to the precrumbled blue and feta cheese in supermarkets. Avoid them all. Cheese loses flavor quickly when it's exposed to air that way.

Cheddar Crackers

Crushed potato chips are the "secret ingredient" that makes these cheese crackers extra crunchy.

1 (5.5-oz.) bag potato chips	**5 TB. unsalted butter, melted**
1½ cups grated sharp cheddar cheese	**⅓ cup all-purpose flour**
	½ tsp. cayenne or to taste

> Yield: 24 crackers
>
> **Active time:** 5 minutes
>
> **Start to finish:** 30 minutes, including 10 minutes for cooling
>
> **Each serving contains:**
>
> 93 calories
>
> 66 calories from fat
>
> 7 g fat
>
> 4 g saturated fat
>
> 2 g protein
>
> 5 g carbohydrates

1. Preheat the oven to 350°F. Place potato chips in a food processor fitted with a steel blade. Chop chips coarsely, using on-and-off pulsing.

2. Scrape potato chip crumbs into a large mixing bowl and add cheese, butter, flour, and cayenne. Stir until mixture is combined and holds together when pressed in the palm of your hand.

3. Form mixture into 1 tablespoon balls. Place balls on an ungreased baking sheet and flatten into circles with the bottom of a floured glass or with your fingers. Repeat with remaining dough, leaving 1 inch between circles.

4. Bake for 15 to 18 minutes or until browned. Cool crackers on the baking sheet for 2 minutes and then transfer to a cooling rack with a spatula to cool completely. Serve at room temperature. (The crackers can be made 2 days in advance and kept at room temperature in a tightly sealed container.)

Variation: Substitute Gruyère or jalapeño Jack for the cheddar.

Fresh Ways

> If you're grating cheese by hand rather than with a food processor, spray the grater with vegetable oil spray before grating. It will be much easier to clean.

Southwest Smoked Salmon Pinwheels

A core of salad greens in the center of layers of smoked salmon and salsa cream cheese makes this a stunning hors d'oeuvre.

Yield: 24 pinwheels

Active time: 15 minutes

Start to finish: 1¼ hours, including 1 hour for chilling

Each serving contains:
65 calories

23 calories from fat

2.5 g fat

1 g saturated fat

3 g protein

7 g carbohydrates

1 cup good-quality refrigerated salsa

1 (3-oz.) pkg. cream cheese, softened

¼ cup chopped fresh cilantro

4 (10-in.) flour tortillas

½ lb. sliced smoked salmon

2 cups mesclun salad mix or other baby greens, rinsed and dried

1. Drain salsa in a strainer, pressing to extract as much liquid as possible. Combine salsa, cream cheese, and cilantro in a mixing bowl, and stir well.

2. Wrap tortillas in plastic wrap and microwave on high (100 percent) for 10 to 20 seconds or until soft and pliable.

3. Place tortillas on a counter, and spread each with cream cheese mixture. Arrange salmon slices on the bottom half of each tortilla. Place ½ cup mesclun at the bottom edge of tortilla on top of salmon. Roll tortillas firmly but gently, starting at the filled edge. Place rolls, seam side down, on a platter or ungreased baking sheet, and refrigerate for 1 hour.

4. Trim end off each roll by cutting on the diagonal to remove the portion of tortilla that does not meet and form a log. Slice each tortilla into 6 slices, and serve chilled. (Tortillas can be filled up to 4 hours in advance and refrigerated, tightly covered. Slice just before serving.)

Variation: You can use thinly sliced smoked turkey, roast beef, or ham instead of the smoked salmon.

Stale Stuff

Do not try to substitute bottled salsa for the fresh, refrigerated salsa you find in the produce section. The success of this dish requires the texture and flavor of the fresh vegetables.

Salmon Tartare on Cucumber Slices

If you're a fan of sushi or shashimi, you'll love this seasoned salmon canapé served on crunchy cucumber slices.

1 (1-lb.) salmon fillet, skinned

1 bunch fresh parsley, rinsed and stemmed

4 anchovy fillets

2 shallots, peeled and quartered

3 TB. capers, drained and rinsed

2 TB. white horseradish

2 TB. grainy mustard

3 TB. freshly squeezed lemon juice

Salt and freshly ground black pepper to taste

2 medium cucumbers

> Yield: 36 slices
>
> **Active time:** 15 minutes
>
> **Start to finish:** 15 minutes
>
> **Each serving contains:**
>
> 24 calories
>
> 6 calories from fat
>
> 1 g fat
>
> 0 g saturated fat
>
> 3.5 g protein
>
> 1 g carbohydrates

1. Rinse salmon and pat dry on paper towels. Cut into ½-inch dice and chop finely by hand. Place salmon in a mixing bowl.

2. Combine parsley, anchovies, and shallots in a food processor fitted with a steel blade. Chop finely using on-and-off pulsing. Scrape mixture into the mixing bowl and add capers, horseradish, mustard, and lemon juice. Stir well, and season to taste with salt and pepper.

3. Rinse cucumbers, and *score* each with the tines of a fork. Slice each cucumber into 18 slices.

4. To serve, top each cucumber slice with 2 teaspoons salmon mixture. (Salmon can be chopped and the remaining mixture can be prepared up to 4 hours in advance. Do not combine them or top cucumber slices until just before serving.)

Variation: Substitute fresh tuna or chopped sea scallops for the salmon. You could also place the mixture on the stem end of Belgian endive spears instead of cucumber slices.

 Fast Talk

To **score** a food is to make shallow cuts at regular intervals. Scoring cucumbers makes them more decorative on a platter, but foods such as flank steak are scored to prevent them from curling when cooked.

Southwest Miniature Crab Cakes

Aromatic fresh cilantro gives these seafood cakes a Hispanic accent.

Yield: 24 cakes

Active time: 15 minutes

Start to finish: 25 minutes

Each serving contains:

36 calories

16 calories from fat

2 g fat

0 g saturated fat

3 g protein

2 g carbohydrates

Stale Stuff

Don't automatically reach for the salt and pepper! Seasoning mixtures such as Old Bay or Cajun seasoning contain both seasonings, so you don't need to add more when using them in recipes.

4 scallions

¾ lb. crabmeat

1 large egg

3 TB. mayonnaise

3 TB. cracker meal

1 to 2 tsp. Old Bay seasoning

2 red bell peppers, seeds and ribs removed, and very finely chopped

3 TB. chopped fresh cilantro

Vegetable oil spray

1. Heat the oven to 450°F. Cover a baking sheet with heavy duty aluminum foil, and spray the foil with vegetable oil spray.

2. Rinse and trim scallions, discarding all but 2 inches of green tops. Chop scallions finely.

3. Place crabmeat on a dark-colored plate. Rub it gently with your fingertips, and discard any bits of shell or cartilage you uncover. Set crabmeat aside.

4. Combine egg, mayonnaise, cracker meal, and Old Bay in a mixing bowl, and whisk until well blended. Gently fold in crabmeat, red bell peppers, scallions, and cilantro.

5. Using a tablespoon, form mixture into balls and then flatten them on the baking sheet into patties. Spray tops of patties with vegetable oil spray.

6. Bake for 10 to 12 minutes, or until lightly brown on top. Serve immediately. (The crabmeat mixture can be made 1 day in advance and refrigerated, tightly covered with plastic wrap. Do not form or bake until just before serving.)

Variation: Larger versions of this hors d'oeuvre can serve 4 as an entrée. Form mixture into 8 patties, and bake them at 400°F for 15 to 20 minutes. Also, you can use finely chopped shrimp or lobster instead of crabmeat.

Baked Shrimp Toast Rolls

These baked rolls are a more healthful version of traditional Chinese shrimp toast.

12 slices white sandwich bread

¾ lb. raw shrimp, peeled and *deveined*

2 TB. chopped fresh ginger

1 TB. Asian sesame oil

1 large egg white

1 TB. dry sherry

2 TB. cornstarch

1 TB. soy sauce

2 scallions, rinsed, trimmed, and sliced into 2-inch sections

⅓ cup finely chopped canned water chestnuts

Salt and freshly ground black pepper to taste

Vegetable oil spray

> Yield: 36 rolls
> **Active time:** 20 minutes
> **Start to finish:** 30 minutes
> **Each serving contains:**
> 40 calories
> 7 calories from fat
> 1 g fat
> 0 g saturated fat
> 3 g protein
> 5 g carbohydrates

1. Preheat the oven to 425°F. Cover a baking sheet with heavy-duty aluminum foil and spray foil with vegetable oil spray.

2. Remove crusts from bread slices using a serrated bread knife. Roll each slice with a rolling pin (or a large glass or a wine bottle) until bread is thin but still pliable. Set aside.

3. Combine shrimp, ginger, sesame oil, egg white, sherry, cornstarch, and soy sauce in a food processor fitted with a steel blade. Purée until smooth, stopping a few times to scrape the sides of the work bowl. Add scallions and chop finely using on-and-off pulsing. Scrape mixture into a mixing bowl and stir in water chestnuts. Season to taste with salt and pepper.

4. Spread bread slices out on a counter, and place 1 heaping tablespoon filling in a line across the long side of each slice. Roll bread around filling so the edges meet, and place rolls, seam side down, on the prepared baking sheet. Spray tops with vegetable oil spray.

5. Bake rolls 5 minutes, turn them over gently with tongs, and bake 4 more minutes or until browned. Cut each roll into 3 sections with a serrated knife, and serve immediately. (Filling can be prepared 1 day in advance and refrigerated, tightly covered. Fill bread and bake the rolls just before serving.)

Variation: Any firm-fleshed white fish such as cod, snapper, or sole will work instead of the shrimp.

> **Fast Talk**
>
> **Deveining** is the process of removing the dark vein (actually the intestinal tract) from the top of shrimp after they are shelled. This is done with a paring knife or with a special gadget called a deveiner.

Asparagus Wrapped in Herbed Cheese and Prosciutto

Asparagus moves from the dinner plate to the hors d'oeuvre tray when wrapped in ham spread with cream cheese.

Yield: 24 spears

Active time: 15 minutes

Start to finish: 20 minutes

Each serving contains:

39 calories

24 calories from fat

3 g fat

2 g saturated fat

2.5 g protein

2 g carbohydrates

 Fresh Ways

Submerging vegetables in ice water performs a number of functions: it stops the vegetables from continuing to cook with residual heat, it cools them down in a jiffy so you can save time, and it sets the green color of vegetables such as asparagus and snow peas.

24 thick asparagus spears (about 2 lb.)

1 (3-oz.) pkg. cream cheese, softened

2 TB. unsalted butter, softened

3 garlic cloves, peeled and minced

2 TB. chopped fresh parsley

1 TB. chopped fresh oregano or ½ tsp. dried

1 TB. chopped fresh basil or ½ tsp. dried

Salt and freshly ground black pepper to taste

¼ lb. thinly sliced prosciutto

1. Rinse asparagus spears, discard woody stem end, and peel ⅓ the way up the stalk with a vegetable peeler. Steam asparagus for 5 to 7 minutes or until crisp-tender. Plunge asparagus into ice water to stop the cooking action. Drain, and pat dry with paper towels.

2. While asparagus is steaming, combine cream cheese, butter, garlic, parsley, oregano, and basil in a mixing bowl. Stir well, and season to taste with salt and pepper.

3. Trim visible fat off prosciutto slices, and cut prosciutto into 2-inch-wide strips.

4. Spread prosciutto slices with cheese mixture and wrap around asparagus spears, beginning at the stem end and wrapping only to the tip. Serve immediately. (Asparagus can be steamed up to 1 day in advance and refrigerated, tightly covered, and they can be wrapped up to 4 hours in advance and refrigerated, tightly covered.)

Variation: If you're not a fan of asparagus, try this recipe with sugar snap peas or broccoli florets.

Vietnamese Spring Rolls (*Cha Gio*)

Delicate rice paper pancakes hold a filling of pork and vegetables in these crispy rolls.

5 large dried shiitake mushrooms

1 oz. *bean thread noodles*

½ lb. ground pork

1 cup bean sprouts, rinsed and cut into 1-inch lengths

½ cup shredded carrot

½ cup chopped scallions, white part and 4 inches of green tops

4 garlic cloves, peeled and minced

3 TB. fish sauce (*nam pla*)

2 large eggs, lightly beaten

½ cup granulated sugar

Salt and freshly ground black pepper to taste

18 rice paper pancakes

Vegetable oil spray

Yield: 36 pieces
Active time: 30 minutes
Start to finish: 1 hour
Each serving contains:
58 calories
15 calories from fat
2 g fat
1 g saturated fat
1 g protein
9 g carbohydrates

1. Soak dried mushrooms and bean thread noodles in separate bowls of very hot tap water for 15 minutes. Remove mushrooms, and squeeze well to extract as much water as possible. Discard stems, and finely chop mushrooms. Drain bean thread noodles. Place on a cutting board in a long log shape, and cut into 1-inch pieces. Measure out ½ cup, and discard any additional noodles.

2. Preheat the oven to 400°F. Cover a baking sheet with heavy-duty aluminum foil, and spray foil with vegetable oil spray.

3. Place mushrooms and noodles in a mixing bowl and add pork, bean sprouts, carrot, scallions, garlic, fish sauce, eggs, and 1 teaspoon sugar. Season to taste with salt and pepper.

4. Fill a wide mixing bowl with very hot tap water, and stir in remaining sugar.

5. Place a damp tea towel in front of you on the counter. Place rice paper pancakes on a plate, and cover with a barely damp towel.

6. Fill 1 rice paper pancake at a time, keeping the remainder covered. Totally immerse pancake in hot water for 2 seconds. Remove, and place it on the damp tea towel; it will become pliable within a few seconds. Gently fold front pancake edge ⅓ of the way to the top. Place about 2 tablespoons filling on

 **Fast Talk**

Bean thread noodles—sometimes called cellophane noodles, glass noodles, or bean thread vermicelli—are translucent strands made from the starch of green mung beans. While they should be soaked before adding to most dishes, they don't need to be soaked if added to soups.

the folded-up portion, and shape it into a log, leaving a 2-inch margin on each side. Lightly spray the unfilled pancake with vegetable oil spray. Fold the sides over filling, and roll tightly but gently, beginning with filled side. Place roll on the baking sheet, and fill remaining rice paper pancakes.

7. Spray tops and sides of rolls with vegetable oil spray. Bake for 12 minutes, turn rolls gently with tongs, and bake an additional 10 to 12 minutes or until rolls are browned. Remove the pan from the oven, and blot rolls with paper towels. Slice each in half on the diagonal, and serve immediately. (Rolls can be made up to 2 days in advance and refrigerated, tightly covered. Reheat in a 375°F oven for 8 to 10 minutes or until crisp.)

Variation: You can use ground turkey or finely chopped raw shrimp for the ground pork in this recipe.

5

Appealing Appetizers

In This Chapter

◆ Hot and cold clam and mussel appetizers

◆ Succulent shrimp dishes

◆ Elegant veggie treats

The dishes in the previous chapter were all finger foods. In this chapter, you'll find recipes for plated appetizers to start a meal. Appetizers are so popular that many restaurants have adopted appetizer-size portions, a.k.a. "little plates," for their entire menu. It's these fast and easy recipes that you'll find in this chapter.

The emphasis in this chapter is on seafood appetizers with a few vegetable dishes in the mix. I think meals should start on a light note. Fish before meat became the norm in classic dining for just that reason. But *light* is hardly synonymous with *dull*. As you'll see, these dishes are vibrantly flavored and draw inspiration from cuisines around the world.

Mad for Mollusks

Mollusks, along with crustaceans, are a large family of seafood that ranges from tiny cockles to massive abalone. But what they all have in common is that they protect their soft bodies with hard shells.

Oysters are identified by their place of origin and have names such as Blue Point (for the waters off New York's Long Island) and Olympia (native to the Pacific Northwest). Clams and scallops are graded by size. Littleneck clams are the smallest, followed in size by cherrystone clams and quahogs. Sea scallops are about four times the size of bay scallops and can be cut into quarters for a recipe calling for the tiny bay scallops.

> **Speedy Solutions**
>
> Removing bivalves from their shells is a labor-intensive process referred to as *shucking*. Increasingly, fish processors are doing this for us. Pints of shucked oysters, scallops by the pound, and minced fresh clams are becoming the rule rather than the exception, so look for preshucked mollusks when you're shopping.

When selecting mollusks, the most critical consideration is whether they are alive. The shells should be closed or should close tightly when handled. To test a mollusk, with your forefinger above and thumb underneath, gently squeeze the mollusk, as if to push the top shell forward. If the shell does not firmly close, the mollusk should be immediately discarded.

Mussel-ing In

While some cultures eat raw mussels, we eat them cooked, so opening them is not a problem. (That happens naturally when they're steamed.) But mussels do require some specialized preparation prior to that trip to the pot.

To clean mussels, first wash and remove the beards. The easiest way is to grasp the mussel between your thumb and a dull knife blade and give the beard a tug to pull it free. Scrape or pull away any that remains. Using a stiff brush or scouring pad, continue to scrub the shell of each mussel to remove every bit of grass and mud. You don't have to remove scales and barnacles, except when the shells are going to be served with the dish.

Black Bean Cakes

These sautéed cakes are flavored with herbs and spices, and they double as a side dish for Mexican or Southwestern meals.

6 TB. olive oil

1 medium onion, peeled and coarsely chopped

3 garlic cloves, peeled and minced

2 serrano chilies, seeds and ribs removed, and diced

2 TB. chili powder

1½ TB. ground cumin

2 (15-oz.) cans black beans, drained and rinsed

½ cup chopped fresh cilantro

½ cup water

Salt and freshly ground black pepper to taste

1 cup sour cream

1 cup good-quality refrigerated tomato salsa

Serves: 6
Active time: 20 minutes
Start to finish: 20 minutes
Each serving contains:
282 calories
194 calories from fat
22 g fat
6 g saturated fat
6 g protein
17 g carbohydrates

---

1. Heat 2 tablespoons olive oil in a large, heavy skillet over medium-high heat. Add onion, garlic, and serrano chilies, and cook, stirring frequently, for 3 minutes or until onion is translucent. Add chili powder and cumin, and cook, stirring constantly, for 1 minute. Add black beans, cilantro, and water. Bring mixture to a boil and simmer, stirring frequently, for 3 minutes.

2. Transfer mixture to a food processor fitted with a steel blade and purée. Scrape mixture into a mixing bowl, and season to taste with salt and pepper.

3. Roll enough mixture into a ball the size of a golf ball. Flatten between two sheets of plastic wrap until patty is ¼ inch thick. Repeat with remaining mixture.

4. Heat remaining 4 tablespoons olive oil in a large, heavy skillet over high heat. Add bean cakes and cook for 1 or 2 minutes per side or until crisp, turning gently with a slotted spatula. Drain cakes on paper towels, and continue until all cakes are cooked.

5. To serve, place 1 or 2 cakes on a plate and top each with 1 tablespoon sour cream and 1 tablespoon salsa. Serve immediately. (Bean mixture can be made up to 1 day in advance and refrigerated, tightly covered. Fry cakes just prior to serving.)

Stale Stuff

You might think it's not necessary to dice and chop ingredients that are destined to become a purée, but it really is important. If the pieces are too large, they won't cook properly and your finished dish will taste like your raw ingredients.

Deviled Leeks

This elegant appetizer conveys the subtle flavor of leeks, the mild member of the onion family.

Serves: 6

Active time: 10 minutes

Start to finish: 25 minutes

Each serving contains:

253 calories

66 calories from fat

7 g fat

4 g saturated fat

9 g protein

39 g carbohydrates

12 to 16 small leeks

2 TB. unsalted butter

½ cup chicken or vegetable stock

⅓ cup dry white wine

2 TB. chopped fresh *marjoram* or 1 tsp. dried

Salt and freshly ground black pepper to taste

3 TB. Dijon mustard

½ cup plain breadcrumbs

½ cup freshly grated Parmesan cheese

1. Preheat the oven to 375°F.

2. Trim off the root end of leeks and discard all but 1 inch of green tops. Split leeks lengthwise, and rinse well under cold running water.

3. Melt butter in a large skillet over medium heat. Add leeks, and cook 5 minutes or until leeks begin to soften, turning them gently with tongs. Add stock, wine, marjoram, salt, and pepper, and bring to a boil. Cover the pan, reduce the heat to low, and cook for 10 minutes, rolling leeks over occasionally.

4. Arrange leeks in a 9×13-inch baking dish, and pour liquid from the skillet over them. Spread leeks evenly with Dijon mustard and sprinkle with breadcrumbs and Parmesan cheese. Bake, uncovered, for 10 minutes. Serve immediately. (Leeks can be prepared for baking up to 6 hours in advance and kept at room temperature. Bake just prior to serving.)

Fast Talk

Marjoram (*MAHR-jur-umm*) is a member of the mint family. The flavor from the long, pale-green leaves is similar to that of oregano but sweeter. If you can't find marjoram, use oregano, but only use half as much as you would marjoram.

Baked Clams Casino

Sautéed onion, sweet red bell pepper, and garlic flavor the bread topping that crowns the clams.

5 TB. unsalted butter

4 garlic cloves, peeled and minced

1 medium onion, peeled and chopped

1 red bell pepper, seeds and ribs removed, and finely chopped

1½ cups *Italian breadcrumbs*

¼ cup freshly grated Parmesan cheese

Salt and freshly ground black pepper to taste

24 littleneck or small cherrystone clams

1. Preheat the oven to 425°F.

2. Melt butter in a large skillet over medium heat. Add garlic and onion and cook, stirring frequently, for 3 minutes or until onion is translucent. Add red bell peppers and cook, stirring frequently, for 5 to 7 minutes or until peppers are soft. Add breadcrumbs and cheese, and stir to combine. Season to taste with salt and pepper. Set aside.

3. Scrub clams well under cold running water with a stiff brush. Discard any clams that do not shut tight while being scrubbed. Place clams in a mixing bowl, and cover them with hot tap water. Within about 2 minutes, the shells will be slightly apart. Insert a clam knife or paring knife between the shells at one corner, and sever the muscles holding the shells together. Discard one shell, release clams from the bottom shell by scraping under meat with a paring knife, and leave meat in the shell.

4. Mound topping on raw clams, using about 1 tablespoon per clam. Bake for 5 to 8 minutes, depending on the size of clam, or until clams are hot and topping is brown. Serve immediately. (Topping can be made up to 2 days in advance and refrigerated in a container or heavy plastic bag.)

Variation: You can use oysters instead of clams for this dish. They bake in the same amount of time.

Serves: 4

Active time: 20 minutes

Start to finish: 25 minutes

Each serving contains:

394 calories

178 calories from fat

20 g fat

11 g saturated fat

16 g protein

38 g carbohydrates

 Fast Talk

Italian breadcrumbs are toasted breadcrumbs that are then seasoned with parsley, other herbs, garlic, and Parmesan cheese. To replicate the flavor if you only have plain breadcrumbs, add 1 teaspoon Italian seasoning, ½ teaspoon garlic powder, and 3 tablespoons Parmesan cheese to each 1 cup plain breadcrumbs.

Garlic-Steamed Clams

This is a very easy dish to make because the clams open during the cooking process, and their juice creates the flavorful broth.

Serves: 6

Active time: 15 minutes

Start to finish: 15 minutes

Each serving contains:

115 calories

66 calories from fat

7 g fat

1 g saturated fat

7.5 g protein

3 g carbohydrates

3 dz. littleneck or small cherrystone clams

3 TB. olive oil

6 garlic cloves, peeled and minced

¼ cup water

¼ cup white wine

¼ cup chopped fresh parsley

Salt and freshly ground black pepper to taste

1. Scrub clams well under cold running water with a stiff brush. Discard any that do not shut tightly while being scrubbed.

2. Heat olive oil in a Dutch oven over medium heat. Add garlic and cook, stirring frequently, for 2 minutes. Raise the heat to high and add water, wine, and clams. Cover the pot and steam clams for 6 to 8 minutes, depending on the size of clams. Shake the pan a few times, without opening it, to redistribute clams.

3. Remove clams from the pan with a slotted spoon, discarding any that did not open. Stir in parsley, salt, and pepper.

4. To serve, place clams in shallow bowls and ladle broth on top. Serve with soup spoons as well as seafood forks.

Variation: If you prefer, you can use fresh mussels instead of clams.

Fresh Ways

Leftover broth from a recipe for steamed mollusks is a treasure trove of flavor for saucing future fish dishes. Freeze it, and be sure to note what dish it's from so you know what flavors you're adding.

Oysters with Green Chili Cilantro Pesto

There's a delicate Southwestern flavor in the cheese topping on these baked oysters.

2 dz. fresh oysters

6 mild green Anaheim chilies, seeds and ribs removed, and cut into 1-inch pieces

3 garlic cloves, peeled

½ cup pine nuts

½ cup firmly packed cilantro leaves

¼ lb. (1 cup) Parmesan cheese, cut into ½-inch cubes

3 TB. olive oil

Salt and freshly ground black pepper to taste

Serves: 6
Active time: 15 minutes
Start to finish: 25 minutes
Each serving contains:
385 calories
222 calories from fat
25 g fat
6 g saturated fat
3 g protein
13 g carbohydrates

1. Preheat the oven to 400°F.

2. Scrub oysters well with a stiff brush under cold running water, and discard any that are not firmly closed. Place oysters on a baking sheet and bake for 5 minutes. Remove oysters and transfer to a bowl of ice water. Pry oysters open, and cut underneath oyster to release the muscle. Discard one shell, arrange oysters on the baking sheet in the remaining shell, and set aside.

3. Increase the oven heat to 500°F.

4. Combine Anaheim chilies, garlic, pine nuts, cilantro, Parmesan cheese, and olive oil in a food processor fitted with a steel blade. Purée until smooth, scraping the sides of the work bowl with a rubber spatula a few times.

5. Spread 1 tablespoon pesto on top of each oyster. Bake oysters for 3 to 5 minutes or until topping is bubbly. Serve immediately. (Pesto can be prepared 1 day in advance and refrigerated, tightly covered.)

Speedy Solutions

It's worth a few dollars to find a fishmonger to open oysters for you but then you should cook them within a few hours. An alternative is to buy preshucked oysters and arrange them in ovenproof gratin dishes (round or oval dishes with low sides). They'll taste just the same, and it saves time and work.

Creole Marinated Shrimp

The sweet shrimp are joined with perky Italian pickled vegetables that create a colorful dish.

Serves: 6

Active time: 15 minutes

Start to finish: 45 minutes, including 30 minutes for chilling

Each serving contains:

309 calories

181 calories from fat

20 g fat

3 g saturated fat

25 g protein

6 g carbohydrates

1½ lb. extra-large (16 to 20 per lb.) cooked shrimp, peeled and deveined

2 celery ribs, rinsed, trimmed, and finely chopped

1 cup pickled Italian *gardiniera* vegetables, drained and chopped

4 garlic cloves, peeled and minced

½ cup chopped fresh parsley

½ cup white wine vinegar

2 TB. freshly squeezed lemon juice

2 TB. chopped fresh oregano

Salt and freshly ground black pepper to taste

½ cup extra-virgin olive oil

3 to 4 cups salad greens or 6 to 8 large leaves Boston lettuce

1. Remove tails from shrimp, if necessary, and place shrimp in a large mixing bowl. Add celery, gardiniera vegetables, garlic, and parsley. Set aside.

2. Combine vinegar, lemon juice, oregano, salt, and pepper in a jar with a tight-fitting lid. Shake well, add olive oil, and shake well again. Add dressing to the bowl, and mix it with shrimp and vegetables. Refrigerate for 30 minutes.

3. To serve, divide mixed greens or lettuce leaves among small plates, and mound shrimp in the center. Serve immediately.

Variation: You could also use cooked bay scallops or 1-inch cubes of cooked halibut, cod, or sole instead of shrimp.

Fast Talk

Gardiniera (*jar-din-YAIR-ah*) vegetables are a mélange of cauliflower, olives, and pepperoncini peppers all pickled together in a jar. They're part of a traditional antipasti spread and can be found in the Italian section of supermarkets.

Bourbon Shrimp

A tomato cream sauce is laced with heady bourbon and scented with aromatic dill in this easy appetizer.

1½ lb. extra large (16 to 20 per lb.) raw shrimp, peeled and deveined

3 TB. unsalted butter

2 TB. olive oil

½ cup bourbon

2 tsp. tomato paste

1 cup heavy cream

1 TB. chopped fresh dill

Salt and freshly ground black pepper to taste

6 dill sprigs for garnish (optional)

Serves: 6
Active time: 20 minutes
Start to finish: 20 minutes
Each serving contains:
400 calories
246 calories from fat
27 g fat
14 g saturated fat
24 g protein
3 g carbohydrates

1. Rinse shrimp and pat dry with paper towels.

2. Heat butter and oil in a large, heavy skillet over medium-high heat. Add shrimp and cook, stirring constantly, for 1 minute or until shrimp just begin to turn pink.

3. Add bourbon, raise the heat to high, and cook for 1 minute or until liquid is reduced to 2 tablespoons.

4. Add tomato paste and cream, and continue to cook for 1 minute. Remove shrimp from the pan with a slotted spoon, and set aside. Raise the heat to high, and reduce sauce by ½. Add chopped dill and season to taste with salt and pepper.

5. To serve, spoon sauce over shrimp and garnish with additional dill sprigs (if using).

Variation: Sea scallops or 1-inch cubes of firm-fleshed whitefish such as cod, halibut, or sea bass work well instead of shrimp.

Stale Stuff

While much of the alcohol is burned off this dish or any dish containing liquor or wine, some residual remains. It's not enough for anyone to feel its effects, but do keep this in mind if you're serving this dish to children.

Crab Cakes with Mustard Sauce

Delicate scallops hold these cakes together, and the sauce is sparked with grainy, sharp mustard.

Serves: 6

Active time: 25 minutes

Start to finish: 25 minutes

Each serving contains:

702 calories

566 calories from fat

63 g fat

28 g saturated fat

22 g protein

10 g carbohydrates

Fresh Ways

Butter sauces are always made at the last minute to keep them emulsified, but here's a trick for some advance preparation: fill an insulated bottle with very hot tap water, drain it, and fill it with the sauce. It will "hold" for up to 2 hours.

¾ lb. crabmeat

10 oz. raw scallops, well chilled

1 egg white

¾ cup heavy cream

Salt and freshly ground black pepper to taste

½ cup cracker crumbs

½ cup dry white wine

2 large shallots, peeled and chopped

4 sprigs fresh thyme

½ lb. (2 sticks) unsalted butter, cut into 1-TB. pieces

3 TB. grainy mustard

½ cup vegetable oil for frying

1. Place crabmeat on a dark-colored plate. Rub it gently with your fingertips, and discard any bits of shell or cartilage you uncover. Set aside.

2. Purée scallops in a food processor fitted with a steel blade until a paste is formed. Slowly add egg white and ½ cup cream through the feed tube, and process until smooth. Season to taste with salt and pepper, and gently fold in crabmeat.

3. Form mixture into 6 to 8 patties, and coat patties in cracker crumbs. Refrigerate cakes loosely covered with plastic wrap.

4. Combine wine, shallots, and thyme in a small saucepan. Cook over high heat until 2 tablespoons remain. Add remaining ¼ cup cream, and cook again until 2 tablespoons remain. Strain sauce and return it to the pan.

5. Place the pan over very low heat, and add pieces of butter, one at a time, swirling with a whisk until a piece is completely incorporated before adding the next. Stir in mustard, and season to taste with salt and pepper.

6. Heat oil in a large skillet over medium-high heat. Add patties and cook for 2 minutes or until lightly brown. Turn gently and cook the other side.

7. To serve, spoon sauce on small plates and top sauce with one crab cake. (Patties can be prepared up to cooking 1 day in advance and refrigerated, tightly covered with plastic wrap.)

Chicken in Lettuce Cups

These Chinese rolls are a healthful version of tacos because the filling is rolled in crunchy lettuce leaves.

2 TB. sesame oil

2 garlic cloves, peeled and minced

1 TB. grated fresh ginger

4 scallions, rinsed, trimmed, and thinly sliced

1 lb. ground chicken

1 (8-oz.) can water chestnuts, drained, rinsed, and chopped

¼ cup soy sauce

2 TB. *hoisin sauce*

1 TB. cider vinegar

1 tsp. cornstarch

Salt and freshly ground black pepper to taste

12 to 16 Boston or iceberg lettuce leaves, rinsed and dried

2 scallions, rinsed, trimmed, and thinly sliced for garnish (optional)

Serves: 6

Active time: 20 minutes

Start to finish: 20 minutes

Each serving contains:

228 calories

135 calories from fat

15 g fat

1 g saturated fat

14.5 g protein

8 g carbohydrates

1. Heat sesame oil in a large skillet over medium-high heat. Add garlic, ginger, and scallions. Stir-fry for 30 seconds, stirring constantly. Add chicken, and stir-fry for 3 or 4 minutes, breaking up lumps with a fork or until chicken has lost all its pink color and is white and beginning to brown. Stir in water chestnuts, and stir-fry 1 minute.

2. Mix soy sauce, hoisin sauce, vinegar, and cornstarch in a small bowl. Add to the pan, and when mixture boils and thickens, reduce heat to low and simmer for 1 minute, stirring frequently. Season to taste with salt and pepper.

3. Spoon mixture into lettuce leaves, and garnish with scallions (if using). Serve immediately.

Variation: Instead of ground chicken, try ground pork or turkey.

Fast Talk

Hoisin (hoy-ZAN) **sauce** is the ketchup of Chinese cooking. This thick, sweet, and spicy reddish-brown sauce is a mixture of soybeans, garlic, chilies, Chinese five-spice powder, and sugar. Like ketchup, it's used both as a condiment and an ingredient.

Chapter 6

The Bountiful Bowl: Soups

In This Chapter

- ◆ Chilled summer soups
- ◆ Creamy chowder creations
- ◆ Hearty winter soups

Soups aid emotional well-being immeasurably. On a hot summer day, a bowl of frosty soup cools like an ocean breeze, and on a chilly winter night, a bowl of steaming soup warms like nothing else. It's easy to see the truth in the old Spanish proverb, "between love and soup, soup is best."

You'll find a potpourri of soups in this chapter, united by the short amount of time it takes to create them. They range from light uncooked summer soups to hearty chowders, perfect for whatever suits your mood or the season.

Taking Stock

Want to know a secret? The reason why so many people think that soups and sauces taste better in restaurants is because they're based on slowly simmered stocks. These stocks form the structure of the soup or sauce and add a depth of flavor.

The *word* fast in the title of this book is antithetical to watching a pot simmer for 8 hours on the stove. But there is a middle ground. If you have the time to make the Quick Chicken Stock in this chapter and have it handy in the freezer, you're much closer to that long-simmered taste.

Quick Chicken Stock

Enriching canned stock quickly with vegetables and herbs replicates the flavor of homemade stock.

2 qt. canned chicken stock

4 celery ribs, rinsed and sliced

1 large onion, peeled and diced

2 carrots, trimmed, scrubbed, and sliced

12 black peppercorns

6 garlic cloves, peeled

4 sprigs parsley

4 sprigs thyme or 1 tsp. dried

2 bay leaves

Makes: 2 quarts
Active time: 5 minutes
Start to finish: 25 minutes
Each serving contains:
289 calories
11 calories from fat
1 g fat
0 g saturated fat
29.5 g protein
47 g carbohydrates

1. Combine stock, celery, onion, carrots, peppercorns, garlic, parsley, thyme, and bay leaves in a large stockpot. Bring to a boil over high heat, reduce heat to low, cover the pan, and simmer for 20 minutes.

2. Strain stock, pressing with the back of a spoon to extract as much liquid as possible. Refrigerate when cool. The stock can be refrigerated and used within 3 days, or it can be frozen for up to 6 months.

 Fresh Ways

If you've got some limp carrots or celery ribs in the refrigerator, don't throw them out. They're still good for making stock.

Gazpacho

Gazpacho is a traditional Spanish vegetable soup flavored with garlic, chilies, and vinegar.

Serves: 8

Active time: 15 minutes

Start to finish: 45 minutes, including 30 minutes for chilling

Each serving contains:

113 calories

64 calories from fat

7 g fat

1 g saturated fat

2 g protein

12 g carbohydrates

1 medium Bermuda or other sweet white onion, peeled and quartered

1 medium cucumber, rinsed, seeded, and cut into 1-inch sections

1 red bell pepper, seeds and ribs removed, and diced

3 medium to large ripe tomatoes, rinsed, cored, seeded, and diced

3 garlic cloves, peeled

1½ cups tomato juice

¼ cup olive oil

1 jalapeño chili, seeds and ribs removed

¼ cup balsamic vinegar

¼ cup chopped fresh cilantro

Salt and freshly ground black pepper to taste

1. Finely chop onion, cucumber, red pepper, and 1 tomato in a food processor fitted with a steel blade using on-and-off pulsing. Scrape mixture into a large mixing bowl.

2. Purée remaining 2 tomatoes with garlic, tomato juice, olive oil, jalapeño, and balsamic vinegar. Stir purée and cilantro into vegetables, and season to taste with salt and pepper. Chill for at least 30 minutes, or until cold. (Soup can be made up to 2 days in advance and refrigerated, tightly covered.)

Speedy Solutions

If you start with all your ingredients chilled, any of these noncooked soups are ready to serve as soon as they're assembled.

Dilled Cream of Cucumber Soup

Aromatic dill makes delicate cucumbers more interesting in this soup that can be served either hot or cold.

2 TB. unsalted butter

1 leek, white part only, trimmed, sliced, and rinsed well

2 large or 3 small cucumbers, rinsed, seeded, and sliced

4 TB. chopped fresh dill or 1 TB. dried

5 cups chicken or vegetable stock

1 cup half-and-half

Salt and freshly ground black pepper to taste

6 to 8 TB. finely chopped cucumber for garnish (optional)

6 to 8 fresh dill sprigs for garnish (optional)

Serves: 8
Active time: 20 minutes
Start to finish: 1 hour if served hot or 3 hours to allow for chilling
Each serving contains:
94 calories
60 calories from fat
7 g fat
4 g saturated fat
3.5 g protein
6 g carbohydrates

1. Melt butter in a heavy 4-quart saucepan over medium heat. Add leek, cucumbers, and 2 tablespoons dill. Cook, stirring frequently, for 5 minutes or until leek is translucent.

2. Add stock and bring to a boil over high heat. Reduce heat to low, and simmer, partially covered, for 25 minutes.

3. Transfer mixture to a blender or food processor fitted with the steel blade. Purée until smooth, and refrigerate soup until chilled, at least 2 hours.

4. Stir in half-and-half and remaining 2 tablespoons dill, and season to taste with salt and pepper. Serve immediately, garnishing each serving with 1 tablespoon cucumber and 1 sprig dill, if using. (Soup can be made up to 2 days in advance and refrigerated, tightly covered.)

Fresh Ways

Although most herbs don't freeze or thaw well, you can freeze leafy herbs such as dill, cilantro, and parsley if you'll later add them to dishes that cook. They'll lose their texture once thawed, but you won't notice it as much in the final dish. Rinse small bundles and freeze wrapped in plastic wrap. "Chop" the frozen herbs using the blunt side of a knife.

Leek and Potato Soup (*Vichyssoise*)

Although this creamy soup has a French name, it was actually invented in New York in the early twentieth century.

Serves: 8

Active time: 15 minutes

Start to finish: 3 hours, including 2 hours for chilling

Each serving contains:

185 calories

76 calories from fat

8 g fat

5 g saturated fat

6 g protein

24 g carbohydrates

 **Fresh Ways**

A huge variation exists in the flavor and composition of canned stocks, with the best-known national brands not very high on the list. Whenever possible, buy organic stocks. The sodium content is much lower, and stocks found in whole foods markets usually have a better flavor.

3 TB. unsalted butter

6 leeks, white part only, trimmed, chopped, and rinsed well

1 lb. boiling potatoes, peeled and thinly sliced

6 cups chicken or vegetable stock

1 cup half-and-half

Salt and freshly ground black pepper to taste

6 to 8 TB. snipped fresh chives for garnish (optional)

1. Melt butter in a heavy 4-quart saucepan over medium heat. Add leeks and cook, stirring frequently, for 5 minutes or until leeks are translucent.

2. Add potatoes and stock, and bring to a boil over high heat. Reduce heat to low and simmer soup, partially covered, for 25 minutes or until potatoes are tender.

3. Transfer mixture to a blender or food processor fitted with the steel blade and purée. (This may have to be done in several batches.)

4. Refrigerate, covered, until cold, at least 2 hours, and then stir in half-and-half. Season to taste with salt and pepper, and serve immediately, garnished with chives, if using. (Soup can be made up to 2 days in advance and refrigerated, tightly covered.)

Variation: This soup can also be served hot, and when served this way, it's frequently not puréed. If serving it hot, omit the half-and-half.

Cream of Celery Soup with Tarragon

Adding rice to the soup as it cooks gives this luxurious dish its thick texture.

8 celery ribs, rinsed, trimmed, and cut into 1-inch lengths

4 cups chicken or vegetable stock

⅓ cup white rice

2 TB. chopped fresh *tarragon* or 2 tsp. dried

1 cup half-and-half

Salt and freshly ground black pepper to taste

6 to 8 sprigs tarragon for garnish (optional)

Serves: 8
Active time: 15 minutes
Start to finish: 50 minutes
Each serving contains:
126 calories
45 calories from fat
5 g fat
3 g saturated fat
6 g protein
14 g carbohydrates

1. Combine celery, stock, rice, and tarragon in a heavy 4-quart saucepan. Bring to a boil over high heat, and simmer soup, partially covered, over low heat for 30 minutes.

2. Place soup in a blender or food processor fitted with the steel blade and purée until smooth. Return soup to the pan, stir in half-and-half, and simmer 2 minutes.

3. Season to taste with salt and pepper, and serve immediately, garnished with tarragon, if using. (Soup can be made up to 2 days in advance and refrigerated, tightly covered.)

 Fast Talk

Tarragon is an aromatic herb used extensively in French cooking. It has long, pointed, dark-green leaves and adds a distinctive aniselike flavor to foods.

Grilled Corn Chowder

The smoky flavor that comes from grilling the corn over aromatic mesquite makes this soup special.

Serves: 8

Active time: 25 minutes

Start to finish: 55 minutes

Each serving contains:

208 calories

81 calories from fat

9 g fat

4.5 g saturated fat

7 g protein

30 g carbohydrates

1 cup mesquite chips

4 garlic cloves, unpeeled

8 to 10 medium ears of fresh corn, unshucked

3 TB. unsalted butter

¼ cup yellow cornmeal

1 (4-oz.) can mild green chilies, drained

2 cups chicken or vegetable stock

2 cups whole milk

Salt and freshly ground black pepper to taste

1. Preheat the oven to 350°F. Light a charcoal or gas grill and soak mesquite chips covered in cold water for 20 minutes.

2. Bake garlic cloves for 15 minutes or until soft. When cool enough to handle, remove pulp and discard skins. Set aside.

3. Remove all but 1 layer of husks from corn, and pull out corn silks. Soak corn covered in cold water for 5 minutes.

4. Drain mesquite chips and place on the fire. Grill corn for 10 to 15 minutes, turning with tongs occasionally. When cool enough to handle, discard husks and cut kernels off cobs using a sharp serrated knife.

5. Melt butter in a large saucepan over low heat. Add kernels and cook for 5 minutes, stirring occasionally. Remove 1 cup kernels and set aside. Purée remaining corn, roasted garlic, cornmeal, chilies, and stock in a food processor fitted with a steel blade or in a blender.

6. Combine purée with milk, and heat to a boil over medium heat, stirring occasionally. Add reserved corn kernels, and season with salt and pepper. Simmer for 5 minutes over low heat, stirring occasionally. Serve immediately. (Soup can be made up to 2 days in advance and refrigerated, tightly covered.)

Speedy Solutions

The most time-consuming part of this recipe is grilling the corn, so there's no reason not to fill the grill with more ears than you'll need for one batch of this chowder. Cut the kernels off the extra cobs and freeze for future batches.

Nantucket Clam Chowder

This version of the New England classic, made with celery and thyme, won contests when I lived on the island!

1¼ lb. red-skinned potatoes, scrubbed and cut into ½-inch dice

3 celery ribs, rinsed, trimmed, and diced

2 (8-oz.) bottles clam juice

2 pt. fresh minced clams, drained with all clam juice reserved

¼ cup chopped fresh parsley

1 TB. fresh thyme or 1 tsp. dried

1 bay leaf

3 TB. unsalted butter

2 medium onions, peeled and diced

¼ cup all-purpose flour

3 cups whole milk or half-and-half

Salt and freshly ground black pepper to taste

Serves: 8
Active time: 25 minutes
Start to finish: 40 minutes
Each serving contains:
255 calories
71 calories from fat
8 g fat
5 g saturated fat
13.5 g protein
32.5 g carbohydrates

1. Combine potatoes, celery, clam juice, reserved clam juice, parsley, thyme, and bay leaf in a heavy 2-quart saucepan. Bring to a boil over high heat. Reduce heat to medium, and cook for 15 minutes or until potatoes are tender and liquid is reduced by half.

2. While potatoes are boiling, melt butter in a small saucepan over medium heat. Add onions and cook, stirring frequently, for 5 minutes or until onions are soft. Reduce heat to low.

3. Stir in flour and cook for 2 minutes, stirring constantly. Whisk in milk, and bring to a boil over medium heat, stirring constantly. Simmer for 2 minutes. Set aside until potatoes are tender.

4. Add cream mixture to potato mixture, and bring to a boil over medium heat. Stir in clams, and simmer for 5 minutes, stirring occasionally. Remove and discard bay leaf. Season to taste with salt and pepper, and serve immediately. (Soup can be made up to 2 days in advance and refrigerated, tightly covered.)

Variation: Many versions of chowder include either corn kernels, crisp crumbled bacon, or both. For this size batch ½ cup corn kernels and 3 tablespoons crumbed bacon would be good additions.

Stale Stuff

It's important to use the additional clam juice for the chowder rather than cooking the potatoes and celery in water. It's this reduction of the clam juice that adds great flavor after the milk is added.

Dilled Corn and Oyster Bisque

Sweet corn and aromatic dill are the perfect foils for the briny taste of oysters in this elegant soup.

Serves: 8
Active time: 20 minutes
Start to finish: 35 minutes
Each serving contains:
252 calories
111 calories from fat
12 g fat
7 g saturated fat
10.5 g protein
28.5 g carbohydrates

 Fresh Ways

Bisque and chowder both contain seafood, but that's where the similarity ends. A bisque is always a puréed cream soup, while chowders are always chunky and can be made with or without cream.

10 ears fresh corn (or 4 cups frozen corn, thawed)

1 pt. fresh oysters

4 TB. unsalted butter

4 cups whole milk

3 TB. chopped fresh dill or 1 TB. dried

1 tsp. hot red pepper sauce

Salt and freshly ground black pepper to taste

6 to 8 sprigs dill for garnish (optional)

1. Shuck corn and discard silks. Cut corn off cobs with a sharp serrated knife.

2. Drain oysters, reserving oyster liquor. Refrigerate oysters, and strain liquor through cheesecloth or a paper coffee filter. Set aside.

3. Melt butter in a heavy 4-quart saucepan. Add corn and cook for 5 minutes, stirring occasionally. Add milk and reserved oyster liquor. Bring to a boil over medium heat, stirring occasionally. Reduce heat to low, and simmer soup uncovered for 15 minutes. Purée soup in a blender or food processor fitted with a steel blade. (Soup can be made up to 2 days in advance and refrigerated, tightly covered.)

3. Before serving, reheat soup to a simmer and add oysters and dill. Bring to a boil, and simmer over low heat, stirring occasionally, for 3 minutes or until edges of oysters start to curl. Stir in hot red pepper sauce, and season to taste with salt and pepper. Serve immediately, garnished with dill sprigs (if using).

Variation: You could use 1 pint minced fresh clams instead of the oysters in this recipe.

Greek Lemon Egg Soup with Chicken and Orzo (*Avgolemono*)

The luxurious texture of this soup comes from being thickened with eggs like a custard.

2 (6-oz.) boneless, skinless chicken breast halves

7 cups chicken stock

⅔ cup orzo

1 large carrot, peeled and grated

2 celery ribs, rinsed, trimmed, and finely chopped

4 large eggs

⅓ cup freshly squeezed lemon juice

1 tsp. grated lemon zest

Salt and freshly ground black pepper to taste

Serves: 8
Active time: 10 minutes
Start to finish: 25 minutes
Each serving contains:
160 calories
36 calories from fat
4 g fat
1 g saturated fat
17 g protein
14 g carbohydrates

1. Rinse chicken and pat dry with paper towels. Trim chicken of all visible fat, and cut into ½-inch cubes.

2. Combine chicken stock, chicken, orzo, carrot, and celery in a heavy 2-quart saucepan. Bring to a boil over high heat, stirring occasionally. Reduce heat to low and simmer, covered, for 10 to 12 minutes or until orzo is tender.

3. While soup is simmering, whisk together eggs and lemon juice. When orzo is tender, remove soup from heat and stir constantly for 1 minute. It should no longer be bubbling at all. Stir in lemon mixture, cover the pan, and allow soup to sit for 5 minutes to thicken.

4. Season to taste with salt and pepper, and serve immediately. (Soup can be made up to 2 days in advance and refrigerated, tightly covered. Reheat over low heat, stirring frequently, until hot. Do not let soup boil.)

Fresh Ways

You want to cool the liquid by stirring before adding the egg to prevent the egg from curdling and turning this into a Greek version of Chinese Egg Drop Soup. Eggs thicken at 160°F, while the boiling point of liquid is 212°F. Be sure to stir!

Tuscan White Bean Soup with Sausage

This thick and hearty soup is a perfect starter on a cold winter night. Swiss chard gives it added color and flavor.

Serves: 8

Active time: 20 minutes

Start to finish: 45 minutes

Each serving contains:

335 calories

62 calories from fat

7 g fat

3 g saturated fat

26 g protein

44 g carbohydrates

 Fresh Ways

Save the rinds from Parmesan cheese and use them for flavoring dishes such as soups and sauces. The rind won't melt into the dishes, but it will impart flavor. Remove and discard it before serving.

1 lb. bulk Italian sausage (sweet or hot)

2 large onions, peeled and diced

4 garlic cloves, peeled and minced

4 celery ribs, rinsed, trimmed, and diced

2 carrots, peeled and diced

4 cups chicken stock

3 (15-oz.) can white beans, drained and rinsed

¼ cup chopped fresh parsley

1½ tsp. dried thyme

1 bay leaf

1 cup water

¾ lb. (8 firmly packed cups) Swiss chard, rinsed, stemmed, and thinly sliced

½ cup freshly grated Parmesan cheese

Salt and freshly ground black pepper to taste

1. Place a heavy 2-quart saucepan over medium-high heat. Add sausage, breaking up lumps with a fork. Cook, stirring occasionally, for 3 minutes or until sausage is browned and no longer pink. Remove sausage from the pan with a slotted spoon, and set aside. Discard all but 1 tablespoon sausage fat from the pan.

2. Add onions, garlic, celery, and carrots to the pan. Cook, stirring occasionally, for 3 minutes or until onion is translucent. Add stock, ½ of beans, parsley, thyme, and bay leaf. Bring to a boil over medium heat. Simmer, partially covered, for 20 minutes or until carrots are soft.

3. While soup begins simmering, combine reserved beans and water in a blender or food processor fitted with a steel blade. Purée until smooth. Stir mixture into soup.

4. Add Swiss chard to soup, and simmer for 5 minutes. Remove and discard bay leaf, and stir Parmesan cheese into soup. Season to taste with salt and pepper, and serve immediately. (You can do this up to 2 days in advance and refrigerate soup, tightly covered. Reheat over low heat, stirring occasionally, until soup comes to a simmer.)

Part 3

Casual Cuisine

Sure you might want to cook a fancy dinner with candles lit and silver gleaming a few nights a week. But what about Sunday brunch? What about those nights when a crusty sandwich or steaming bowl of pasta is what will hit the spot? These are the times you'll turn to the recipes in Part 3.

Here you'll find a chapter with goodies for breakfast and brunch—but don't relegate them to the morning. Many of them can do double duty as a light supper, too. The other chapters in this part contain recipes for those great stalwarts of casual cooking—sandwiches, pastas, and pizza. But do look closely. While the categories are casual, the dishes are sophisticated as well as delicious.

Chapter 7

Sunny Starts: Breakfast

In This Chapter

- ◆ Sweet and savory pancakes
- ◆ Fancy frittatas
- ◆ Exotic egg dishes

Nutritionists are quick to point out that breakfast is the most important meal of the day, but we all know that the morning is also the most hectic part of the day. The recipes in this chapter are here to solve that dilemma.

Foods like pancakes can be on the table in a matter of minutes. And it's much more efficient to cook one frittata that serves the whole table rather than worrying about individual omelets. So breakfast need not be a reason for stress, and these recipes start the day with a treat.

Pancake Pointers

Pancakes couldn't be easier to make, and nearly everyone loves them. To save time in the morning, start the pancake-making process the night before by combining the dry ingredients in one bowl and whisking the wet ingredients in another. In the morning, all you have to do is stir them together as the griddle heats. (Don't over mix the batter or whisk it. Pancake batters *should* be somewhat lumpy.)

Getting your griddle or skillet to the proper temperature is important. The ideal pancake-cooking temperature is 375°F. To test and see if it's 375°F, drop a few drops of water onto it. If they "dance" across the griddle as they turn to steam, then you're ready to cook.

If you use a ¼-cup measure, your pancakes will all be relatively the same size. If you're really particular about perfectly round pancakes, use a bulb baster filled with batter.

Pancakes are ready to turn when you see bubbles appearing on the surface and the edges turn brown. It's at this time that you can add some additional ingredients like chocolate chips, dried fruit, or granola. Use a wide spatula when flipping pancakes so the whole bottom of the pancake is supported.

The Fine Points of Frittatas

Frittatas are Italian-style omelets. Unlike their French counterparts, which are cooked in single portions entirely on the stove, frittatas start on the stovetop and finish in the oven. It's much easier to make one frittata for two people rather than two individual omelets, and frittatas don't require the careful turning that can lead to omelets becoming scrambled eggs with other ingredients folded in. Plus you only have the one skillet to wash.

> **Fresh Ways**
>
> Only have skillets with plastic handles? Wrap the handle in a double layer of aluminum foil before you place the skillet into the oven to prevent the plastic from cracking or even melting.

Cutting Cholesterol

Eggs have gotten a bad nutritional reputation because of the fat and cholesterol in the yolk. But the white is the "good egg." The white, made up primarily of protein and water, is what gives eggs their ability to bind.

> **Stale Stuff**
>
> Never rinse eggs before using them. The water makes the shells porous and can cause the eggs to spoil faster and allow bacteria to enter.

If you want to be judicious about cutting cholesterol, you can use an egg substitute product. (The best-known one is Egg Beaters.) These products are essentially egg whites tinted yellow. But you can also make your own by using 2 egg whites for each whole egg, or if a recipe calls for several eggs, use 2 egg whites and 1 whole egg for every 2 whole eggs listed.

Oven-Baked Apple Pancakes

These puffy pancakes are like small apple cakes—children adore them!

6 TB. unsalted butter

2 Golden Delicious apples, peeled, cored, and thinly sliced

⅓ cup firmly packed dark brown sugar

¼ tsp. ground cinnamon

3 TB. freshly squeezed lemon juice

6 large eggs, lightly beaten

1 cup whole milk

1 cup all-purpose flour

Pinch salt

Maple syrup or apple butter for serving

Serves: 6
Active time: 15 minutes
Start to finish: 30 minutes
Each serving contains:
354 calories
169 calories from fat
19 g fat
10 g saturated fat
10 g protein
37 g carbohydrates

1. Preheat the oven to 425°F. Place 6 (1-cup) custard cups on a baking sheet.

2. Melt butter in a small saucepan over low heat. Pour 1 tablespoon butter into each custard cup.

3. Toss apples with brown sugar and cinnamon and drizzle with lemon juice. Combine eggs, milk, flour, and salt in a mixing bowl, and stir until just blended. Divide batter among cups on top of butter. Arrange apple slices on top of batter.

4. Bake for 15 minutes or until pancakes are puffed and golden. Unmold the pancakes onto plates, and serve immediately with maple syrup or apple butter.

Variation: You could also try pears or peaches instead of apples.

 Stale Stuff

Don't use 2 percent or skim milk here. This is one recipe that really does require whole milk. The fat is necessary to make the pancakes puff.

Gingerbread Pancakes

If you love the flavor of gingerbread cookies, these are the way to start your day.

Serves: 6

Active time: 20 minutes

Start to finish: 30 minutes

Each serving contains:

636 calories

258 calories from fat

29 g fat

12 g saturated fat

11 g protein

85 g carbohydrates

3 cups all-purpose flour

1 cup firmly packed dark brown sugar

1 TB. baking powder

1½ tsp. baking soda

¾ tsp. salt

1 tsp. ground cinnamon

1 tsp. ground ginger

½ tsp. grated nutmeg

½ cup water

½ cup brewed coffee, cold or at room temperature

4 large eggs

¼ lb. (1 stick) unsalted butter, melted and cooled

¼ cup vegetable oil

Maple syrup or sweetened whipped cream for serving

1. Preheat the oven to 200°F, and cover a baking sheet with aluminum foil.

2. Combine flour, brown sugar, baking powder, baking soda, salt, cinnamon, ginger, and nutmeg in a large mixing bowl, and whisk well. Combine water, coffee, eggs, and butter in another mixing bowl, and whisk well. Pour liquid mixture into flour mixture, and stir until just combined. Allow batter to sit for 10 minutes.

3. Place a griddle or 12-inch skillet over medium heat. Brush with oil. Pour ¼ cup measures of batter into the skillet, and cook for 1 or 2 minutes or until bubbles appear on the surface. Turn pancakes with a spatula and cook for 1 or 2 more minutes or until pancakes are cooked through. Place pancakes on a baking sheet and keep warm in the oven. Repeat with remaining batter, brushing the griddle with oil between batches.

4. Serve immediately, topping pancakes with maple syrup or sweetened whipped cream.

Fresh Ways

Although it's a shelf-stable product, baking powder does have an expiration date; check it before buying. And because you use so little of it for any recipe, hunt for the cans with the date farthest in the future.

Whole-Wheat Blueberry Pancakes

The inclusion of whole-wheat flour makes these blueberry pancakes hardier than most.

¾ cup all-purpose flour

½ cup whole-wheat flour

¼ cup wheat germ

¼ cup granulated sugar

2 tsp. baking powder

1½ tsp. baking soda

½ tsp. salt

2 cups buttermilk, well shaken

3 large eggs

6 TB. unsalted butter, melted and cooled

2 cups blueberries, rinsed

¼ cup vegetable oil

Maple syrup or blueberry syrup for serving

Serves: 6
Active time: 20 minutes
Start to finish: 30 minutes
Each serving contains:
426 calories
229 calories from fat
25 g fat
10 g saturated fat
10 g protein
42 g carbohydrates

1. Preheat the oven to 200°F, and cover a baking sheet with aluminum foil.

2. Combine all-purpose flour, whole-wheat flour, wheat germ, sugar, baking powder, baking soda, and salt in a large mixing bowl, and whisk well. Combine buttermilk, eggs, and butter in another mixing bowl, and whisk well. Pour liquid into flour mixture, and stir until just combined. Stir in blueberries.

3. Place a griddle or 12-inch skillet over medium heat. Brush with oil. Pour ¼ cup measures of batter into the skillet, and cook for 1 or 2 minutes or until bubbles appear on the surface. Turn pancakes with a spatula and cook 1 or 2 more minutes or until pancakes are cooked through. Place pancakes on a baking sheet and keep warm in the oven. Repeat with remaining batter, brushing the griddle with oil between batches.

4. Serve immediately, topping pancakes with maple or blueberry syrup.

Variation: Feel free to substitute sliced strawberries or raspberries for the blueberries.

Stale Stuff

All the "butter" of buttermilk tends to rise to the top of the carton, it's important to shake it vigorously. And shake it often if you're using it at different times when preparing a recipe.

Banana Pancakes with Banana Syrup

These pancakes are rich and luscious. In fact, on occasion, I serve them for dessert with vanilla ice cream.

Serves: 6

Active time: 25 minutes

Start to finish: 25 minutes

Each serving contains:

907 calories

352 calories from fat

39 g fat

19 g saturated fat

18 g protein

124 g carbohydrates

 Fresh Ways

If you have bananas that are past their prime, toss them into the freezer still in their peels. Defrosted, they're perfect for any recipe calling for mashed bananas such as this one or banana bread.

12 TB. (1½ sticks) unsalted butter, melted

1 cup firmly packed dark brown sugar

½ cup water

¾ tsp. pure vanilla extract

4 large very ripe bananas

4 cups all-purpose flour

⅔ cup granulated sugar

2 tsp. baking powder

1 tsp. baking soda

½ tsp. ground cinnamon

½ tsp. salt

3 cups buttermilk, well shaken

4 large eggs

¼ cup vegetable oil

1. Preheat the oven to 200°F, and cover a baking sheet with aluminum foil.

2. Combine 8 tablespoons butter, brown sugar, water, and vanilla extract in a medium saucepan. Bring to a boil over medium-high heat and simmer mixture, stirring occasionally, for 5 minutes.

3. While syrup is simmering, peel bananas. Cut 2 bananas into ¼-inch slices, and mash remaining 2 bananas in a large mixing bowl. Stir sliced bananas into syrup, and set aside.

4. Combine flour, granulated sugar, baking powder, baking soda, cinnamon, and salt in a large mixing bowl. Whisk well. Add buttermilk, eggs, and remaining 4 tablespoons butter to bowl with mashed bananas, and whisk well. Pour liquid into flour mixture, and stir until just combined.

5. Place a griddle or 12-inch skillet over medium heat. Brush with oil. Pour ¼ cup measures of batter into the skillet, and cook for 1 or 2 minutes or until bubbles appear on the surface. Turn pancakes with a spatula and cook 1 or 2 more minutes or until pancakes are cooked through. Place pancakes on a baking sheet and keep warm in the oven. Repeat with remaining batter, brushing the griddle with oil between batches.

6. Serve immediately, topping pancakes with banana syrup.

Raspberry French Toast with Raspberry Sauce

This dish takes French toast to the next level by filling slices with fruity cream cheese.

12 slices *challah* **or other egg bread, sliced ½-inch thick**

4 large eggs

2½ cups whole milk

¾ cup granulated sugar

½ tsp. pure vanilla extract

¼ tsp. salt

1 (8-oz.) pkg. cream cheese, well chilled

3 cups fresh raspberries, rinsed

2 TB. unsalted butter, or as necessary

Serves: 6
Active time: 20 minutes
Start to finish: 25 minutes
Each serving contains:
630 calories
261 calories from fat
29 g fat
15 g saturated fat
19 g protein
75.5 g carbohydrates

1. Trim crusts from challah, and cut slices into a uniform shape. Arrange bread slices in a 9×13-inch baking pan, and set aside.

2. Whisk eggs in a large mixing bowl until frothy. Add milk, ½ cup sugar, vanilla extract, and salt. Whisk again, and pour liquid over bread slices in baking pan. Allow bread to soak for 5 minutes, turning slices occasionally with a slotted spatula.

3. While bread is soaking, cut cream cheese into 12 slices, and set aside.

4. Purée 1½ cups raspberries with remaining ¼ cup sugar in a blender or food processor fitted with a steel blade. Set aside.

5. Heat 2 tablespoons butter in a large, heavy skillet over medium heat. Remove 6 bread slices from liquid, and allow excess to drain back into the pan. Add slices to the skillet, and cook for 3 minutes or until lightly browned. Place 2 cream cheese slices on each bread slice, and top cream cheese with ¼ cup raspberries. Place remaining bread slices on top of raspberries, and press gently to enclose filling. Turn gently with a slotted spatula, and cook for an additional 3 minutes or until browned. (This may have to be done in batches if 6 slices cannot fit into the skillet. If so, keep the first batch warm in a 200°F oven while the second batch cooks.) Serve immediately.

Variation: No raspberries? Try blueberries, blackberries, or sliced strawberries instead.

Fast Talk

Challah is an egg-rich ceremonial Jewish bread served on the Sabbath and holidays. It has a light, airy texture and is traditionally braided into an oval loaf that tapers at the ends.

Potato, Onion, and Bacon Frittata

This combination of omelet additions comes from the Lyon region of France, and all the elements add great flavor to the dish.

Serves: 4

Active time: 20 minutes

Start to finish: 30 minutes

Each serving contains:

513 calories

335 calories from fat

37 g fat

19 g saturated fat

21 g protein

22 g carbohydrates

½ **lb. bacon, cut into 1-inch lengths**

2 large red-skinned potatoes, scrubbed and cut into ¼-inch dice

1 large onion, peeled and diced

1 garlic clove, peeled and minced

8 large eggs

¼ **cup half-and-half**

2 TB. chopped fresh parsley

Salt and freshly ground black pepper to taste

1. Preheat the oven to 425°F.

2. Place bacon in a 12-inch ovenproof skillet over medium-high heat. Cook for 5 to 7 minutes or until bacon is crisp. Remove bacon from the pan with a slotted spoon and set aside.

3. Discard all but 3 tablespoons bacon fat from the skillet. Add potatoes, and cook until tender, scraping them occasionally with a heavy spatula. Add onion and garlic to the skillet and cook for 5 minutes, stirring occasionally, or until onion is soft.

4. Whisk eggs with half-and-half and parsley, and season to taste with salt and pepper. Pour egg mixture into the skillet. Cook for 4 minutes over medium heat.

5. Transfer the skillet to the oven, and bake for 10 minutes or until top is browned. Remove the skillet from the oven, and run a spatula around the sides of the skillet and underneath frittata to release it from the pan. Slide frittata onto a platter, and cut it into wedges. Serve immediately.

Variation: You can substitute ham or sausage for the bacon, and ½ cup diced red bell pepper works well cooked along with the onion and garlic.

Speedy Solutions

If you have trouble separating individual slices of bacon when they're cold, here's an easy solution: peel off the total number of slices you need, and place the block into the hot pan. Within a few minutes, the slices will naturally separate due to the heat and then you can pull them apart with a meat fork.

Western Frittata

This is an easier version of a Western omelet—filled with a combination of ham, onions, and bell peppers—to feed a crowd in a hurry.

3 TB. unsalted butter

1 large onion, peeled and cut into ½-inch dice

1 red bell pepper, seeds and ribs removed, and cut into ½-inch dice

½ lb. baked ham, trimmed of all visible fat, and cut into ½-inch dice

8 large eggs

¼ cup half-and-half

Salt and freshly ground black pepper to taste

Serves: 4

Active time: 20 minutes

Start to finish: 30 minutes

Each serving contains:

321 calories

204 calories from fat

23 g fat

11 g saturated fat

23 g protein

7 g carbohydrates

1. Preheat the oven to 425°F.

2. Heat butter in a 12-inch ovenproof skillet over medium heat. Add onion and red bell pepper, and cook, stirring frequently, for 3 minutes or until onion is translucent. Add ham and cook for 2 minutes, stirring frequently. Remove the pan from the heat.

3. Whisk eggs with half-and-half, and season to taste with salt and pepper. Pour egg mixture into the skillet. Cook for 4 minutes over medium heat.

4. Transfer the skillet to the oven, and bake for 10 minutes or until top is browned. Remove the skillet from the oven, and run a spatula around the sides of the skillet and underneath frittata to release it from the pan. Slide frittata onto a platter, and cut it into wedges. Serve immediately.

Variation: Instead of ham, try it with cooked and crumbled bacon, sausage, or poultry sausage. You can sub mushrooms for the bell pepper, too.

Speedy Solutions

To save time when dicing ham, ask the deli clerk to cut the meat into ½-inch-thick slices. When you get home, all you have to do is stack them and they're ready to dice.

Vegetable Frittata with Pasta

This dish can easily be served room temperature on a picnic or at a brunch with a tossed salad.

Serves: 4

Active time: 25 minutes

Start to finish: 35 minutes

Each serving contains:

514 calories

247 calories from fat

27 g fat

8 g saturated fat

26 g protein

41 g carbohydrates

 **Fast Talk**

Al dente is Italian for "against the teeth" and refers to pasta (or another ingredient such as rice) that is neither soft nor hard, but just slightly firm when you bite it.

1 (6-oz.) pkg. fresh angel hair pasta, cut into 2-inch sections

4 scallions

3 TB. olive oil

2 small zucchini, trimmed and thinly sliced

1 garlic clove, peeled and minced

2 ripe medium tomatoes, cored, seeded, and finely chopped

3 TB. chopped fresh basil or 2 tsp. dried

1 TB. chopped fresh oregano or ½ tsp. dried

¼ cup sliced green olives

Salt and freshly ground black pepper to taste

8 large eggs

¾ cup freshly grated Parmesan cheese

2 TB. half-and-half

1. Preheat the oven to 425°F.

2. Cook pasta according to package directions until *al dente*. Drain and set aside to cool.

3. Rinse and trim scallions, discarding all but 2 inches of green tops. Cut scallions into thin slices.

4. Heat olive oil in a heavy 12-inch skillet over medium-high heat. Add zucchini, scallions, and garlic. Cook, stirring frequently, for 3 minutes or until zucchini is tender. Add tomatoes, basil, oregano, and olives. Cook, stirring occasionally, for 5 minutes or until liquid from tomatoes has evaporated. Season to taste with salt and pepper, and let cool for 10 minutes. (You can prepare this a day in advance and refrigerate, tightly covered. Before baking, reheat vegetables to room temperature in a microwave-safe dish or over low heat.)

5. Whisk eggs with Parmesan and half-and-half, and season to taste with salt and pepper. Stir in pasta, and pour egg mixture into the skillet. Cook for 4 minutes over medium heat.

6. Transfer the skillet to the oven, and bake for 10 minutes or until top is browned. Remove the skillet from the oven, and run a spatula around the sides of the skillet and underneath frittata to release it from the pan. Slide frittata onto a platter, and cut it into wedges. Serve immediately.

Baked Eggs with Herbed Cheese

Shirred eggs were the epitome of elegance in the Victorian era, and this easy recipe is an updated version.

3 TB. unsalted butter

½ cup heavy cream

12 large eggs

½ cup herbed chèvre or Boursin cheese

3 TB. chopped fresh chives or parsley

Salt and freshly ground black pepper to taste

Serves: 6
Active time: 5 minutes
Start to finish: 15 minutes
Each serving contains:
304 calories
235 calories from fat
26 g fat
13 g saturated fat
15 g protein
2 g carbohydrates

1. Preheat the oven to 450°F, and bring a kettle of water to a boil.

2. Divide butter and cream into the bottom of 12 (6-ounce) oven-proof ramekins. Break 1 egg into the center of each ramekin, and dot the top of each egg with 2 teaspoons cheese. Sprinkle eggs with chives, salt, and pepper.

3. Arrange ramekins in a baking pan, and pour boiling water into the pan so it comes halfway up the sides of the ramekins for a *bain marie*. Bake eggs for 7 to 10 minutes or until whites are set. Serve immediately.

Variation: Grated cheddar, dilled Havarti, or jalapeño Jack work well in this dish, too.

Fast Talk

Bain marie is the French term for a simmering water bath that cooks food gently. The water temperature is actually lower than the oven temperature, as water only reaches 212°F, so delicate egg dishes and custards set without getting rubbery.

Chapter 8

Convertible Cooking: Casual Meals for Brunch or Supper

In This Chapter

◆ Hearty hashes

◆ Fancy pancakes

◆ Filling pepper and other veggie dishes

◆ Egg additions

After you've cooked a recipe and liked the results, you're likely to want to cook it again. You've come to the right place, because the recipes in this chapter serve double duty on the brunch table or as a casual supper.

Brunch is the composite word for "breakfast and lunch" and is most often a savory dish that might or might not contain eggs. The same definition holds true for a casual supper. What changes are the side dishes for different times of the day.

Many dishes in this chapter are some sort of hash. *Hash* comes from the French *hacher*, which means "to chop." And what's chopped can range from standards such as corned beef and grilled chicken to succulent smoked salmon.

Brunch Bonuses

Think about the breakfast part of the day when planning for tag-alongs for brunch. Fruit salads are always welcomed, and beverages can be either fruit juices or juices blended with sparkling wine for a mimosa or wine and fruit for a version of sangria.

Breads and other side dishes should also carry on the early morning theme. Muffins, croissants, quick breads, and Danish pastries pair with coffee following or during the meal to anchor the dish to the early part of the day.

Don't feel obligated to make anything other than the main course yourself. After all, it's early in the day and there's bound to be a good bakery within a few miles.

Sides for Supper

The crunchy dinner side dishes could be a tossed salad or some sort of raw or cooked vegetable salad. Take a peek at the recipes for small salads in Chapter 11 for inspiration.

What to serve to drink? It is supper time, so the same wine or beer you'd serve with other meals would work here, too.

For dessert, anything goes. It can be a light fruit dessert from Chapter 20 or a rich chocolate concoction found in the pages of Chapter 21.

Southwest Sweet Potato Pancakes with Salsa Cream

Potato pancakes go from homey to haute when they're made with sweet potatoes and topped with spicy salsa.

4 large sweet potatoes (about 3½ lb. total), scrubbed and cut into 1-inch dice

1 medium onion, peeled and cut into 1-inch dice

2 large eggs

3 TB. all-purpose flour

½ cup chopped fresh cilantro

1 jalapeño chili, seeds and ribs removed, and finely chopped

1 TB. ground cumin

Salt and freshly ground black pepper to taste

½ cup vegetable oil

1 cup crème fraîche

2 cups Three Tomato Salsa (recipe in Chapter 18) or good-quality refrigerated salsa

6 sprigs cilantro for garnish (optional)

Serves: 6
Active time: 25 minutes
Start to finish: 25 minutes
Each serving contains:
432 calories
318 calories from fat
35 g fat
12 g saturated fat
6 g protein
26 g carbohydrates

1. Preheat the oven to 200°F, and line a baking sheet with aluminum foil.

2. Place 1 cup sweet potato cubes in a food processor fitted with the steel blade. Chop finely using on-and-off pulsing. Scrape potatoes into a colander, and repeat until all sweet potatoes and onion are finely chopped. (You can also do this through the large holes of a box grater.) Press on sweet potatoes and onion with the back of a heavy spoon to extract as much liquid as possible.

3. Whisk eggs, flour, cilantro, jalapeño, cumin, salt, and pepper in a large mixing bowl. Add sweet potato and onion mixture, and stir well.

4. Heat oil in a heavy 12-inch skillet over medium-high heat. Add batter by ¼-cup measures and flatten with a slotted spatula. Cook for 4 minutes or until browned and crisp. Turn gently with a slotted spatula and fry other side. Remove pancakes from the skillet and drain on paper towels. Place pancakes in the warm oven with the door ajar, and repeat with remaining batter.

5. To serve, spread tops of pancakes with crème fraîche and top with salsa. Garnish with cilantro sprigs (if using) and serve immediately.

Stale Stuff

When using a food processor for puréeing food, never fill it more than ⅔ way up so there's room for the food to move. When you're chopping food finely, it needs a lot more space than that. Don't fill it more than ¼ full.

Summertime Baked Eggs

A mélange of fresh vegetables form the base for baked eggs. Feel free to experiment with different vegetables.

Serves: 6

Active time: 18 minutes

Start to finish: 30 minutes

Each serving contains:

416 calories

290 calories from fat

32 g fat

12 g saturated fat

22 g protein

11 g carbohydrates

 Fresh Ways

When buying mushrooms, it's best to choose loose ones rather than prepackaged. Look for tightly closed mushrooms. If the brown gills on the bottom are showing, the mushrooms are past their prime.

½ lb. white mushrooms

¼ cup olive oil

2 TB. unsalted butter

6 scallions, rinsed, trimmed, and thinly sliced

1 red bell pepper, seeds and ribs removed, and chopped

3 garlic cloves, peeled and minced

6 ripe plum tomatoes, rinsed, cored, seeded, and chopped

2 tsp. Herbes de Provence

Salt and freshly ground black pepper to taste

12 large eggs

1½ cups grated Monterey Jack cheese

1. Preheat the oven to 350°F, and grease a 9×13-inch baking dish.

2. Wipe mushrooms with a damp paper towel. Discard stems, and slice mushrooms thinly.

3. Heat olive oil and butter in a medium skillet over medium heat. Add scallions, red bell pepper, mushrooms, and garlic. Cook, stirring frequently, for 3 minutes or until scallions are translucent. Add tomatoes and Herbes de Provence, raise the heat to medium-high, and cook, stirring frequently, for 5 minutes or until mixture has slightly thickened and liquid has almost evaporated. Season vegetables to taste with salt and pepper.

4. Spread vegetables in the baking dish in an even layer. Make 12 depressions in the vegetables with the back of a spoon, and break an egg into each. Sprinkle eggs with salt and pepper and sprinkle cheese over the top of eggs and vegetables.

5. Bake for 12 to 15 minutes or until eggs are just set. Serve immediately. (Vegetable mixture can be prepared 1 day in advance and refrigerated, tightly covered. Reheat over low heat before adding eggs and baking.)

Smoked Salmon Hash with Poached Eggs

"Cheating" by using frozen hash-brown potatoes gets this dish on the table fast—a boon to morning meals.

½ lb. sliced smoked salmon, cut into ½-in. strips

1 small red onion, peeled and finely chopped

¼ cup capers, drained and rinsed

⅓ cup sour cream

2 TB. prepared white horse-radish

2 TB. Dijon mustard

3 TB. unsalted butter

2 TB. olive oil

½ lb. (2 cups) frozen hash-brown potatoes

Salt and freshly ground black pepper to taste

12 large eggs, cold

2 TB. distilled white vinegar

Serves: 6
Active time: 20 minutes
Start to finish: 30 minutes
Each serving contains:
355 calories
222 calories from fat
25 g fat
9 g saturated fat
22 g protein
12 g carbohydrates

1. Combine smoked salmon, onion, capers, sour cream, horserad-ish, and Dijon mustard in a mixing bowl and set aside.

2. Heat butter and oil in a large, heavy skillet over medium-high heat. Add potatoes and cook for 10 to 12 minutes or until golden brown. Reduce heat to low, and stir in salmon mixture. Cook, stirring gently, for 2 minutes or until heated through. Season to taste with salt and pepper.

3. While potatoes are cooking, poach eggs. Bring a saucepan of water to a simmer and add vinegar. Break eggs, one at a time, into a custard cup or saucer. Holding the dish close to water's surface, slip egg into water. Cook eggs for 3 to 5 minutes, depending on desired doneness, keeping water at just a bare simmer. Remove eggs with a slotted spoon and place them in a bowl of cold water for 10 seconds to remove vinegar and stop the cooking. Place eggs gently on a kitchen towel to drain.

4. To serve, place a portion of hash onto each plate and top with 2 poached eggs. (Hash can be prepared 3 hours in advance and reheated gently over low heat. If you're not serving eggs imme-diately, leave them in cold water for up to 3 hours. Reheat eggs by holding them in simmering water in a slotted spoon for 20 seconds.)

 Fresh Ways

If you're not sure about the freshness of your eggs, float them in a bowl of cold water. Fresh eggs sink to the bottom of the bowl, because as eggs age, air pockets form that cause them to float. If the eggs are floating high on the surface of the water, it's best to get a fresh dozen.

Grilled Chicken Hash

The smoky nuances from the grilled chicken meld with the sweet flavor of caramelized onions to create a memorable dish.

Serves: 6

Active time: 20 minutes

Start to finish: 1 hour, including 30 minutes for marinating

Each serving contains:

436 calories

214 calories from fat

24 g fat

8 g saturated fat

27.5 g protein

28 g carbohydrates

4 (6-oz.) boneless, skinless chicken breast halves

⅓ cup olive oil

3 garlic cloves, peeled and minced

1 TB. herbes de Provence

Salt and freshly ground black pepper to taste

4 TB. unsalted butter

2 large sweet onions, such as Vidalia or Bermuda, peeled and diced

1 tsp. granulated sugar

1½ lb. red-skinned potatoes, scrubbed and cut into ½-inch dice

1. Light a charcoal or gas grill.

2. Trim any visible fat off chicken breasts and pound chicken between 2 sheets of plastic wrap to an even thickness of ½ inch using the flat side of a meat mallet or the bottom of a heavy skillet.

3. Place 3 tablespoons olive oil in a mixing bowl and add garlic, herbes de Provence, salt, and pepper. Add chicken breasts, turning them to coat with mixture. Marinate chicken for 30 minutes. Grill chicken for 3 or 4 minutes on each side or until cooked through and no longer pink. When cool, dice chicken into ½-inch pieces and set aside.

4. While chicken is marinating, heat butter and remaining olive oil in a large saucepan over low heat. Add onions, toss to coat with fats, and cover the pan. Cook over low heat for 10 minutes, stirring occasionally. Uncover the pan, raise the heat to medium, sprinkle with salt, and stir in sugar. Cook for 15 to 20 minutes, stirring frequently, until onions are medium brown.

5. Preheat the oven to 450°F, and grease a 9×13-inch baking pan.

6. While onions are cooking, place potato cubes in a large saucepan of salted water. Bring to a boil over high heat, and boil for 10 to 12 minutes or until potatoes are very tender when tested with the tip of a paring knife. Drain potatoes and mash roughly with a potato masher. Set aside.

⏱ Speedy Solutions

The smaller the cubes of hard foods like potatoes or carrots, the faster they cook. If you want to rush a recipe and it specifies potatoes that are quartered, feel free to cut them into smaller pieces.

7. Add chicken and onions to potatoes and mix well. Season to taste with salt and pepper. Spread hash into prepared pan, and bake for 10 minutes or until top is lightly brown. Serve immediately. (Hash can be prepared 2 days in advance and refrigerated, tightly covered. Reheat covered with aluminum foil for 10 minutes and then remove foil and bake for 10 more minutes.)

Variation: You can substitute diced cooked ham or roast beef for the grilled chicken—or any leftover roasted chicken.

Welsh Rarebit with Tomatoes and Bacon

Welsh rarebit is a traditional "high tea" meal for British laborers; it was their evening meal because lunch was the heavy meal of the day.

1 lb. bacon

3 large ripe tomatoes, rinsed, cored, seeded, and thinly sliced

Salt and freshly ground black pepper to taste

6 to 8 slices white or whole-wheat bread

1 (12-oz.) can lager beer

1 TB. prepared mustard, preferably English

2 tsp. paprika

½ tsp. cayenne

1 lb. (4 cups) sharp cheddar cheese, coarsely grated

1 TB. cold water

1 TB. cornstarch

Serves: 6
Active time: 15 minutes
Start to finish: 15 minutes
Each serving contains:
779 calories
543 calories from fat
60 g fat
27.5 g saturated fat
31 g protein
24 g carbohydrates

1. Place bacon in a large heavy skillet. Cook over medium-high heat, turning as necessary with tongs, for 5 to 7 minutes or until bacon is crisp. Remove bacon from the pan with a slotted spoon, and drain on paper towels.

2. While bacon is cooking, sprinkle tomatoes with salt and pepper, and set aside. Toast bread slices, and set aside.

3. Combine beer, mustard, paprika, and cayenne in a heavy 2-quart saucepan, and stir well. Bring to a simmer over medium heat.

Fresh Ways

Sprinkling tomatoes with salt and pepper in advance of eating them, even by a few minutes, increases the taste of the tomato. The salt absorbs into the fruit so it tastes succulent but not salty.

4. Add cheddar cheese to beer by ½-cup measures, stirring constantly with a whisk in a figure-eight pattern. Add additional cheese only after the previous addition is melted.

5. Combine water and cornstarch in a small bowl, and stir to dissolve cornstarch. Add to cheese mixture, and bring to a simmer, stirring constantly. Cook over low heat for 1 or 2 minutes or until thickened. Season to taste with salt and pepper.

6. To serve, place toast slices on individual plates and top with sliced tomatoes and bacon. Spoon cheese mixture over all, and serve immediately.

Variation: Sliced turkey, roast beef, or ham can be used in place of bacon.

Baked Macaroni and Cheese with Ham

If you omit the ham, this creamy mac and cheese becomes a side dish for 10 for any simple entrée.

Serves: 6
Active time: 15 minutes
Start to finish: 50 minutes
Each serving contains:
818 calories
354 calories from fat
39 g fat
24 g saturated fat
48 g protein
67 g carbohydrates

1 (1-lb. pkg.) elbow macaroni

4 TB. unsalted butter

4 TB. all-purpose flour

1 tsp. paprika

¼ tsp. cayenne

1 cup chicken stock

2 cups whole milk

1 lb. (4 cups) grated sharp cheddar cheese

1 TB. Dijon mustard

Salt and freshly ground black pepper to taste

1 lb. cooked ham, trimmed of fat and cut into ½-inch cubes

1. Preheat the oven to 400°F, and grease a 10×14-inch baking pan.

2. Bring a large pot of salted water to a boil. Add macaroni, and cook for 2 minutes less than the package directions indicate. Drain and set aside.

3. Melt butter in a saucepan over low heat. Stir in flour, paprika, and cayenne, and stir constantly for 2 minutes. Whisk in chicken stock, and bring to a boil over medium-high heat, whisking constantly. Reduce heat to low, and simmer for 2 minutes. Stir in whole milk and all but ½ cup grated cheese, stirring until cheese is melted. Stir in Dijon mustard, and season to taste with salt and pepper.

4. Stir ham and macaroni into sauce, and transfer mixture to the prepared baking pan. Cover with aluminum foil and bake for 10 minutes. Remove foil, sprinkle with remaining ½ cup cheese, and bake for 15 to 20 more minutes or until bubbly. Allow to sit for 5 minutes before serving.

Variation: Replace the ham with cooked sausage, chicken, or turkey, or make this dish vegetarian by using sautéed mushrooms and peppers instead of the ham and vegetable stock instead of the chicken stock.

 Fresh Ways

When pasta is going to be baked in a sauce after its initial boiling it's best to undercook it by a few minutes. It will absorb moisture from the sauce and finish cooking in the oven without overcooking.

Sausage and Pepper Hash

A dramatic way to serve this dish individually is in halved bell peppers that are blanched for 5 minutes before baking.

1½ lb. bulk pork sausage

10 shallots, peeled and minced

6 garlic cloves, peeled and minced

2 yellow bell peppers, seeds and ribs removed, and finely chopped

2 red bell peppers, seeds and ribs removed, and finely chopped

2 green bell peppers, seeds and ribs removed, and finely chopped

1 jalapeño chili, seeds and ribs removed, finely chopped

½ cup chopped fresh parsley

1 TB. chopped fresh sage or 1 tsp. dried

1 TB. fresh thyme leaves or 1 tsp. dried

1 TB. chopped fresh rosemary leaves or 1 tsp. dried

2 tsp. chopped fresh oregano or ½ tsp. dried

3 bay leaves

Salt and freshly ground black pepper to taste

12 large eggs

Serves: 6

Active time: 20 minutes

Start to finish: 45 minutes

Each serving contains:

580 calories

413 calories from fat

46 g fat

16 g saturated fat

31 g protein

11 g carbohydrates

1. Preheat the oven to 350°F.

2. Place a large skillet over medium-high heat. Add sausage, breaking up any lumps with a fork, and brown sausage for 5 minutes or until no pink remains. Remove sausage from the pan with a slotted spoon and set aside. Discard all but 2 tablespoons sausage fat from the skillet.

3. Add shallots, garlic, yellow bell peppers, red bell peppers, green bell peppers, and jalapeño to the pan. Cook over medium-high heat, stirring frequently, for 3 minutes or until shallots are translucent. Return sausage to the pan, and add parsley, sage, thyme, rosemary, oregano, and bay leaves. Simmer mixture over low heat, stirring occasionally, for 15 to 20 minutes or until vegetables are soft. Remove and discard bay leaves. Tilt the pan and skim off as much grease as possible. Season mixture to taste with salt and pepper.

4. Spread sausage mixture in a 9×13-inch baking dish. Make 12 indentations in mixture with the back of a spoon, and break 1 egg into each. Sprinkle eggs with salt and pepper, and bake for 12 to 15 minutes or until egg whites are set. Serve immediately. (Sausage mixture can be made 2 days in advance and refrigerated, tightly covered. Reheat over low heat or in a microwave oven before adding eggs and baking.)

Stale Stuff

Bay leaves have an extremely bitter flavor and should always be removed from a dish before serving. They're left whole when included in a recipe because it makes them easier to spot at the end.

Stuffed Peppers

Sausage in tomato sauce sits beneath a baked egg when these are brought to the table.

Serves: 6
Active time: 15 minutes
Start to finish: 35 minutes
Each serving contains:
302 calories
159 calories from fat
18 g fat
5 g saturated fat
22 g protein
15 g carbohydrates

6 small red, yellow, or orange bell peppers that sit evenly when placed on a flat surface

2 TB. olive oil

¼ cup Italian breadcrumbs

1 lb. bulk sweet Italian sausage

½ cup marinara sauce

1 TB. chopped fresh parsley

1 TB. chopped fresh basil or ½ tsp. dried

6 large eggs

Salt and freshly ground black pepper to taste

3 TB. freshly grated Parmesan cheese

1. Bring a large pot of salted water to a boil over high heat. Preheat the oven to 375°F, and grease a 9×13-inch baking pan.

2. Cut tops off peppers. Discard tops and seeds, and pull out ribs with your fingers. Boil peppers for 4 minutes. Remove from water with tongs and place upside down on paper towels to drain.

3. While peppers are blanching, heat olive oil in a heavy skillet over medium heat. Add breadcrumbs and cook, stirring constantly, for 2 minutes or until brown. Scrape crumbs into a small bowl, and set aside.

4. In the same pan, cook sausage over medium-high heat, breaking up lumps with a fork. Cook, stirring frequently, for 5 minutes or until brown with no trace of pink. Remove sausage from the pan with a slotted spoon, and drain on paper towels. Discard all grease from the pan. Return sausage to the pan, and add marinara sauce, parsley, and basil. Bring to a boil and simmer, stirring occasionally, for 2 minutes.

5. Place peppers in the baking dish. Evenly divide sausage mixture into the bottom of each pepper. Break 1 egg on top of sausage, and sprinkle eggs with salt and pepper, toasted breadcrumbs, and Parmesan cheese. Bake for 20 minutes, or until egg whites are set. Serve immediately. (Peppers can be prepared for cooking up to 2 hours in advance and kept at room temperature. Bake them just before serving.)

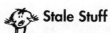 **Stale Stuff**

Green peppers are immature red bell peppers; they're less expensive because they're not as perishable to ship. Green peppers have a harsher flavor than their brightly colored cousins and should not be substituted.

Bacon, Egg, and Arugula Salad

Soft-scrambled eggs and crunchy bacon are tossed along with greens for this all-in-one meal.

Serves: 6

Active time: 20 minutes

Start to finish: 20 minutes

Each serving contains:

455 calories

368 calories from fat

41 g fat

14 g saturated fat

18 g protein

3.5 g carbohydrates

¾ lb. bacon

2 TB. unsalted butter

10 large eggs

⅓ cup sour cream

Salt and freshly ground black pepper to taste

6 cups arugula leaves, rinsed and stemmed

⅓ cup Balsamic Vinaigrette (recipe in Chapter 11)

1. Place bacon in a large, heavy skillet, and cook over medium-high heat for 5 to 7 minutes or until bacon is crisp. Drain and crumble bacon. Set aside. Pour bacon grease out of the skillet.

2. Melt butter in the same skillet over low heat.

3. Whisk eggs with sour cream, salt, and pepper. When butter has melted, pour eggs into the skillet and then cover the pan. After 3 minutes, stir eggs and cover the pan again. Cook for another 2 or 3 minutes or until eggs are ¾ set.

4. While eggs are cooking, place arugula in a salad bowl. Toss with Balsamic Vinaigrette. Add reserved bacon and hot eggs to salad bowl, and toss gently. Serve immediately. (Balsamic Vinaigrette can be made 2 days in advance and refrigerated, tightly covered.)

Speedy Solutions

An alternative to frying bacon is to bake it on a baking pan in a 325°F oven for 15 minutes or until crisp. The baking time depends on the thickness of the bacon.

Corned Beef Hash with Baked Eggs

Buying the corned beef precooked from the supermarket makes this hash that much easier to prepare.

1½ lb. red-skinned potatoes, scrubbed and cut into ½-inch dice

1 TB. unsalted butter

2 TB. vegetable oil

1 large sweet onion, such as Bermuda or Vidalia, peeled and diced

1 red bell pepper, seeds and ribs removed, and chopped

2 garlic cloves, peeled and minced

1½ lb. cooked corned beef, coarsely chopped

1 TB. fresh thyme or 1 tsp. dried

Salt and freshly ground black pepper to taste

6 to 8 large eggs

> Serves: 6
>
> **Active time:** 28 minutes
>
> **Start to finish:** 40 minutes
>
> **Each serving contains:**
>
> 535 calories
>
> 309 calories from fat
>
> 34 g fat
>
> 11 g saturated fat
>
> 31 g protein
>
> 25 g carbohydrates

1. Preheat the oven to 350°F. Grease a 9×13-inch baking pan.

2. Place potato cubes in a large saucepan of salted water. Bring to a boil over high heat, and boil for 10 to 12 minutes or until potatoes are very tender when tested with a knife. Drain potatoes and mash roughly with a potato masher. Set aside.

3. While potatoes are cooking, heat butter and oil in a large skillet over medium heat. Add onion, red bell pepper, and garlic. Cook, stirring frequently, for 10 minutes or until vegetables are soft. Add corned beef, mashed potatoes, and thyme, and mix well. Season to taste with salt and pepper. (You can do this a day in advance and refrigerate, tightly covered. Add 15 minutes to the initial covered baking if chilled.)

4. Spread hash in the prepared baking pan, and create 6 to 8 evenly spaced indentations in top of hash. Break 1 egg into each indentation, and sprinkle eggs with salt and pepper. Bake for 12 to 15 minutes or until whites are set. Serve immediately.

Stale Stuff _____

When making a dish that contains corned beef, ham, prosciutto, sausage, or any cured or spiced meat, use salt sparingly, if at all, because all these foods already have a high salt content. In a dish such as this one with potatoes, chances are you'll need to add additional salt, but that's not usually the case.

Chapter 9

Crusty Creations:
Hot Sandwiches and Quiches

In This Chapter

◆ Creative quesadillas

◆ Panini with panache

◆ Quick-cooking quiches

There's something so appealing about crunchy textures, be it from a sand-wich or an actual crust. And those are the recipes you'll find in this chapter. Hot sandwiches elevate everyone's favorite finger food into a more elegant meal, and you'll find ones made crisp by grilling and others that top toast with luscious sauces.

Egg custard tarts are usually lumped under the "quiche" moniker. They bake quickly and can be flavored in myriad ways. You'll find classic and contemporary fillings for quiches here, too.

Great Grill!

One of the greatest small appliances to come on the market in the past decade is the sloping double-sided grill. Boxing great George Foreman is famous in this field, although many companies now manufacture such grills. I love these grills for indoor cooking because they cook both sides at the same time, which cuts down on cooking time.

I've recently discovered how great these grills are for making sandwiches. There are some expensive panini presses on the market, but they're really superfluous unless you want every gadget in the aisle

Sophisticated Sandwiches

It used to be that quesadillas (*case-ah-DEE-yas*) were only found on Mexican menus; the word *quesadilla* comes from the Spanish word *queso*, which means "cheese." But that's all changed today. Quesadillas now mean any hot sandwich made in a flour tortilla.

While some recipes are fried, I prefer to bake them to cut back on the fat. If you don't want to wait for the stove to preheat, heat 2 tablespoons vegetable oil in a heavy 12-inch skillet over medium-high heat. Add the quesadillas, and cook for 2 minutes per side or until browned and the cheese has melted. Turn the quesadillas gently with a slotted spatula, and blot them with paper towels before serving.

If you've never heard of panini (*pah-NEE-nee*), you're missing out! You must acquaint yourself with these grilled Italian sandwich snacks that traditionally have stripe marks on both sides from the grill.

Quiche Quickie

Quiche (*KEESH*) originated in the Alsace-Lorraine region in northeastern France. The only common denominator to call something a quiche is that the base is an egg and cream custard and it's baked as an open-faced tart. Other than that, it's all up to you.

Fresh Ways

While quiches can be fully baked in advance and reheated, they look so pretty coming to the table lightly puffed right from the oven that it's a shame to miss that visual part of the experience.

One step you should not skip when making quiches is partially baking the crust before adding the filling. This ensures a crispy crust. You can pre-bake the pie shell and make the filling in advance, and relax during the final 30-minute-or-less baking time.

Quiches are done when the egg mixture no longer jiggles in any way and a knife inserted into the center comes out clean, without any egg particles clinging to it.

Eggplant and Red Pepper Panini

This healthful sandwich is reminiscent of eggplant Parmesan, with melted cheese layered with vegetables.

6 red bell peppers (or 6 jarred roasted red peppers)

6 Italian eggplant, rinsed, trimmed, and cut into ¼-inch slices

Salt and freshly ground black pepper to taste

½ cup olive oil

12 slices Italian bread, ¼ inch thick and 8 inches wide

¾ lb. thinly sliced fontina cheese

Serves: 6
Active time: 30 minutes
Start to finish: 40 minutes
Each serving contains:
661 calories
349 calories from fat
39 g fat
14 g saturated fat
25 g protein
59 g carbohydrates

1. Preheat an oven broiler. Place red peppers on the rack of a broiler pan and broil 4 inches from the broiler element until skin is charred and black. Turn peppers with tongs to char all sides. Plunge peppers into ice water, and when cool enough to handle, remove and discard cap, skin, and seeds. Slice peppers into thin slices, and set aside.

2. Season eggplant slices to taste with salt and pepper. Arrange slices on the rack of the broiler pan, and brush slices with olive oil. Broil eggplant for 3 minutes per side, turning gently with a slotted spatula. (You might have to do this in batches.) Remove eggplant from the broiler and set aside.

3. Preheat a two-sided grill (if using). Brush one side of bread slices with remaining olive oil. Place bread slices, oiled sides down, on the counter or a plate. Place half of eggplant slices on a slice of bread, and top with half of cheese, roasted peppers, remaining cheese, and remaining 2 bread slices, oiled sides up.

4. Grill sandwiches in a two-sided grill for 3 or 4 minutes or until bread is brown and cheese is melted. Alternately fry sandwiches for 3 minutes per side in a ridged grill pan or any large skillet, turning it once, weighted down by a pan. Cut sandwiches in half, and serve immediately.

 Fresh Ways

Like all fruits, eggplants have male and female gender, and the males are preferable because they are less bitter and have fewer seeds. To tell a male from a female, look at the stem end. The male is rounded and has a more even hole, and the female hole is indented.

Grilled Chicken, Sun-Dried Tomato, and Mozzarella Panini

Sun-dried tomatoes are a miracle food in the way they give foods an intense flavor without juice, so they're perfect for this sandwich.

Serves: 6

Active time: 25 minutes

Start to finish: 50 minutes, including 15 minutes for marinating

Each serving contains:

728 calories

360 calories from fat

40 g fat

12 g saturated fat

55 g protein

35 g carbohydrates

Speedy Solutions

As long as you're pounding chicken breasts, do a few extra. Freeze them flat, wrapping each one in plastic wrap and placing the group into a heavy resealable plastic bag. Pounded breasts defrost very quickly.

6 (6-oz.) boneless, skinless chicken breast halves

Salt and freshly ground black pepper to taste

½ cup olive oil

4 garlic cloves, peeled and minced

3 TB. chopped fresh rosemary or 2 tsp. dried

12 slices Italian bread, ¼ inch thick and 8 inches wide

¾ cup sun-dried tomatoes packed in olive oil, drained and chopped

¾ lb. fresh mozzarella, drained and sliced

1. Rinse chicken, pat dry with paper towels, and trim of all visible fat. Place chicken between two sheets of plastic wrap and pound to an even ¼-inch thickness. Place chicken on a platter, and season both sides to taste with salt and pepper. Combine ¼ cup olive oil, garlic, and 1 tablespoon rosemary in a small bowl. Rub mixture on both sides of chicken. Let chicken sit at room temperature for 15 minutes, covered with plastic wrap.

2. Preheat a grill or oven broiler. Grill or broil chicken for 4 minutes on a side, turning it gently with tongs, or until chicken is cooked through and no longer pink. Set aside.

3. Preheat a two-sided grill (if using). Brush one side of bread slices with remaining olive oil. Place bread slices, oiled sides down, on the counter or a plate. Place 1 chicken breast on a slice of bread, and top with ⅙ of sun-dried tomatoes, ⅙ of mozzarella, and remaining 6 bread slices, oiled sides up.

4. Grill sandwiches in a two-sided grill for 3 or 4 minutes or until bread is brown and cheese is melted. Alternately fry sandwiches for 3 minutes per side in a ridged grill pan or any large skillet, turning them once, weighted down by a pan. Cut sandwiches in half, and serve immediately.

Variation: This recipe works equally well with leftover roast chicken or a thin fish fillet such as sole or tilapia.

Cuban Quesadillas

The traditional combination of ham, pork, pickles, mustard, and Swiss cheese is the filling for these crispy sandwiches.

6 (10-in.) flour tortillas

6 TB. *Dijon mustard*

1 lb. thinly sliced roast pork

1 lb. baked ham

1 cup thinly sliced dill pickles

3 cups grated Swiss cheese

Vegetable oil spray

Serves: 6
Active time: 10 minutes
Start to finish: 20 minutes
Each serving contains:
662 calories
262 calories from fat
29 g fat
15 g saturated fat
49 g protein
52 g carbohydrates

1. Preheat the oven to 450°F. Cover 2 baking sheets with heavy-duty aluminum foil, and spray foil with vegetable oil spray.

2. Place tortillas on a counter. Spread Dijon mustard on each tortilla. Layer roast pork, baked ham, and pickle slices on one half of each tortilla. Sprinkle Swiss cheese over filling. Fold blank side of tortillas over filling, and press closed with the palm of your hand or a spatula. Arrange tortillas on prepared baking sheets, and spray tops with vegetable oil spray.

3. Bake quesadillas for 10 minutes. Turn them gently with a spatula, and press them down if the top has separated from the filling. Bake for an additional 5 minutes or until crispy.

4. Allow quesadillas to sit for 3 minutes and then cut each in half and serve immediately. (You can do this up to 6 hours in advance and refrigerate the quesadillas, covered with plastic wrap. Add 3 minutes to the baking time if chilled.)

Variation: Try thinly sliced chicken or roast beef instead of roast pork.

Fast Talk

Dijon mustard, known for its clean, sharp flavor, was actually invented in Dijon, France. It is made from a combination of brown and black mustard seeds, and the essential ingredients are white wine and unfermented grape juice.

Springtime Quesadillas

Have ham, hard-cooked eggs, and asparagus left over from Easter dinner? Here's a great way to use them up!

Serves: 6

Active time: 15 minutes

Start to finish: 25 minutes

Each serving contains:

576 calories

238 calories from fat

26.5 g fat

13 g saturated fat

37 g protein

48 g carbohydrates

Speedy Solutions

If you don't have any hard-cooked eggs in the house, pick some up at the supermarket salad bar. The salad bar is also a great place if all you need is a small amount of any ingredient contained in its bins.

1 lb. fresh asparagus spears

6 (10-in.) flour tortillas

4 oz. Boursin cheese with garlic and herbs, softened

1 lb. baked ham, thinly sliced

6 hard-cooked eggs, peeled and cut into 6 slices each

3 ripe plum tomatoes, rinsed, cored, seeded, and thinly sliced

Freshly ground black pepper to taste

1½ cups grated sharp cheddar

Vegetable oil spray

1. Preheat the oven to 450°F. Cover 2 baking sheets with heavy-duty aluminum foil, and spray the foil with vegetable oil spray. Have a bowl of ice water handy.

2. Break woody stems off asparagus, and place spears in a microwave-safe dish. Sprinkle with water, and cover dish tightly with plastic wrap. Microwave on high (100 percent) for 1 minute. Remove asparagus, cut slit in plastic wrap to allow steam to escape, and plunge asparagus into ice water to stop the cooking action. Drain, and set aside.

3. Place tortillas on the baking sheets, and spread Boursin on half of each tortilla. Layer ham, eggs, tomatoes, and asparagus on top of cheese. Season with pepper, and spread ¼ cup cheddar on each quesadilla. Fold empty half of tortillas over filled sides, pressing with the palm of your hand to seal tightly. Spray tops with vegetable oil spray.

4. Bake quesadillas for 5 minutes, turn gently with a spatula, and bake for 4 or 5 minutes more or until browned. Allow quesadillas to sit for 3 minutes and then cut into 2 or 3 wedges. Serve immediately. (Quesadillas can be prepared for baking up to 1 day in advance and refrigerated, tightly covered.)

Variation: Instead of ham, try this recipe with sliced turkey, chicken, or roast beef. Instead of cheddar, try Gruyère.

Tuna Melt with Olives

Mellow kalamata olives added to the tuna salad make this fast meal special.

3 (6-oz.) can light tuna, drained and flaked

¾ cup mayonnaise

3 celery ribs, rinsed, trimmed, and chopped

¾ cup pitted kalamata or other pitted brine-cured black olives, chopped

3 TB. chopped fresh parsley

2 TB. freshly squeezed lemon juice

Freshly ground black pepper to taste

6 slices rye bread, lightly toasted

1½ cups grated sharp cheddar cheese

Serves: 6
Active time: 15 minutes
Start to finish: 17 minutes
Each serving contains:
520 calories
315 calories from fat
35 g fat
11 g saturated fat
32 g protein
18 g carbohydrates

1. Preheat an oven broiler, and cover a baking sheet with heavy-duty aluminum foil. Combine tuna, mayonnaise, celery, olives, parsley, lemon juice, and pepper in medium mixing bowl. Stir well.

2. Place toast slices on the baking sheet, and divide tuna mixture among them. Spread tuna evenly, and top with grated cheese.

3. Broil sandwiches 6 inches from the broiling element for 2 minutes or until cheese is melted and bubbly. Serve immediately.

Stale Stuff _____

Due to the high amount of salt in canned tuna, plus the salt added to commercial mayonnaise, you shouldn't add salt to a tuna salad—at least before tasting it.

Kentucky Hot Brown Sandwich

This is a knife-and-fork sandwich with ham, turkey, and asparagus topped with a cheddar cheese sauce.

Serves: 6

Active time: 15 minutes

Start to finish: 20 minutes

Each serving contains:

548 calories

287 calories from fat

32 g fat

18.5 g saturated fat

41 g protein

24 g carbohydrates

6 slices thick white bread

1 lb. fresh asparagus spears

3 TB. unsalted butter

3 TB. all-purpose flour

1½ cups half-and-half

2 cups grated sharp or mild cheddar cheese

Salt and cayenne to taste

⅓ lb. smoked ham, sliced

3 cups shredded cooked turkey

3 ripe tomatoes, rinsed, cored, seeded, and sliced

¼ cup freshly grated Parmesan cheese

1. Preheat the oven broiler, and cover a baking sheet with heavy-duty aluminum foil. Have a bowl of ice water handy.

2. Toast bread slices and set aside.

3. Break woody stems off asparagus, and place spears in a microwave-safe dish. Sprinkle with water, and cover dish tightly with plastic wrap. Microwave on high (100 percent) for 1 minute. Remove asparagus, cut slit in plastic wrap to allow steam to escape, and plunge asparagus into ice water to stop the cooking action. Drain, and set aside.

4. Melt butter in a saucepan over low heat. Stir in flour, and cook *roux* for 2 minutes, stirring constantly. Whisk in half-and-half and bring to a boil. Simmer, stirring frequently, for 2 minutes. Stir in cheddar cheese until melted, and season to taste with salt and cayenne. Set aside.

5. Arrange toast slices on the baking sheet. Layer ham, turkey, tomatoes, and asparagus on top of toast. Ladle sauce over asparagus, and sprinkle with Parmesan cheese.

6. Broil 8 inches from the broiler element for 5 minutes or until bubbly and Parmesan is browned. Serve immediately.

Variation: Not a fan of asparagus? Try broccoli or cauliflower florets or green beans instead. Love Gruyère? Used it instead of cheddar.

Fast Talk

Roux (pronounced *ROO*, like in kangaroo) is a French term for a mixture of fat and flour used as a thickening agent for soups and sauces. The first step in all roux preparation is to cook the flour so the dish doesn't taste like library paste.

Grilled Reuben Sandwich

The combination of corned beef, sauerkraut, Swiss cheese, and Russian dressing is what defines a classic Reuben, named for a deli in New York.

1½ cups sauerkraut, drained

3 TB. unsalted butter, softened

12 slices rye bread or pumpernickel

¾ cup Russian or Thousand Island dressing

¾ lb. thinly sliced Swiss cheese

1 lb. thinly sliced corned beef

Serves: 6

Active time: 15 minutes

Start to finish: 18 minutes

Each serving contains:

717 calories

399 calories from fat

44 g fat

20 g saturated fat

41 g protein

40 g carbohydrates

1. Place sauerkraut in a large mixing bowl of cold water, and swirl it around well. Drain and repeat three more times. Press dry after the last draining, and set aside.

2. Preheat a two-sided grill (if using). Butter one side of each slice of bread. Spread Russian dressing on the nonbuttered sides. Layer the sauerkraut, Swiss cheese, and corned beef on 2 slices. Enclose filling by topping it with remaining bread slices, buttered side up.

3. Grill sandwiches in a two-sided grill for 3 or 4 minutes or until bread is brown and cheese is melted. Alternately, fry sandwiches for 3 minutes per side in a ridged grill pan or any large skillet, turning it once, weighted down by a pan. Cut sandwiches in half and serve immediately.

Fresh Ways

What most people find objectionable about sauerkraut is the salty brine in which it's pickled. By repeatedly rinsing it, you wash away most of this brine.

Crab Quiche

The sweet flavor of fresh crab is enhanced with fresh herbs in this easy and elegant recipe.

Serves: 6

Active time: 15 minutes

Start to finish: 40 minutes

Each serving contains:

564 calories

407 calories from fat

45 g fat

24 g saturated fat

21 g protein

18.5 g carbohydrates

Stale Stuff

Stay away from dried chives. Like parsley and cilantro, chives lose all flavor when dried. If you don't have fresh chives, you can always substitute finely chopped green scallion tops, but don't use dried chives.

1 (9-in.) pie shell, thawed if frozen

3 scallions

2 TB. unsalted butter

½ lb. crabmeat

3 large eggs

1¼ cups heavy cream

2 TB. chopped fresh chives

2 TB. chopped fresh cilantro

1 TB. chopped fresh rosemary or 1 tsp. dried

1½ cups grated Swiss cheese

Salt and freshly ground black pepper to taste

1. Preheat the oven to 400°F. Prick pie shell all over with the tines of a fork, and bake for 8 or 9 minutes or until pastry is set and just starting to brown. Remove crust from the oven, and set aside.

2. While crust is baking, rinse and trim scallions, discarding all but 2 inches of green tops. Slice scallions thinly. Heat butter in a small skillet over medium-high heat. Add scallions and cook, stirring frequently, for 4 minutes or until scallions are soft. Cool for 5 minutes.

3. Place crabmeat on a dark-colored plate. Rub it gently with your fingertips, and discard any bits of shell or cartilage you uncover. Set aside.

4. Reduce the oven temperature to 375°F. Whisk eggs with cream and add chives, cilantro, rosemary, and Swiss cheese. Season to taste with salt and pepper. Stir in crabmeat, fill pie shell, and bake quiche for 25 to 30 minutes or until it's browned and eggs are set. Serve immediately. (Filling can be prepared 1 day in advance and refrigerated, tightly covered. Add 5 to 7 minutes to the baking time if filling is chilled.)

Variation: Substitute diced cooked shrimp or chicken for the crab.

Herbed Sausage and Tomato Quiche

Now here's a hearty quiche with aromatic herbs, sweet tomatoes, and your choice of sausage that's sure to please any carnivore for supper as well as lunch.

1 (9-in.) pie shell, thawed if frozen

¾ lb. bulk pork sausage

3 garlic cloves, peeled and minced

2 shallots, peeled and minced

6 ripe plum tomatoes, rinsed, cored, seeded, and finely chopped, or 1 (14.5-oz.) can petite cut canned tomatoes, drained

1 TB. herbes de Provence

3 large eggs

1¼ cups heavy cream

Salt and freshly ground black pepper to taste

Serves: 6
Active time: 20 minutes
Start to finish: 45 minutes
Each serving contains:
588 calories
443 calories from fat
49 g fat
21 g saturated fat
15 g protein
22.5 g carbohydrates

1. Preheat the oven to 400°F. Prick pie shell all over with the tines of a fork and bake for 8 or 9 minutes or until pastry is set and just starting to brown. Remove crust from the oven, and set aside.

2. While crust is baking, place a large skillet over medium-high heat and crumble sausage into it, breaking up any lumps with a fork. Cook sausage, stirring occasionally, for 5 minutes or until sausage is brown and no pink remains. Add garlic and shallots, and cook, stirring frequently, for 3 minutes or until shallots are translucent. Add tomatoes and herbes de Provence, and cook, stirring occasionally, for 5 to 7 minutes or until tomato juice has evaporated. Cool mixture for 5 minutes.

3. Reduce the oven temperature to 375°F. Whisk eggs with cream, and season to taste with salt and pepper. Stir in sausage mixture, fill pie shell, and bake quiche for 25 to 30 minutes or until it's browned and eggs are set. Serve immediately. (Filling can be prepared 1 day in advance and refrigerated, tightly covered. Add 5 to 7 minutes to the baking time if filling is chilled.)

Variation: Try chopped ham or poultry sausage instead of pork sausage.

 Fresh Ways

All the quiche fillings in this chapter can also be used to make about 4 dozen mini-quiches for hors d'oeuvres. Use Athens Foods' prebaked phyllo shells (found in the freezer section of supermarkets), and bake the mini-quiches for 12 to 15 minutes or until the tops are browned.

Classic Quiche Lorraine

This bacon and cheese quiche is the one that started it all in France centuries ago.

Serves: 6

Active time: 15 minutes

Start to finish: 40 minutes

Each serving contains:

625 calories

496 calories from fat

55 g fat

25 g saturated fat

17 g protein

16 g carbohydrates

1 (9-in.) pie shell, thawed if frozen

½ lb. thick sliced bacon, cut into *lardons*

3 large eggs

1¼ cups heavy cream

1 cup grated Gruyère

Pinch ground nutmeg

Salt and freshly ground black pepper to taste

1. Preheat the oven to 400°F. Prick pie shell all over with the tines of a fork, and bake for 8 or 9 minutes or until pastry is set and just starting to brown. Remove crust from the oven, and set aside.

2. While crust is baking, place a skillet over medium-high heat. Cook bacon for 5 to 7 minutes or until crisp. Remove bacon from the pan with a slotted spoon, and drain on paper towels.

3. Reduce the oven temperature to 375°F. Whisk eggs with cream, Gruyère, and nutmeg and season to taste with salt and pepper. Stir in bacon, fill pie shell, and bake quiche for 25 to 30 minutes or until it's browned and eggs are set. Serve immediately. (Filling can be prepared 1 day in advance and refrigerated, tightly covered. Add 5 to 7 minutes to the baking time if filling is chilled.)

Fast Talk

Lardons (*LAHR-don*) is the French term for bacon that's been cut into pieces about the size of matchsticks. It's easiest to do if you buy thick-sliced bacon and then just cut it into very thin slices.

10

A Potpourri of Pasta and Pizza

In This Chapter

- ◆ Lightning-fast pasta recipes
- ◆ Easy vegetarian pastas
- ◆ Pizzas with panache

As long as you've got a few boxes of dried pasta in the pantry, dinner is a certainty. There's always something around in the cupboard or in the refrigerator to use as a sauce or toss. And as you'll see by the recipes in this chapter, sauces need not take hours to simmer away.

And then there's pizza. Making pizza at home is becoming almost as common as boiling a pot of pasta. And what you top your pizza with can be homey or haute—the choice is up to you. In this chapter, I give you some recipes that are sure to get you thinking about what else you can top your pie with.

Pasta Power

Good-quality dried pasta is made with a high percentage of high-gluten semolina, the inner part of the grain of hard durum wheat. The gluten gives the pasta resilience and allows it to cook while remaining somewhat firm, thus reaching the state of al dente.

Pasta is merely flour and water, so it's high in carbohydrates. The higher a pasta's semolina content, the more protein it contains. The protein in pasta is an incomplete protein, like that of rice, which can be completed by eating it with foods such as beans.

Eggless pasta contains little fat, and other nutrients are added if spinach or tomato flour is used. Each ounce of pasta is approximately 100 calories.

Perfect Pasta Tips

As a general rule, pasta imported from Italy is superior to American factory-made products due to its higher semolina content. Try to purchase pasta you can see through a cellophane window in the box. The pasta should be smooth and shiny, not crumbly.

Traditional dried Italian pastas are named according to their shape. For example, fusilli are twists, and fiochetti are bows. You could fill an entire kitchen with boxes of different-shaped pasta if you wanted a complete selection. Not many people have such a pantry luxury, so instead look at the cooking times and sizes in the following table to determine alternatives you might have on hand to make a recipe.

Fresh Ways

Store pasta in a sealed plastic bag after you open the box, and it will stay fresh for at least 6 months. You can still use pasta if it's stale; just add a few minutes to the cooking time.

Pasta	Cooking Time
Farfalle, fiochetti, fusilli, orecchiette, penne, rigatoni, ziti	10 to 12 minutes
Anelli, cavatappi, macaroni, manicotti, mostaccioli, orzo, rotelle	8 to 10 minutes
Fettuccine, linguine, spaghetti, tagliatelli	6 to 9 minutes

While the table serves as a guideline, each brand of pasta can vary slightly both in pasta composition and size. It's best to take the manufacturer's advice as to how long to cook each one.

Fresh from the Refrigerator Case

Until the past few years, it was rare to find fresh dough in supermarkets. Some pizza parlors might sell you a ball, or you could find frozen shells, which never really delivered the product you wanted.

But that's all changed today. In almost all cities, you can now purchase ready-to-bake balls of pizza dough. They're right there in the dairy case. Look for a brand made locally, and look at the condition of the ball. It should be shiny but not too puffy. If it shows signs of liquid inside the plastic bag, it means the dough might have been frozen, so don't purchase it.

With a few balls of pizza dough handy, any pizza can be on the table in less time than it takes to have one delivered!

 **Fresh Ways**

Pizzas are best if baked on pizza stones that have been heated in the oven as it preheats. A pizza pan that has holes in the bottom so the heat penetrates also yields a crispy crust.

Spaghetti with Escarole, Pine Nuts, and Raisins

Bitter greens, sweet raisins, and crunchy nuts blend masterfully in this quickly prepared dish.

Serves: 8

Active time: 25 minutes

Start to finish: 25 minutes

Each serving contains:

481 calories

164 calories from fat

18 g fat

3 g saturated fat

14.5 g protein

65 g carbohydrates

1¼ lb. spaghetti

½ cup golden raisins

1 lb. *escarole*

⅓ cup olive oil

½ cup pine nuts

4 garlic cloves

¼ cup dry white wine

¼ cup water

Salt and freshly ground black pepper to taste

¾ cup freshly grated Parmesan cheese

Fast Talk

Escarole is a member of the endive family of vegetables. It has broad, pale green leaves that are slightly curved, and it's more mild in flavor than Belgian or curly endive.

1. Bring a large pot of salted water to a boil. Add pasta and cook according to package directions until al dente. Drain, reserving ½ cup cooking liquid, and set aside.

2. Soak raisins in very hot tap water for 15 minutes and then drain and set aside.

3. Rinse escarole well, discard the core, and cut it into thin shreds. Set aside.

4. While water is heating, heat olive oil in a large, heavy skillet over medium heat. Add pine nuts and cook, stirring constantly, for 1 minute or until nuts are browned. Remove nuts from the skillet with a slotted spoon and set aside. Add garlic to the skillet and cook, stirring constantly, for 1 minute. Add escarole, wine, and water to the skillet. Stir well, cover the skillet, and cook, stirring occasionally, for 10 minutes or until escarole is soft. Season to taste with salt and pepper.

5. Add drained pasta to the skillet, and add some reserved cooking water if mixture seems dry. Cook for 2 minutes. Serve immediately, sprinkled with pine nuts. Pass Parmesan cheese separately.

Variation: For a little something extra, try adding about 1 pound sautéed Italian sausage or ground turkey to this recipe. Add it to the oil along with the garlic, and it will continue to cook from that point.

Pasta with Garlic and Oil
(*Pasta Aglio e Olio*)

This is a classic Italian recipe, and if you're a garlic fan, it's a natural for your repertoire.

1¼ lb. spaghetti or linguine

⅔ cup olive oil

10 garlic cloves, peeled and minced

2 to 3 tsp. crushed red pepper flakes

Salt to taste

¾ cup freshly grated Parmesan cheese

Serves: 8
Active time: 15 minutes
Start to finish: 15 minutes
Each serving contains:
462 calories
193 calories from fat
21 g fat
4 g saturated fat
12 g protein
55 g carbohydrates

1. Bring a large pot of salted water to a boil. Add pasta and cook according to package directions until al dente. Drain, reserving ½ cup cooking liquid, and set aside.

2. While pasta is cooking, heat olive oil in a heavy 12-inch skillet over medium-high heat. Add garlic and red pepper flakes. Reduce heat to low, and cook, stirring constantly, for 1 minute or until garlic is golden brown.

3. Remove the pan from the heat and add pasta. Toss well, adding some reserved cooking liquid if mixture seems dry. Season to taste with salt, and serve immediately, offering Parmesan cheese separately.

Speedy Solutions

Reserving some of the pasta cooking water is a traditional step in Italian cooking for pastas cooked in relatively dry sauces. It can moisten the sauce with the same innate flavor without making the dish taste "watery."

Fusilli with Porcini Puttanesca Sauce

There's a spicy bite to this hearty tomato sauce from Southern Italy.

Serves: 8

Active time: 20 minutes

Start to finish: 40 minutes

Each serving contains:

413 calories

89 calories from fat

10 g fat

2 g saturated fat

15 g protein

68 g carbohydrates

1¼ lb. fusilli

½ cup dried porcini mushrooms, chopped

1 cup boiling water

3 TB. olive oil

1 large onion, peeled and chopped

4 garlic cloves, peeled and minced

3 lb. ripe plum tomatoes, rinsed, cored, and chopped, or 2 (14.5-oz.) cans diced tomatoes, undrained

½ cup Niçoise olives, pitted and chopped

2 TB. tomato paste

2 TB. capers, drained and rinsed

2 TB. anchovy paste (optional)

2 tsp. dried oregano

2 tsp. dried basil

¼ tsp. red pepper flakes or to taste

Salt to taste

¾ cup freshly grated Parmesan cheese

 **Fresh Ways**

Any food that comes in a tube like anchovy paste or tomato paste can be hard to extract fully, even if you roll up the tube. One way to be sure you're getting it all out is to use a rolling pin on the metal tube before turning the tube forward.

1. Bring a large pot of salted water to a boil. Add pasta and cook according to package directions until al dente. Drain and set aside.

2. Soak mushrooms in boiling water for 10 minutes, pushing them down into the water with the back of a spoon. Drain mushrooms, reserving soaking liquid. Strain soaking liquid through a sieve or coffee filter and set aside.

3. While mushrooms are soaking, heat olive oil in a heavy 2-quart saucepan over medium-high heat. Add onion and garlic, and cook, stirring frequently, for 3 minutes or until onion is translucent. Add tomatoes, olives, tomato paste, capers, anchovy paste (if using), oregano, basil, and red pepper flakes. Bring to a boil over medium-high heat.

4. Add mushrooms and strained soaking liquid to the saucepan when available. Reduce heat to low, and simmer sauce, uncovered, for 20 minutes or until slightly thickened. Season to taste with salt.

5. To serve, top pasta with sauce and pass Parmesan cheese separately.

Linguine with White Clam Sauce

Garlic, herbs, and tomatoes join with clams and white wine in this light sauce.

1¼ lb. linguine

2 pt. fresh minced clams

¼ cup olive oil

2 large shallots, peeled and minced

6 garlic cloves, peeled and minced

1 (8-oz.) bottle clam juice

¾ cup dry white wine

¼ cup chopped fresh parsley

¼ cup chopped fresh basil

½ tsp. red pepper flakes or to taste

4 ripe plum tomatoes, rinsed, cored, seeded, and diced

Salt and freshly ground black pepper to taste

¾ cup freshly grated Parmesan cheese

Serves: 8

Active time: 15 minutes

Start to finish: 40 minutes

Each serving contains:

456 calories

94 calories from fat

10.5 g fat

2 g saturated fat

21 g protein

65 g carbohydrates

1. Bring a large pot of salted water to a boil. Add pasta and cook according to package directions until al dente. Drain, and set aside.

2. Place clams in a colander over a mixing bowl. Press with the back of a spoon to extract as much liquid as possible. Refrigerate clams if not using immediately. Reserve clam juice, and refrigerate it also if not cooking immediately.

3. Heat olive oil in a heavy 2-quart saucepan over medium-high heat. Add shallots and garlic, and cook, stirring frequently, for 3 minutes or until shallots are translucent. Add reserved clam juice, bottled clam juice, wine, parsley, basil, and red pepper flakes. Bring to a boil, stirring occasionally. Simmer sauce uncovered for 20 minutes or until reduced by half.

3. Add tomatoes and clams to sauce. Bring to a boil and simmer for 5 minutes. Season to taste with salt and pepper. Add pasta to sauce, and serve immediately, offering Parmesan cheese separately.

Variation: For red clam sauce, use red wine in place of white.

Fresh Ways

Clams cook so quickly that they should be added to dishes at the end of cooking time. However, a sauce should not be seasoned until after the clams are cooked because they give off liquid into the food.

Spaghetti with Egg and Bacon (*Pasta Carbonara*)

Recipes don't get any faster than this! And there's a lot of black pepper and Parmesan cheese, too.

Serves: 6

Active time: 15 minutes

Start to finish: 15 minutes

Each serving contains:

706 calories

337 calories from fat

37 g fat

14 g saturated fat

31 g protein

59 g carbohydrates

1 lb. spaghetti

¾ lb. bacon, sliced into ½-inch strips

6 garlic cloves, peeled and minced

Freshly ground black pepper to taste (at least 1½ tsp.)

6 large eggs, beaten

1½ cups freshly grated Parmesan cheese

Salt to taste

1. Bring a large pot of salted water to a boil. Add pasta and cook according to package directions until al dente. Drain and set aside.

2. Place bacon in a heavy 12-inch skillet over medium-high heat. Cook, stirring occasionally, for 5 to 7 minutes or until crisp. Remove bacon from the skillet with a slotted spoon and set aside.

3. Discard all but 2 tablespoons bacon grease from the pan. Add garlic and black pepper, and cook for 30 seconds. Return bacon to the pan and turn off heat.

4. Add drained pasta, and cook over medium heat for 1 minute. Remove the pan from the stove, and stir in eggs. Allow eggs to thicken, but do not put the pan back on the stove or they will scramble. Add cheese, and season to taste with salt and additional pepper. Serve immediately.

Stale Stuff

Don't pour bacon grease down the kitchen sink! Bacon grease is notorious for clogging kitchen plumbing, even if it's put down the sink with the hot water running. To better dispose of it, pour it in empty cans or half-pint cream containers after it's cool and dispose of it in the container.

Basic Pizza Dough

This is my favorite recipe, given to me years ago by famed chef Wolfgang Puck, and it's foolproof.

3 cups all-purpose flour

1 (¼-oz.) pkg. dry or fresh yeast

1 tsp. salt

1 TB. honey

2 TB. olive oil

¾ cup water

2 TB. yellow cornmeal

1. Place flour and yeast in a mixing bowl or the bowl of an electric mixer fitted with a dough hook. Add salt, honey, olive oil, and water, and mix well until dough forms a soft ball.

2. Transfer dough to a lightly floured surface and *knead* for 5 minutes or until smooth. Place dough in a buttered deep bowl and allow dough to rest, covered with a clean dry towel, for 30 minutes.

3. Preheat the oven to 450°F, and if using a baking stone or tiles, place them in the oven now.

4. Divide dough into 4 equal parts for individual pizzas, and roll each piece into a smooth, tight ball. Place them on a flat dish, covered with a damp towel, and refrigerate until baking time. For 1 large pizza, leave dough as a large ball. (This can be done up to 6 hours in advance, but dough should be removed from the refrigerator 1 hour before baking to reach room temperature.)

5. Lightly flour a work surface, and using the fleshy part of your fingertips, flatten each dough ball into a circle, approximately 6 inches in diameter, leaving the outer edge thicker than the center. Lift dough from the work surface and gently stretch the edges, working clockwise, to form 8-inch circles.

6. Sprinkle cornmeal on pizza paddles or baking sheets, and place pizza on cornmeal. Brush surface with olive oil, and top as desired.

7. Bake pizzas for 10 to 12 minutes, or as directed, until crust is golden brown and topping is bubbly.

Makes: dough for 4 (8-inch) pizzas

Active time: 15 minutes

Start to finish: 50 minutes, including 30 minutes for rising

Each serving contains:

411 calories

69 calories from fat

8 g fat

1 g saturated fat

10 g protein

76 g carbohydrates

Fast Talk

To **knead** is to work dough to make it pliable so it holds the gas bubbles from the leavening agent and expands when heated. Kneading is done with a pressing-folding-turning action. Press down into the dough with the heels of both hands and then push your hands away from your body. Fold the dough in half, give it a quarter turn, and repeat the process.

Pizza Margherita

This is a authentic Italian combination of mozzarella, fresh basil, and tomatoes.

Serves: 4

Active time: 10 minutes

Start to finish: 30 minutes

Each serving contains:

386 calories

252 calories from fat

28 g fat

10 g saturated fat

16 g protein

22 g carbohydrates

1 batch Basic Pizza Dough (recipe on previous page) or purchased pizza dough

½ lb. whole milk mozzarella cheese, thinly sliced

8 ripe plum tomatoes, rinsed, cored, seeded, and chopped

½ cup firmly packed fresh basil leaves

Salt and freshly ground black pepper to taste

4 TB. extra-virgin olive oil

2 TB. yellow cornmeal

1. Make Basic Pizza Dough according to recipe instructions.

2. Preheat the oven to 450°F, and if using a baking stone or tiles, place them in the oven now.

3. Shape pizza dough into 1 large round or 4 individual rounds. Cover with mozzarella and then tomatoes. Scatter basil over the top. Season to taste with salt and freshly ground black pepper, and drizzle 3 tablespoons oil over the top.

4. Sprinkle cornmeal on the baking sheet. Bake pizza for 10 minutes. Reduce the oven temperature to 400°F and bake for an additional 10 minutes or until crust is golden. Drizzle with remaining 1 tablespoon oil, and serve immediately.

Variation: Either fresh oregano or fresh chopped rosemary can be substituted for basil.

Fresh Ways

To ensure that the tomatoes don't create a soggy pizza crust, spin them in a salad spinner before placing them on the unbaked pie.

Smoked Salmon Pizza

This prebaked pizza crust is topped with a combination of succulent smoked salmon nestled on creamy sour cream. Try cutting it into small pieces for an hors d'oeuvre.

1 batch Basic Pizza Dough (recipe earlier in this chapter) or purchased dough

6 oz. sliced smoked salmon

3 TB. minced fresh chives

4 TB. extra-virgin olive oil

2 TB. yellow cornmeal

6 TB. sour cream

4 TB. golden *caviar*

4 TB. salmon caviar

Serves: 4

Active time: 10 minutes

Start to finish: 20 minutes

Each serving contains:

332 calories

233 calories from fat

26 g fat

6 g saturated fat

17 g protein

11.5 g carbohydrates

1. Make Basic Pizza Dough according to recipe instructions.

2. Preheat the oven to 500°F, and if using a baking stone or tiles, place them in the oven now.

3. Slice smoked salmon into thin strips, and set aside.

4. Knead 2 tablespoons minced chives into pizza dough. Shape pizza dough into 1 large round or 4 individual rounds. Brush center with olive oil.

5. Sprinkle cornmeal on baking sheet, and bake crusts for 8 to 10 minutes or until golden. Transfer pizzas to 4 serving plates. (Crusts can be baked up to 6 hours in advance. Reheat in a 400°F oven for 5 minutes.)

6. Spread crust with sour cream, and arrange salmon slices decoratively over top of sour cream. Place 1 tablespoon golden caviar in the center of each pizza, sprinkle salmon caviar around circumference, and sprinkle remaining chives over top of salmon. Serve immediately.

Fast Talk

Caviar is just fish roe (eggs from female fish) that's been pressed through a sieve and salted. When most people think of caviar, they're thinking of the eggs from three species of Caspian Sea sturgeon—beluga, osetra, and sevruga. But American golden whitefish caviar and the bright red eggs of salmon caviar are also authentic for those species.

Prosciutto Pizza

This is a robust recipe, with red bell peppers, basil, and two cheeses added to the Italian meat topping.

Serves: 4

Active time: 15 minutes

Start to finish: 30 minutes

Each serving contains:

895 calories

616 calories from fat

68.5 g fat

28 g saturated fat

48 g protein

25 g carbohydrates

 **Fresh Ways**

You can greatly reduce garlic's pungency if you blanch it a few minutes or roast it in the oven. Both methods of taming it render it sweet. With a few cloves it's easier to blanch; a whole head can be roasted in a 375°F oven for 30 to 45 minutes.

1 batch Basic Pizza Dough (recipe earlier in this chapter) or purchased pizza dough

4 garlic cloves, peeled

½ cup olive oil

2 red bell peppers, seeds and ribs removed, and thinly sliced

1 TB. crushed red pepper flakes

¾ lb. (3 cups) fresh whole-milk mozzarella, grated

¼ lb. (1 cup) fontina cheese, grated

½ cup chopped fresh basil

6 ripe plum tomatoes, rinsed, cored, and thinly sliced

6 oz. prosciutto, cut into fine julienne strips

1 medium red onion, peeled and thinly sliced

4 oz. (1 cup) fresh goat cheese, crumbled

1. Make Basic Pizza Dough according to recipe instructions.

2. Preheat the oven to 450°F, and if using a baking stone or tiles, place them in the oven now.

3. Bring a small saucepan of water to a boil over high heat. Add garlic cloves and blanch for 3 minutes. Drain, slice, and set aside.

4. Heat ¼ cup olive oil in a large skillet over medium-high heat. Add red bell peppers and cook, stirring frequently, for 5 minutes or until peppers are soft.

5. Mix remaining ¼ cup oil with crushed red pepper flakes, and set aside.

6. Combine mozzarella and fontina cheeses, and set aside.

7. Brush dough with pepper oil. Spread mixed cheeses on top, reserving 1 cup cheese and leaving a ½-inch margin. Sprinkle with basil, top with tomatoes, prosciutto, red peppers, red onion, and garlic. Dot with goat cheese, and finish by sprinkling with reserved cheese.

8. Sprinkle cornmeal on baking sheets. Bake pizzas for 15 to 17 minutes or until crust is golden brown and toppings are bubbly. Serve immediately.

Part 4

Salad Daze

Salad is synonymous with "fast and fresh cooking." In fact, *cooking* might be a misnomer; it's often fast and fresh *slicing* and *dicing!*

Two chapters in this part are for small salads that serve as an elegant touch if your entrée is something that's simple. There are small salads that could be served as appetizers or as a side dish, and there's a chapter of chilled salads made from carbohydrates, including new twists on old-fashioned pasta and potato salads.

The last chapter in this part is for main dish salads, which continue to grow in popularity because they combine so many colors, textures, and flavors of produce with proteins. You'll find options featuring all types of aquatic species as well as meats and poultry.

11

On the Side:
Small Vegetable Salads

In This Chapter

◆ Cooked and raw salads

◆ Crispy slaws

◆ Distinctive dressings

When the entrée is a simple grilled or broiled food, it's the little touches—like the salad—that give the meal style. You'll find recipes for just such salads in this chapter.

While we think of salads as a mélange of raw vegetables, that need not be the case. Some of the salads in this chapter are cooked and served either warm or at room temperature. Some star a certain food like cucumbers or cabbage, and a number mix a cornucopia of vegetables.

The chapter ends with some simple dressings that have delicious flavor and a fraction of the fat of conventional dressings. They're the salad equivalent of having your cake and eating it, too!

Olive Oil Savvy

Olive oil is made from ripe, crushed olives. Two types of olive oil are available commercially—extra virgin and pure. Extra-virgin olive oil is made from the first pressing of the olives, which have been cold pressed (no heat added) with no chemicals added to the mixture. Olive oil must have less than 1 percent acidity in most countries to be called extra-virgin.

Pure olive oil is a blend of virgin and refined olive oil, which is oil that's been extracted from the olives by means other than mechanical or physical. Olives that are damaged—bruised or too ripe—are mixed with chemicals such as caustic soda which generates heat and "cooks" the olives to remove characteristic bitterness and soften them.

Stale Stuff

Extra-virgin olive oil is sensitive to light and heat and should be in dark bottles, ideally with a coating. Do not buy olive oil that's been sitting on a shelf near a window exposed to light.

Extra-virgin olive oil is primarily a condiment and is used for dressings and other cold dishes. It is a waste of money to use it for cooking, plus some extra-virgin oils burn at a lower temperature than pure oils if they contain olive particles.

Store all olive oil in a cool, dark place away from heat. If a bottle is unopened, a wine cellar is the perfect storage spot. Refrigerating olive oil can extend its life, but the oil will become cloudy and solidify. It will liquefy again when warmed to room temperature.

Warm Vegetable Salad

A cornucopia of fresh vegetables are blanched and served warm in a light vinaigrette dressing.

2 medium tomatoes, rinsed, cored, seeded, and finely chopped

2 shallots, peeled and finely chopped

2 garlic cloves, peeled and minced

¼ cup freshly squeezed lemon juice

2 TB. chopped fresh parsley

1 TB. chopped fresh tarragon or 1 tsp. dried

1 TB. chopped fresh basil or 1 tsp. dried

Salt and freshly ground black pepper to taste

½ cup extra-virgin olive oil

¼ lb. green beans, rinsed, stemmed, and cut into 1-in. sections

1 carrot, peeled and cut into *julienne* strips

¼ lb. asparagus, rinsed, woody stems discarded, and cut into 1-in. sections

1 cup cauliflower florets

1 cup broccoli florets

6 leaves Boston or iceberg lettuce

Serves: 6
Active time: 10 minutes
Start to finish: 15 minutes
Each serving contains:
199 calories
171 calories from fat
19 g fat
3 g saturated fat
2 g protein
9 g carbohydrates

1. Bring a large pot of salted water to a boil, and have a bowl of ice water handy.

2. Combine tomatoes, shallots, garlic, lemon juice, parsley, tarragon, basil, salt, and pepper in a jar with a tight-fitting lid. Shake well, add olive oil, and shake well again. Set aside.

3. Add green beans, carrot, asparagus, cauliflower, and broccoli to boiling water. Cook for 3 to 5 minutes or until vegetables are crisp-tender. Drain, and plunge vegetables into ice water to stop the cooking action. Drain again, and toss with dressing. Arrange lettuce leaves on plates, and divide vegetable mixture into leaves. Serve immediately.

 **Fast Talk**

Julienne (*julie-EN*) is the French word for very thin sticks of vegetables that can cook very quickly. To cut a vegetable julienne style, first cut into long, thin slices, about ⅛ inch thick or smaller. Stack these layers, and cut into thin strips. Then cut the strips into any length, as determined by the recipe.

Stir-Fried Vegetable Salad

This salad has all the flavors of a traditional Chinese stir-fry including sesame, scallions, ginger, and soy sauce.

Serves: 6

Active time: 15 minutes

Start to finish: 30 minutes, including 15 minutes for chilling

Each serving contains:

169 calories

113 calories from fat

12.5 g fat

2 g saturated fat

5 g protein

11 g carbohydrates

¼ cup sesame seeds

1 bunch bok choy

½ lb. snow peas

½ lb. fresh shiitake mushrooms

2 TB. vegetable oil

2 TB. Asian sesame oil

3 garlic cloves, peeled and minced

2 TB. finely minced fresh ginger

4 scallions, rinsed, trimmed, and thinly sliced

½ cup oyster sauce

¼ cup vegetable stock

2 TB. soy sauce

2 TB. dry sherry

1. Place sesame seeds in a small dry skillet over medium heat. Toast seeds for 2 minutes, or until browned, shaking the pan frequently. Set aside.

2. Trim root end off bok choy, and separate head into ribs. Rinse ribs under cold running water and pat dry with paper towels. Slice ribs on the diagonal into ½-inch slices, and set aside.

3. Remove tips from snow peas, rinse in a colander, and set aside.

4. Trim and discard stems from shiitake mushrooms. Wipe mushroom caps with a damp paper towel, and set caps aside.

5. Heat vegetable oil and sesame oil in a wok or large skillet over medium-high heat. Add garlic, ginger, and scallions. Stir-fry 30 seconds or until fragrant. Add mushroom caps, and stir-fry for 2 minutes or until caps are soft. Add bok choy, and stir-fry for 1 minute. Add snow peas, and stir-fry for 1 minute. Add oyster sauce, stock, soy sauce, and sherry. Stir well and bring to a boil. Boil for 1 minute and then remove pan from heat.

6. Transfer vegetables to a mixing bowl or serving dish with a slotted spoon. Chill for at least 15 minutes to reach room temperature, or refrigerate, tightly covered, and serve chilled. Sprinkle vegetables with toasted sesame seeds just before serving. (Salad can be prepared up to 1 day in advance and refrigerated, tightly covered.)

 Fresh Ways

Store wild mushrooms, such as fresh shiitakes, in a paper bag rather than a plastic bag. Plastic causes mushrooms to become moist and soggy. You could also line a bowl with paper towels, add the mushrooms, and then cover the bowl with more paper towels.

Green Bean and Tomato Salad

Here, bright green beans and vivid red tomatoes are tossed with a creamy dressing. This salad can also be served for summer picnics.

2 garlic cloves, peeled and minced

½ cup sour cream

2 TB. freshly squeezed lemon juice

1 TB. dry mustard

1 tsp. granulated sugar

Salt and freshly ground black pepper to taste

1 lb. green beans, rinsed, stemmed, and cut into 2-in. segments

1 pt. cherry tomatoes, rinsed, stemmed, and halved

Serves: 6
Active time: 15 minutes
Start to finish: 15 minutes
Each serving contains:
80 calories
33 calories from fat
4 g fat
2 g saturated fat
3 g protein
11 g carbohydrates

1. Bring a large pot of salted water to a boil, and have a bowl of ice water handy.

2. Combine garlic, sour cream, lemon juice, mustard, sugar, salt, and pepper in a jar with a tight-fitting lid. Shake well, and set aside.

3. Add green beans to boiling water. Cook for 3 to 5 minutes or until crisp-tender. Drain and plunge vegetables into ice water to stop the cooking action. Drain again, and place beans in a mixing bowl. Add tomatoes, toss with dressing, and serve immediately.

Variation: For a dish lower in fat and calories, use plain nonfat yogurt instead of sour cream.

Fresh Ways

To make this salad into a kaleidoscope of color, use yellow and orange cherry tomatoes as well as red ones. These bright tomatoes are becoming more available in supermarkets as well as farmers' markets.

Asian Eggplant Salad

Baked eggplant is moistened with a sesame seed dressing in this easy salad.

Serves: 4

Active time: 10 minutes

Start to finish: 25 minutes

Each serving contains:

316 calories

263 calories from fat

29 g fat

4 g saturated fat

4 g protein

14 g carbohydrates

---

4 to 6 Japanese eggplants (about 1¼ lb. total)

3 TB. vegetable oil

Salt and freshly ground black pepper to taste

¼ cup sesame seeds

2 TB. soy sauce

2 garlic cloves, peeled and minced

1 tsp. granulated sugar

2 TB. Asian sesame oil

2 TB. extra-virgin olive oil

¼ tsp. hot red pepper sauce

4 to 6 cups salad greens, rinsed and dried

1. Preheat the oven to 400°F, and cover 2 baking sheets with heavy-duty aluminum foil.

2. Cut eggplants into ¼-inch slices. Spread vegetable oil on baking sheets, and arrange eggplant slices. Sprinkle with salt and pepper. Bake eggplants for 15 to 20 minutes or until soft.

3. While eggplants are baking, place sesame seeds in a small dry skillet over medium heat. Toast seeds for 2 minutes or until browned, shaking the pan frequently. Set aside.

4. Combine soy sauce, garlic, and sugar in a jar with a tight-fitting lid. Shake well, add sesame oil, olive oil, and hot red pepper sauce and shake well again. Set aside.

5. Arrange salad greens on serving plates, and top with warm eggplant slices. Drizzle with dressing, sprinkle with sesame seeds, and serve immediately.

Stale Stuff

Don't use salt in a dressing that contains soy sauce. The soy sauce is very high in sodium and serves the same purpose.

Tomato and Mozzarella Salad with Oregano

This salad with aromatic oregano, delicate cheese, and vivid tomatoes is a variation on the Italian classic *caprese* and is great for a buffet, as it uses small cherry tomatoes.

2 pt. cherry tomatoes, rinsed, stemmed, and halved

Salt and freshly ground black pepper to taste

1 lb. fresh mozzarella cheese, drained and cut into ½-inch dice

3 TB. chopped fresh oregano

2 TB. capers, drained and rinsed

¼ cup balsamic vinegar

¼ cup extra-virgin olive oil

Serves: 6
Active time: 10 minutes
Start to finish: 20 minutes, including 10 minutes for chilling
Each serving contains:
348 calories
239 calories from fat
27 g fat
11 g saturated fat
18 g protein
10.5 g carbohydrates

1. Place cherry tomatoes in a mixing bowl and sprinkle with salt and pepper. Refrigerate for 10 minutes. Drain tomatoes and return them to the mixing bowl.

2. Add mozzarella, oregano, and capers to tomatoes. Sprinkle salad with vinegar and oil, and toss well. Serve immediately.

Variation: The traditional way to make this salad is with basil, and it can be substituted for oregano.

Fresh Ways

Fresh mozzarella is very perishable, and the best way to keep it fresh is to change the water that covers it daily. The same process will prolong the freshness of tofu.

Fennel Salad

Fresh fennel has the crunch of celery with a light taste of licorice, and it's dressed simply in this easy salad.

Serves: 6

Active time: 10 minutes

Start to finish: 10 minutes

Each serving contains:

134 calories

113 calories from fat

12.5 g fat

2 g saturated fat

1 g protein

7 g carbohydrates

2 fennel bulbs, well chilled

¼ cup chopped fresh parsley

⅓ cup extra-virgin olive oil

3 TB. freshly squeezed lemon juice

2 tsp. anchovy paste, or ½ tsp. salt

2 garlic cloves, peeled and minced

Freshly ground black pepper to taste

1. Trim stalks and root ends from fennel bulbs. Slice fennel using a thin slicing disc of a food processor, or a very sharp knife. Place fennel in a salad bowl, and toss with parsley.

2. Place olive oil, lemon juice, anchovy paste, garlic, and pepper in a jar with a tight-fitting lid and shake well.

3. Toss dressing with fennel, and serve immediately.

Fresh Ways

This salad uses the bulb of the fennel, so save the stalks and use them as an alternative to celery in chicken and tuna salad.

Three-Pepper Gazpacho Salad

Imagine all the healthful vegetables used to make gazpacho soup tossed in a salad bowl.

2 red bell peppers, seeds and ribs removed, and thinly sliced

2 yellow bell peppers, seeds and ribs removed, and thinly sliced

1 green bell pepper, seeds and ribs removed, and thinly sliced

⅓ cup chopped red onion

2 medium cucumbers, rinsed, seeded, and thinly sliced

1 pt. cherry tomatoes, rinsed, stemmed, and halved

2 garlic cloves, peeled and minced

¼ cup chopped fresh cilantro

¼ cup balsamic vinegar

Salt and cayenne to taste

⅓ cup extra-virgin olive oil

Serves: 6

Active time: 15 minutes

Start to finish: 30 minutes, including 15 minutes for chilling

Each serving contains:

178 calories

116 calories from fat

13 g fat

2 g saturated fat

2 g protein

16 g carbohydrates

1. Combine red bell peppers, yellow bell peppers, green bell pepper, onion, cucumbers, and tomatoes in a large mixing bowl.

2. Combine garlic, cilantro, vinegar, salt, and cayenne in a jar with a tight-fitting lid. Shake well, add olive oil, and shake well again.

3. Toss salad with dressing, and refrigerate for 15 minutes. Serve well chilled.

Speedy Solutions

Save time by buying English cucumbers rather than conventional ones. The seeds are so small that seeding them isn't really necessary. They're larger, so 1 English cucumber is the equivalent of 1½ to 2 conventional ones.

Black Bean and Papaya Salad

Colorful, sweet ripe papaya and earthy black beans are a great combination in a dressing with Caribbean flavors.

Serves: 6

Active time: 15 minutes

Start to finish: 15 minutes

Each serving contains:

258 calories

114 calories from fat

13 g fat

2 g saturated fat

6 g protein

32 g carbohydrates

Fast Talk

Jicama (*HEE-kam-ah*) is a root vegetable with crunchy flesh that tastes reminiscent of an apple. It's covered with a thin brown skin that should be peeled just prior to cutting it.

2 (15-oz.) cans black beans, drained and rinsed

1 ripe papaya, peeled, seeded, and cut into ½-inch dice

1 medium *jicama*, peeled and cut into ½-inch dice

½ red bell pepper, seeds and ribs removed, and cut into ½-inch dice

¼ cup chopped fresh cilantro

3 garlic cloves, peeled and minced

3 shallots, peeled and chopped

1 tsp. ground cumin

¼ tsp. ground cinnamon

⅓ cup freshly squeezed orange juice

3 TB. freshly squeezed lime juice

3 TB. sherry vinegar

Salt and cayenne to taste

⅓ cup olive oil

1. Combine beans, papaya, jicama, red bell pepper, and cilantro in a mixing bowl.

2. Combine garlic, shallots, cumin, cinnamon, orange juice, lime juice, vinegar, salt, and cayenne in a jar with a tight-fitting lid. Shake well, add olive oil, and shake well again.

3. Toss salad with dressing, and refrigerate salad for at least 15 minutes before serving. (Salad can be made 1 day in advance and refrigerated, tightly covered.)

Variation: For some substitutions, try mango instead of papaya and white beans instead of black beans.

Gingered Asian Red Cabbage Slaw

This colorful slaw is dotted with golden raisins in an easy sweet and sour dressing.

½ cup golden raisins

1 (2-lb.) head red cabbage, cored and shredded

2 carrots, peeled and grated

½ red onion, peeled and thinly sliced

2 TB. grated fresh ginger

¾ cup cider vinegar

2 TB. honey

3 TB. vegetable oil

Salt and freshly ground black pepper to taste

3 scallions, rinsed, trimmed with all but 2 inches of green tops discarded, and thinly sliced

Serves: 6

Active time: 15 minutes

Start to finish: 45 minutes, including 30 minutes for marinating

Each serving contains:

183 calories

67 calories from fat

7.5 g fat

1 g saturated fat

4 g protein

29 g carbohydrates

1. Place raisins in a mixing bowl and cover with very hot tap water. Allow raisins to plump for 15 minutes. Drain, and set aside.

2. Combine cabbage, carrots, and onion in a vegetable steamer over boiling water. Steam for 5 minutes, drain, and place in a glass or stainless-steel bowl.

3. Combine ginger, vinegar, honey, oil, salt, and pepper in a jar with a tight-fitting lid. Shake well, and pour dressing over steamed vegetables. Add raisins and scallions, and marinate at room temperature for at least 30 minutes, tossing occasionally. (Slaw can be made 1 day in advance and refrigerated, tightly covered.)

Fresh Ways

Slaw always tastes better if the cabbage has been wilted in some way to lose its bitterness. In this case, it's steamed and then tossed with a room temperature dressing, but an alternative, as in the next recipe, is to pour hot dressing over cold cabbage.

Dilled Cucumbers

Mild rice wine vinegar creates a delicate pickling for these healthful cucumbers.

Serves: 6

Active time: 10 minutes

Start to finish: 2 hours, 10 minutes, including 2 hours for marinating

Each serving contains:

66 calories

2 calories from fat

0 g fat

0 g saturated fat

11 g protein

13 g carbohydrates

3 medium cucumbers, rinsed, seeded, and thinly sliced

½ large sweet onion, such as Vidalia or Bermuda, peeled and thinly sliced

1 cup rice wine vinegar

3 TB. chopped fresh dill

2 TB. granulated sugar

Salt and freshly ground white pepper to taste

1. Combine cucumbers and onion in a heavy resealable plastic bag.

2. Combine vinegar, dill, sugar, salt, and pepper in a jar with a tight-fitting lid. Shake well to dissolve sugar.

3. Add cucumbers and onion to dressing, and marinate for at least 2 hours, refrigerated.

4. Drain salad from marinade, and serve chilled. (Salad can be made up to 2 days in advance and refrigerated, tightly covered.)

Variation: You can use zucchini or yellow squash in place of cucumbers. They need to marinate for 3 hours.

Stale Stuff

All rice wine vinegar is not created equal. Some have been seasoned and are sometimes referred to as "sushi vinegar." That's not what you want. Always be sure you see "unseasoned" on the label if you plan on cooking with it.

Thai Cucumber Salad

If you like spicy food, this is the dish for you, with lots of red pepper in the pickling liquid.

¾ cup distilled white vinegar

¼ cup firmly packed light brown sugar

1 TB. fish sauce (*nam pla*)

1 to 2 tsp. crushed red pepper

3 medium cucumbers, rinsed, halved, seeded, and thinly sliced

3 plum tomatoes, cored, seeded, and diced

Serves: 6
Active time: 10 minutes
Start to finish: 2½ hours, including 2 hours, 20 minutes for marinating
Each serving contains:
73 calories
4 calories from fat
0 g fat
0 g saturated fat
2 g protein
17.5 g carbohydrates

1. Combine vinegar, brown sugar, fish sauce, and red pepper in a heavy resealable plastic bag. Mix well to dissolve sugar.

2. Add cucumbers, and marinate for 2 hours, refrigerated. Add tomatoes, and marinate an additional 20 minutes.

3. Drain salad from marinade, and serve chilled. (Salad can be made up to 2 days in advance and refrigerated, tightly covered.)

Variation: Instead of cucumbers, try zucchini or yellow squash. And then up the marinade time to 3 hours.

Fast Talk

Fish sauce (nam pla), a salty sauce with an extremely pungent odor, is made from fermented fish. It's used as a dipping sauce/condiment and seasoning ingredient throughout Southeast Asia. *Nam pla* is the Thai term; it's known as *nuoc nam* in Vietnam and *shottsuru* in Japan.

Pear Dressing

Luscious ripe pears and cashew nuts give this dressing a creamy appearance.

Makes: 8 (2-ounce) servings

Active time: 10 minutes

Start to finish: 10 minutes

Each serving contains:

175 calories

147 calories from fat

16 g fat

2 g saturated fat

1 g protein

8 g carbohydrates

2 ripe pears, peeled, cored, and diced

¼ cup unsalted cashews

5 TB. raspberry vinegar

⅓ cup vegetable oil

3 TB. walnut oil

1 TB. Dijon mustard

2 sprigs parsley

1 TB. fresh thyme or 1 tsp. dried

Salt and freshly ground black pepper to taste

1. Combine pears, cashews, vinegar, vegetable oil, walnut oil, Dijon mustard, parsley, thyme, salt, and pepper in a blender or food processor fitted with a steel blade. Purée until smooth.

2. Transfer dressing to a container, and refrigerate for up to 5 days.

Fresh Ways

While pears, like apples and bananas, discolor when exposed to the air, there's no need to rub them with lemon juice for use in this recipe. The vinegar in the dressing serves that purpose.

Balsamic Vinaigrette

Sweet fresh orange juice cuts the acidity of the vinegar in this great all-purpose dressing.

½ cup freshly squeezed orange juice

6 TB. *balsamic vinegar*

4 TB. freshly squeezed lemon juice

1 TB. chopped fresh oregano or ½ tsp. dried

Salt and freshly ground black pepper to taste

⅓ cup extra-virgin olive oil

1. Combine orange juice, vinegar, lemon juice, oregano, salt, and pepper in a jar with a tight-fitting lid. Shake well, add olive oil, and shake well again. Refrigerate for up to 5 days.

Fast Talk

Balsamic vinegar is traditionally made from white Trebbiano grapes grown in the Modena region of Italy. It gets its rich, dark color and mellow flavor from being aged for many years in wooden barrels, similar to aging a wine.

> Makes: 6 (2-ounce) servings
>
> **Active time:** 5 minutes
>
> **Start to finish:** 5 minutes
>
> **Each serving contains:**
>
> 131 calories
>
> 105 calories from fat
>
> 12 g fat
>
> 2 g saturated fat
>
> 0 g protein
>
> 7 g carbohydrates

Sesame Ginger Dressing

This flavorful dressing can also be used as a marinade for meats, chicken, or seafood.

¼ cup sesame seeds

½ cup rice wine vinegar

3 TB. grated fresh ginger

2 garlic cloves, peeled and minced

2 TB. soy sauce

2 TB. hoisin sauce

1 TB. dry sherry

Red pepper flakes to taste

¼ cup Asian sesame oil

3 TB. vegetable oil

1. Place sesame seeds in a small dry skillet over medium heat. Toast seeds for 2 minutes, or until browned, shaking the pan frequently. Set aside.

> Makes: 6 (2-ounce) servings
>
> **Active time:** 8 minutes
>
> **Start to finish:** 8 minutes
>
> **Each serving contains:**
>
> 206 calories
>
> 173 calories from fat
>
> 19 g fat
>
> 3 g saturated fat
>
> 2 g protein
>
> 6 g carbohydrates

2. Combine sesame seeds, vinegar, ginger, garlic, soy sauce, hoisin sauce, sherry, and red pepper flakes in a jar with a tight-fitting lid. Shake well, add sesame oil and vegetable oil, and shake well again. Refrigerate for up to 5 days.

Fresh Ways

An easy way to peel fresh ginger without losing a lot of its flesh is with the edge of a measuring spoon. The thin brown skin scrapes off easily.

Celery Seed Dressing

The distinctive flavor of celery seeds blends well with fruity raspberry vinegar and honey in this dressing.

Makes: 6 (2-ounce) servings

Active time: 5 minutes

Start to finish: 5 minutes

Each serving contains:

185 calories

115 calories from fat

13 g fat

2 g saturated fat

1 g protein

18 g carbohydrates

½ **cup raspberry vinegar**

⅓ **cup vegetable stock**

¼ **cup honey**

2 TB. **celery seed**

Salt and freshly ground black pepper to taste

⅓ **cup vegetable oil**

1. Combine vinegar, stock, honey, celery seed, salt, and pepper in a jar with a tight-fitting lid. Shake well, add oil, and shake well again. Refrigerate for up to 5 days.

Speedy Solutions

If you coat a measuring spoon or measuring cup with vegetable oil spray, sticky ingredients like honey or molasses won't stick to it.

Cold Carb Salads

In This Chapter

- ◆ Chilly pastas
- ◆ Cold Asian rice dishes
- ◆ Super spuds

Salads don't only encompass leafy green things, as you see when cooking the recipes in this chapter. All these frosty side dishes are made with carbohydrates flavored in myriad ways. For example, potato salad is an all-American summer favorite, but it can be made with European flair as well. And rice, native to Asia, takes on Asian seasonings for this group of yummy recipes. And of course, no roster of cold carbs would be complete without some pastas added.

Whether you're looking for a salad to take to a pitch-in or something for your dinner table, you'll find the salad in this chapter.

Rice Size Specifics

Rice is classified by the length of individual grains. Perhaps the most popular is white long-grain rice, in which the length of the grain is four or five times the size of the width. When cooked, it produces light, dry grains that separate easily.

Along with white long-grain rice, other species are popular:

Basmati and *jasmine rice* are both long-grain varieties from Asia and produce an aromatic fragrance when cooked. The aroma is created by a high concentration of acetyl pyroline, a compound naturally found in all rice.

Brown rice is the entire grain with only the inedible outer husk removed. The nutritious, high-fiber bran coating gives it a light tan color, nutlike flavor, and chewy texture. The presence of the bran means brown rice is subject to rancidity, which limits its shelf life to only about 6 months. It also takes slightly longer to cook (up to 50 minutes total) than regular white long-grain rice.

Arborio rice, almost all of which is imported from Italy, is a medium-grain rice (a softer rice that is two to three times as long as it is wide). Arborio rice has a high starch content. This natural carbohydrate is released as the rice is stirred to create a creamy texture in risotto dishes.

Potato Pointers

Potatoes are tubers, which are the swellings of the root of the plant, which is why they're so nutritious. It's in the roots that the plant's valuable nutrients are stored.

Fresh Ways

Always choose firm, well-shaped potatoes free of blemishes, bruises, discolorations, or sprouting eyes. Especially avoid those with green spots, which indicate the presence of a toxic alkaloid called solanine that results from exposure to light.

Broadly speaking, potatoes are divided into "bakers," "boilers," and "all-purpose." Baking potatoes have more starch so they're light and fluffy when cooked. In addition to baking, they're wonderful for mashing and french fries. "Boilers" have less starch but more moisture. That's why they're the ones to use for potato salads and sautéeing. They have thin skin yet hold their shape quite well when sliced. "All-purpose" potatoes can be either baked or boiled and are generally white or red.

Sesame Noodles with Asian Vegetables

In addition to sesame, the dressing for this salad contains peanut butter and Asian seasonings.

1 lb. linguine, broken into 2-in. sections

¼ cup sesame seeds

¼ cup peanut butter

¼ cup very hot tap water

4 TB. Asian sesame oil

2 TB. soy sauce

2 TB. rice wine vinegar

2 TB. firmly packed dark brown sugar

3 garlic cloves, peeled and minced

2 TB. grated fresh ginger

2 TB. chopped fresh cilantro

1 to 2 TB. *Chinese chili paste with garlic*

6 scallions, rinsed, trimmed, and thinly sliced

1 medium cucumber, rinsed, halved lengthwise, seeded, and thinly sliced

1 carrot, peeled and thinly sliced

1 cup bean sprouts, rinsed

Serves: 8
Active time: 15 minutes
Start to finish: 25 minutes
Each serving contains:
377 calories
128 calories from fat
14 g fat
2 g saturated fat
11 g protein
52 g carbohydrates

1. Bring a large pot of salted water to a boil. Add pasta and cook according to package directions until al dente. Drain pasta, and rinse under cold running water until pasta is cool. Drain and refrigerate.

2. Place sesame seeds in a small dry skillet over medium heat. Toast seeds for 2 minutes or until browned, shaking the pan frequently. Set aside.

3. Combine peanut butter and water in a mixing bowl, and whisk until smooth. Add sesame oil, soy sauce, vinegar, brown sugar, garlic, ginger, cilantro, and Chinese chili paste. Whisk well again.

4. Add sauce, scallions, cucumber, carrot, and bean sprouts to pasta. Mix well and serve immediately, sprinkled with toasted sesame seeds.

Variation: Add cold shredded chicken or pork to make this a main dish salad that will serve 4 to 6.

Fast Talk

Chinese chili paste with garlic is a fiery thick paste made from fermented fava beans, red chilies, and garlic. It's available in jars in the Asian aisle of supermarkets.

Rigatoni with Vegetables and Mozzarella

This is a cooling salad that's perfect for summer when tomatoes and herbs are all grown locally.

Serves: 8

Active time: 20 minutes

Start to finish: 20 minutes

Each serving contains:

433 calories

165 calories from fat

18 g fat

6 g saturated fat

17.5 g protein

51 g carbohydrates

 **Fresh Ways**

You don't mix the vegetables in step 2 because while salt adds to the flavor of tomatoes, it draws moisture out of the other vegetables.

---

1 lb. rigatoni

1 lb. ripe plum tomatoes, rinsed, cored, and chopped

Salt and freshly ground black pepper to taste

1 orange or yellow bell pepper, seeds and ribs removed, and chopped

2 small zucchini, rinsed, trimmed, and chopped

1 small cucumber, rinsed, seeded, and chopped

6 scallions, rinsed, trimmed, and chopped

1 cup chopped fresh basil leaves

½ lb. fresh mozzarella, drained and cut into ½-inch dice

⅓ cup extra-virgin olive oil

½ cup freshly grated Parmesan cheese

1. Bring a large pot of salted water to a boil. Add pasta and cook according to package directions until al dente. Drain pasta and rinse under cold running water until pasta is cool. Drain and refrigerate.

2. While pasta is cooking, place tomatoes in a large mixing bowl and season to taste with salt and pepper. Add orange bell pepper, zucchini, cucumber, and scallions to the bowl but *do not mix.*

3. Add chilled pasta, basil, mozzarella, olive oil, and Parmesan. Toss to mix, season to taste with salt and pepper, and serve immediately.

Gemelli with White Beans, Tomatoes, and Sage

The pungent and musky taste of fresh sage melds with the sweetness of the tomatoes in this hearty salad.

1 lb. gemelli

⅓ cup extra-virgin olive oil

4 garlic cloves, peeled and minced

¼ cup chopped fresh sage or 2 TB. dried

1½ lb. ripe plum tomatoes, rinsed, cored, and chopped

1 (15-oz.) can cannellini beans, drained and rinsed

Salt and freshly ground black pepper to taste

Serves: 8
Active time: 10 minutes
Start to finish: 20 minutes
Each serving contains:
162 calories
87 calories from fat
10 g fat
1 g saturated fat
5 g protein
16 g carbohydrates

1. Bring a large pot of salted water to a boil. Add pasta and cook according to package directions until al dente. Drain pasta and rinse under cold running water until pasta is cool. Drain and refrigerate.

2. While water is heating, heat olive oil in a large skillet over medium-high heat. Add garlic and sage, and cook, stirring constantly, for 1 minute. Scrape mixture into a large mixing bowl, and add tomatoes and beans.

3. Add pasta to mixing bowl, season to taste with salt and pepper, and serve at room temperature or chilled.

Fresh Ways

The purpose of cooking the garlic and herbs in oil for a minute is to infuse the oil with the herb and garlic flavors. And it also mellows the garlic flavor and makes it less pungent.

Coconut Rice and Vegetable Salad

Here, aromatic jasmine rice is cooked in coconut milk and Asian seasonings and then tossed with crunchy vegetables.

Serves: 8

Active time: 30 minutes

Start to finish: 2½ hours, including 2 hours for chilling

Each serving contains:

290 calories

133 calories from fat

15 g fat

7 g saturated fat

5 g protein

36.5 g carbohydrates

½ cup unsweetened shredded coconut

2¾ cups water

Salt and freshly ground black pepper to taste

1½ cups jasmine rice

1 cup chopped fresh cilantro

¾ cup coconut milk

4 tsp. grated fresh ginger

1 TB. freshly squeezed lime juice

2 garlic cloves, peeled and minced

1 TB. Asian sesame oil

1 TB. vegetable oil

6 scallions, rinsed, trimmed, and thinly sliced

1 tsp. ground cumin

½ tsp. crushed red pepper flakes or to taste

¼ lb. snow peas, rinsed and stemmed

1 pt. cherry tomatoes, rinsed, stemmed, and halved

½ cup salted peanuts, coarsely chopped

Fresh Ways

If you're cutting back on fat in your diet, use light coconut milk. It delivers the same flavor but has less fat.

1. Stir shredded coconut in a small nonstick skillet over medium heat for 5 minutes or until light golden. Set aside.

2. Bring water, salt, and pepper to boil in a saucepan. Stir in rice, and bring to a boil. Reduce heat to low, cover the saucepan, and simmer for about 18 minutes or until water is absorbed and rice is tender.

3. While rice is cooking, combine cilantro, ½ cup coconut milk, 1 teaspoon ginger, lime juice, and ½ of the garlic in a blender. Purée until smooth, and stir purée and toasted coconut into rice. Set aside.

4. Heat sesame oil and vegetable oil in a large skillet over medium-high heat. Add remaining garlic, remaining ginger, ½ scallions, cumin, and red pepper flakes. Cook, stirring constantly, for 1 minute. Stir in snow peas and remaining coconut milk. Cover and cook for 1 minute or until snow peas are bright green.

5. Stir vegetables into rice, and season to taste with salt and pepper. Chill for at least 2 hours or until cold. (Salad can be prepared up to 1 day in advance and refrigerated, tightly covered.) Stir in remaining scallions and tomatoes, and sprinkle with peanuts before serving.

Variation: Add cold shredded chicken or diced shrimp to make this a main dish salad that will serve 4 to 6.

Thai Rice Salad

This sweet and sour rice salad contains a confetti of vegetables.

1½ cups jasmine rice

6 TB. vegetable oil

4 garlic cloves, peeled and minced

1 large shallot, peeled and minced

3 cups water

Salt and freshly ground black pepper to taste

½ cup rice wine vinegar

¼ cup firmly packed dark brown sugar

2 TB. fish sauce (*nam pla*)

1 to 2 tsp. Chinese chili paste with garlic

1 large carrot, peeled and shredded

1 red bell pepper, seeds and ribs removed, and finely chopped

6 scallions, rinsed, trimmed, and finely chopped

Serves: 8
Active time: 30 minutes
Start to finish: 2 hours, including 1½ hours for chilling
Each serving contains:
258 calories
95 calories from fat
11 g fat
1.5 g saturated fat
2 g protein
38 g carbohydrates

1. Rinse rice in a colander under cold running water.

2. Heat 2 tablespoons oil in a large saucepan over medium heat. Add garlic and shallot, and cook, stirring frequently, for 3 minutes or until shallot is translucent. Add rice, water, salt, and pepper and cover the pan. Bring rice to a boil over high heat. Reduce heat to low, and simmer rice for 20 minutes or until liquid is absorbed. Remove the pan from heat. Allow rice to rest, covered, for 10 minutes, and then fluff with a fork.

3. While rice is cooking, combine vinegar, brown sugar, fish sauce, and Chinese chili paste in a jar with a tight-fitting lid. Shake well until sugar is dissolved. Add remaining 4 tablespoons oil, and shake well again.

4. Place rice in a mixing bowl or serving dish. Pour dressing over hot rice. Add carrot, red bell pepper, and scallions. Mix well to combine. Refrigerate salad for at least 2 hours or until chilled, tightly covered with plastic wrap. (Salad can be made up to 2 days in advance.)

Variation: If you want, replace the carrot and red bell pepper with sliced raw celery or cooked asparagus.

⏱ Speedy Solutions

Burning rice is a common problem. To get rid of the burnt taste—and save the rice—scoop it out into a clean pot, leaving the burnt layer behind. Then cover the top of the rice with a layer of onion skins, and cover the pot for 10 minutes. Discard the onion peels, and your rice won't taste burnt.

Spicy Asian Brown Rice Salad

While brown rice might not be Asian, its nutty flavor takes well to the assertive seasonings in this salad.

Serves: 8

Active time: 15 minutes

Start to finish: 45 minutes, including 30 minutes for chilling

Each serving contains:

252 calories

61 calories from fat

7 g fat

1 g saturated fat

7 g protein

42 g carbohydrates

¼ lb. fresh shiitake mushrooms

3 TB. Asian sesame oil

3 garlic cloves, peeled and minced

4 TB. grated fresh ginger

2 carrots, peeled and thinly sliced

2 medium zucchini, rinsed, trimmed, and thinly sliced

¼ lb. snow peas, rinsed, stemmed, and halved lengthwise

⅓ cup *tamari*

¼ cup water

2 TB. hoisin sauce

1 tsp. Chinese chili paste with garlic or to taste

6 cups cold cooked brown rice

Freshly ground black pepper to taste

3 scallions, rinsed, trimmed, and thinly sliced

Fast Talk

Tamari, like soy sauce, is a dark sauce made from soybeans, but its flavor is more mellow and less salty than that of soy sauce.

1. Wipe mushrooms with a damp paper towel. Discard stems, and cut mushrooms into thin strips.

2. Heat oil in a large skillet over high heat. Add garlic and ginger, and stir-fry 1 minute. Add carrots, zucchini, shiitake mushrooms, and snow peas, and cook, stirring frequently, for 2 minutes or until vegetables are crisp-tender. Add tamari, water, hoisin sauce, and Chinese chili paste, and cook for 1 minute. Scrape mixture into a large mixing bowl.

3. Stir in rice, and season to taste with pepper. Chill for at least 30 minutes. Serve sprinkled with scallions.

Tabbouleh with Feta

This lemony bulgur salad with chopped cucumber, tomato, and onion is a staple in the Middle East.

1 lb. bulgur wheat

¾ cup freshly squeezed lemon juice

3 cups hot water

1 medium cucumber, rinsed, seeded, and chopped

4 ripe plum tomatoes, rinsed, cored, seeded, and chopped

1 small red onion, peeled and minced

2 garlic cloves, peeled and minced

1 cup chopped fresh parsley

3 TB. chopped fresh mint

1 cup crumbled feta cheese

½ cup olive oil

Salt and freshly ground black pepper to taste

Serves: 8

Active time: 20 minutes

Start to finish: 1½ hours, including 1 hour for chilling

Each serving contains:

395 calories

173 calories from fat

19 g fat

5 g saturated fat

12 g protein

49.5 g carbohydrates

---

1. Place bulgur in a large mixing bowl, and add lemon juice and hot water. Let stand for 30 minutes or until bulgur is tender. Drain off any excess liquid.

2. Add cucumber, tomatoes, onion, garlic, parsley, mint, and feta to bulgur, and toss to combine. Add olive oil a few tablespoons at a time to make salad moist but not runny. Season to taste with salt and pepper.

3. Refrigerate *tabbouleh* for at least 1 hour. Serve cold or at room temperature.

Fast Talk

Tabbouleh (*ta-BOOL-a*) is a salad dish of the Middle East; it's served as an accompaniment to almost every-thing. The characteristic ingredients are bulgur, parsley, and lemon juice. From that base, it's open to interpretation.

Janet's Potato Salad

The inclusion of delicate and crunchy cucumber is a welcomed addition to this classic summer potato salad.

Serves: 8

Active time: 20 minutes

Start to finish: 2 hours, including 1½ hours for chilling

Each serving contains:

200 calories

101 calories from fat

11 g fat

2 g saturated fat

3 g protein

22 g carbohydrates

2 lb. small red-skinned potatoes, scrubbed

1 medium cucumber, peeled

1 green bell pepper, seeds and ribs removed

1 small red onion, peeled

3 celery ribs, rinsed and trimmed

½ cup mayonnaise

2 TB. white wine vinegar

Salt and freshly ground black pepper to taste

1. Place potatoes in a large saucepan of cold, salted water. Bring to a boil over high heat, and boil potatoes for 10 to 20 minutes or until they're tender when pierced with the tip of a paring knife. Drain potatoes and chill well. Cut potatoes into 1-inch cubes, and place them in a large mixing bowl.

2. Cut cucumber in half lengthwise and scrape out seeds with a teaspoon. Slice cucumber into thin arcs, and add to potatoes.

3. Cut green bell pepper into 1-inch sections, and slice each section into thin strips. Add peppers to the mixing bowl.

4. Cut onion in half through the root end, and cut each half into thirds. Cut into thin slices, and add to the mixing bowl.

5. Cut each celery rib in half lengthwise, and thinly slice celery. Add to the mixing bowl.

6. Toss potato salad with mayonnaise and vinegar, and season to taste with salt and pepper. Serve well chilled. (Salad can be made 1 day in advance and refrigerated, tightly covered.)

 Fresh Ways

To keep onions from overpowering other ingredients in a salad after a few hours, before adding them to a salad, soak the cut onions for about 10 minutes in a bowl of cold water with a few tablespoons of vinegar added.

Garlicky Potato Salad

The dressing for this salad dotted with colorful vegetables is an aïoli from Provence.

2 lb. small red-skinned potatoes, scrubbed

3 carrots, peeled and cut into ¼-inch dice

1 cup fresh green peas (or frozen peas, thawed)

1 red bell pepper, seeds and ribs removed, and finely chopped

6 garlic cloves, peeled

2 egg yolks, at room temperature

¾ cup extra-virgin olive oil

1 TB. freshly squeezed lemon juice

Salt and freshly ground black pepper to taste

Serves: 8

Active time: 20 minutes

Start to finish: 2 hours, including 1½ hours for chilling

Each serving contains:
306 calories

202 calories from fat

22 g fat

3.5 g saturated fat

4 g protein

51 g carbohydrates

1. Place potatoes in a large saucepan of cold, salted water. Bring to a boil over high heat, and boil potatoes for 10 to 20 minutes or until they're tender when pierced with the tip of a paring knife. After 5 minutes, add carrots to the pan. When potatoes are almost tender, add peas to the pan. Drain vegetables and chill well. Cut potatoes into 1-inch cubes, and add red bell pepper to the mixing bowl.

2. Combine garlic and egg yolks in a food processor fitted with a steel blade or in a blender. Purée and then very slowly add olive oil through the feed tube of the food processor or the top of the blender. When sauce has thickened, add lemon juice, and season to taste with salt and pepper.

3. Combine sauce and vegetables, and serve chilled. (Salad can be made 1 day in advance and refrigerated, tightly covered.)

Speedy Solutions

Potatoes cooked whole rather than chopped retain their shape better in salads such as this. If you don't want to take the time to cook whole potatoes, add some white distilled vinegar to the salted water and boil the potatoes cubed.

Sweet Potato Salad with Mustard Dressing

Sweet pickles balance the Dijon mustard in the dressing for this colorful sweet potato salad.

Serves: 8

Active time: 20 minutes

Start to finish: 35 minutes, including 15 minutes for cooling

Each serving contains:

210 calories

122 calories from fat

14 g fat

2 g saturated fat

2 g protein

21 g carbohydrates

1½ lb. sweet potatoes, scrubbed

3 TB. white wine vinegar

2 TB. Dijon mustard

Salt and freshly ground black pepper to taste

1 shallot, peeled and finely chopped

2 garlic cloves, peeled and minced

½ cup olive oil

¼ small red onion, peeled and finely chopped

½ red bell pepper, seeds and ribs removed, and finely chopped

¼ cup finely chopped sweet pickles

1. Quarter sweet potatoes lengthwise, and cut quarters into 2-inch sections. Place sweet potatoes in a saucepan of cold, salted water. Bring potatoes to a boil over high heat, and boil for 10 minutes or until potatoes are tender. Drain well and peel potatoes when cool enough to handle. Cut potatoes into 1-inch cubes, and place in a mixing bowl.

2. Combine vinegar, Dijon mustard, salt, pepper, shallots, and garlic in a jar with a tight-fitting lid, and shake well. Add oil and shake well again.

3. Add dressing to potatoes along with onion, red bell pepper, and pickles. Toss gently, and season to taste with salt and pepper. Serve at room temperature or chilled. (Salad can be made 1 day in advance and refrigerated, tightly covered with plastic wrap.)

Speedy Solutions

It's much faster to peel potatoes after they're cooked rather than when they're raw. That's why these sweet potatoes were cooked and then peeled. (And that's why red-skinned potatoes are such a time-saver; they don't need peeling at all!)

The Main Event: Entrée Salads

In This Chapter

- ◆ Salads with hot toppings
- ◆ Fruity salads
- ◆ New life for leftovers

Salads are a great way to give second life to cooked foods. Maybe that's the reason why the entrée salad is one category that continues to grow in popularity, especially during the warm summer months. These visually attractive and colorful mixtures of raw lettuces and other greens with cooked chicken, seafood, or meats are refreshing as well as healthful to eat. Those are the recipes you'll find in this chapter.

Entrée salads are also a delicious way to ensure you're getting all nine daily servings of fruits and vegetables in your diet. As a bonus, they can be on the table in a matter of minutes.

Savvy Greens Subbing

Making substitutions for some ingredients is difficult if you want to retain the character of the finished dish, but this is hardly a problem with lettuces. It's more important to have the freshest lettuce than a specific one. Use the following table to pick a lettuce that has the same characteristics as the one specified in a recipe.

Name	Texture	Flavor
Arugula	tender	pungent
Belgian endive	crisp	slightly bitter
Curly endive	crisp	bitter
Escarole	crisp	bitter
Frisée	crisp	bitter
Lettuce		
Butter	very tender	mild
Iceberg	crisp	very mild
Leaf	crisp tender	mild
Romaine	mainly crisp with tender outer leaves	fairly mild
Radicchio	tender leaves with crisp veins	slightly bitter
Watercress	tender leaves on crisp stalks	peppery, pungent

Thai Shrimp Salad

This salad is emblematic of Thai cuisine; it uses both fiery chilies and aromatic basil.

8 oz. thin *rice noodles*

⅓ cup freshly squeezed lime juice

¼ cup fish sauce (*nam pla*)

¼ cup vegetable oil

2 TB. granulated sugar

2 (¼-inch-thick) slices fresh ginger, about the size of a quarter

2 to 3 jalapeño chilies, stemmed and seeded

3 cloves garlic, peeled

¾ cup firmly packed basil leaves

1½ lb. cooked shrimp, peeled and deveined

1 English cucumber, rinsed, trimmed, halved lengthwise, and thinly sliced

1 small red onion, peeled and thinly sliced

10 oz. baby spinach, rinsed and dried

Serves: 6
Active time: 30 minutes
Start to finish: 1 hour, including 30 minutes for chilling
Each serving contains:
379 calories
100 calories from fat
11 g fat
2 g saturated fat
28 g protein
42 g carbohydrates

1. Cook rice noodles according to package directions and chill.

2. Combine lime juice, fish sauce, oil, sugar, ginger, jalapeños, garlic, and basil in a food processor fitted with a steel blade or in a blender. Purée until smooth. Refrigerate dressing.

3. Combine shrimp with cooked rice noodles, cucumber, and red onion in a mixing bowl. Toss with dressing, and chill 30 minutes.

4. To serve, arrange spinach on individual plates or on a platter. Mound salad in the center.

Variation: Instead of shrimp, try cooked lobster, chicken, turkey, or pork.

 Fast Talk

Rice noodles are Asian noodles made from rice flour, so they are a boon to people who are gluten-intolerant. They have a delicate flavor and are very quick-cooking.

Scallop and Asparagus Salad

Citrus flavors and herbs are the subtle seasonings in this delicate and colorful salad.

Serves: 6

Active time: 30 minutes

Start to finish: 45 minutes, including 15 minutes for chilling

Each serving contains:

204 calories

54 calories from fat

6 g fat

1 g saturated fat

23 g protein

16 g carbohydrates

1½ lb. bay scallops or sea scallops, cut into quarters and rinsed

Water or fish stock

1½ lb. fresh asparagus spears, rinsed ¼ small red onion, peeled and finely chopped

½ cup freshly squeezed orange juice

2 TB. white wine vinegar

2 TB. chopped fresh parsley

1 TB. grated lemon zest

1 TB. grated orange zest

2 tsp. fresh thyme or ½ tsp. dried

1 tsp. granulated sugar

Salt and freshly ground black pepper to taste

2 TB. extra-virgin olive oil

6 to 8 cups baby salad greens, rinsed and dried

1 large cucumber, rinsed and sliced

½ pt. cherry tomatoes, rinsed and stemmed

1. Place scallops in a small saucepan with water or fish stock to cover. Bring to a boil over high heat, cover the pan, and remove the pan from heat. Allow scallops to sit undisturbed in the covered pan for 5 minutes. Drain, place scallops in a mixing bowl, and chill for at least 15 minutes.

2. Bring a large pot of salted water to a boil, and have a bowl of ice water handy. Break woody stems off asparagus spears, and cut asparagus into 1-inch sections on the diagonal. Blanch asparagus for 3 to 5 minutes or until crisp-tender. Drain and plunge asparagus into ice water to stop the cooking action. Drain again, and add asparagus to the mixing bowl with scallops along with red onion.

3. Combine orange juice, vinegar, parsley, lemon zest, orange zest, thyme, sugar, salt, and pepper in a jar with a tight-fitting lid. Shake well, add oil, and shake well again. Set aside. Combine dressing with salad 5 minutes before serving.

4. Arrange greens, cucumber, and tomatoes on individual plates or a serving platter, and mound salad in the center. Serve immediately. (Salad can be prepared 1 day in advance and refrigerated, tightly covered. Do not add dressing until just prior to serving.)

Variation: You can substitute cooked shrimp, ½-inch cubes of cooked chicken, turkey, or pork for the scallops.

 Stale Stuff _____

If you buy organic cucumbers, there's no reason to peel them. This saves time, plus the peel contains many nutrients. If you're using a conventional cucumber, it should be peeled because there's a good chance it's been waxed.

Salmon and Cucumber Salad

Poached salmon with dill sauce is a classic combination that's transformed to a salad in this recipe.

2 cups water or fish stock

1½ lb. salmon fillets, skinned

3 medium cucumbers

1 cup sour cream

2 scallions, rinsed, trimmed, and cut into 1-inch segments

Salt and freshly ground black pepper to taste

¼ cup chopped fresh dill or 1 TB. dried

6 to 8 cups baby salad greens, rinsed and dried

1 pt. cherry tomatoes, rinsed and stemmed

Serves: 6
Active time: 25 minutes
Start to finish: 1¼ hours, including 50 minutes for chilling
Each serving contains:
363 calories
201 calories from fat
22 g fat
8 g saturated fat
29 g protein
12 g carbohydrates

1. Bring water or fish stock to a boil in a large skillet. Add salmon fillets, reduce heat to a simmer, and _poach_ fillets for 7 to 10 minutes, depending on the size. Remove fillets from the pan with a slotted spatula, and break fillets with a fork into 1-inch chunks. Place salmon chunks in a mixing bowl, and chill until cold, at least 50 minutes.

2. Rinse cucumbers, cut them in half lengthwise, scrape out seeds, and cut cucumbers into ¼-inch slices. Set aside ⅓ cup cucumber slices, and add remaining slices to the mixing bowl with salmon.

3. Combine sour cream, scallions, and remaining cucumber in a blender or food processor fitted with the steel blade. Purée until smooth. Scrape dressing into a bowl, season to taste with

salt and pepper, and stir in dill. Gently toss salmon and cucumbers with dressing.

4. Arrange greens and tomatoes on individual plates or a serving platter, and mound salad in the center. Serve immediately. (Salad can be prepared 1 day in advance and refrigerated, tightly covered.)

Variation: To lower the fat content of this salad, you can use plain nonfat yogurt instead of sour cream.

 Fresh Ways

Certain herbs, such as the chopped dill in this recipe, add visual interest to the finished dish. That's the reason they're not puréed along with the other dressing ingredients.

Gazpacho Chicken Salad

All the crisp vegetables comprising gazpacho soup are represented in this refreshing chicken salad.

Serves: 6

Active time: 20 minutes

Start to finish: 30 minutes, including 10 minutes for chilling

Each serving contains:

444 calories

157 calories from fat

17 g fat

3 g saturated fat

41 g protein

32 g carbohydrates

1½ lb. cooked chicken, cut into ½-inch dice

2 red bell peppers, seeds and ribs removed, and cut into ½-inch dice

2 cucumbers, rinsed, seeded, and cut into ½-inch dice

1 small red onion, peeled and cut into ½-inch dice

3 large ripe tomatoes, rinsed, cored, seeded, and cut into ½-inch dice

⅓ cup chopped fresh cilantro

1 jalapeño chili, seeds and ribs removed, and finely chopped

3 garlic cloves, peeled and minced

¼ cup balsamic vinegar

Salt and freshly ground black pepper to taste

6 to 8 cups baby salad greens, rinsed and dried

⅓ cup extra-virgin olive oil

6 to 8 cups baby salad greens, rinsed and dried

1. Combine chicken, red bell peppers, cucumbers, red onion, and tomatoes in a large mixing bowl.

2. Combine cilantro, jalapeño, garlic, vinegar, salt, and pepper in a jar with a tight-fitting lid. Shake well, add olive oil, and shake well again. Pour dressing over salad, and refrigerate 10 minutes.

3. Arrange greens on individual plates or a serving platter, and mound salad in the center. Serve immediately. (Salad can be prepared 1 day in advance and refrigerated, tightly covered. Do not add dressing until 10 minutes before serving.)

Variation: You could substitute cooked shrimp or turkey for the chicken.

 **Stale Stuff**

Don't add the dressing until a recipe says to. Some salads are only dressed at the last minute to ensure that the assertive flavors in the dressing don't overpower the delicate flavors of the salad.

Stir-Fried Chicken and Papaya Salad

Warm chicken in a citrus dressing is contrasted with buttery avocado and luscious tropical fruit in this recipe.

6 (6-oz.) boneless skinless chicken breast halves

3 navel oranges

6 TB. sesame seeds

3 shallots, peeled

3 garlic cloves, peeled

⅓ cup sherry vinegar

2 TB. fresh ginger, peeled and sliced

Salt and freshly ground black pepper to taste

1 cup vegetable oil

2 or 3 heads Boston lettuce, rinsed, dried, and broken into 1-inch pieces

3 ripe avocadoes, peeled and sliced

2 ripe papayas, peeled, seeds discarded, and thinly sliced

3 red bell peppers, seeds and ribs removed, and thinly sliced

3 TB. soy sauce

Serves: 6
Active time: 25 minutes
Start to finish: 25 minutes
Each serving contains:
808 calories
518 calories from fat
57.5 g fat
8 g saturated fat
46 g protein
35 g carbohydrates

1. Rinse chicken and pat dry with paper towels. Trim chicken of all visible fat, and slice chicken into ¼-inch slices against the grain.

2. Cut all rind and white pith off oranges, and cut between the sections to free orange segments from membranes.

3. Place sesame seeds in a small dry skillet over medium heat. Toast seeds for 2 minutes, or until browned, shaking the pan frequently. Set aside.

4. Place orange segments, shallots, garlic, sherry vinegar, ginger, salt, and pepper in a blender or food processor fitted with a steel blade. Purée until smooth. Add ¾ cup vegetable oil, and blend again. Set aside.

5. Arrange lettuce, avocadoes, and papayas on individual plates or a large platter.

6. Add remaining ¼ cup oil to the skillet, and heat over medium-high heat. Add chicken and red bell peppers, and cook, stirring constantly, for 3 minutes or until chicken is cooked through and no longer pink. Add soy sauce and stir well. Turn off heat, and add dressing to the skillet. Stir to warm dressing, but do not let mixture boil.

7. To serve, mound chicken mixture on top of greens and fruits, and sprinkle with toasted sesame seeds. Serve immediately.

Variation: Instead of chicken, you could use 1½ pounds of extra large (16 to 20 per pound) shrimp, peeled and deveined. The shrimp will take the same time. Instead of papaya, try mango.

Smoked Turkey Salad

Eggs, beans, and a barbecue-flavored dressing join turkey in this quick and easy salad.

Fresh Ways

Always add granular seasonings like salt or sugar to a salad dressing before adding the oil. These ingredients dissolve in liquid but not in oil.

Serves: 6

Active time: 15 minutes

Start to finish: 15 minutes

Each serving contains:

412 calories

185 calories from fat

21 g fat

3 g saturated fat

31 g protein

30 g carbohydrates

1½ lb. smoked turkey, cut into ½-inch dice

4 hard-cooked eggs, peeled and diced

1 cup cooked corn kernels

1 (15-oz.) can red kidney beans, drained and rinsed

1 small red onion, peeled and chopped

2 celery ribs, rinsed, trimmed, and thinly sliced

½ cup barbecue sauce

2 garlic cloves, peeled and minced

2 TB. chopped fresh cilantro

⅓ cup mayonnaise or to taste

6 to 8 cups baby greens, rinsed and dried

3 to 4 ripe beefsteak tomatoes, rinsed, cored, and sliced

1. Combine turkey, eggs, corn, beans, onion, and celery in a mixing bowl.

2. Whisk together barbecue sauce, garlic, cilantro, and mayonnaise. Toss dressing with salad and refrigerate.

3. Arrange greens and tomatoes on individual plates or a serving platter, and mound salad in the center. Serve immediately. (Salad can be prepared 1 day in advance and refrigerated, tightly covered.)

Variation: Smoked chicken or roasted turkey or chicken can be substituted for the smoked turkey.

> **⊘ Speedy Solutions**
>
> The large celery ribs around the outside of a bunch can be tough and fibrous. Starting at the tip, break off the top inch. It will be attached to the strings, which you can then easily pull off.

Asian Chicken Salad

Aromatic sesame oil adds its flavor to this simple salad made with crunchy Chinese cabbage.

⅓ **cup soy sauce**

⅓ **cup rice wine vinegar**

⅓ **cup vegetable oil**

3 TB. **Asian sesame oil**

3 TB. **Dijon mustard**

3 TB. **grated fresh ginger**

¾ tsp. **dried hot red pepper flakes**

1½ lb. **cooked chicken, coarsely shredded**

6 cups **shredded Napa cabbage**

3 medium **cucumbers, rinsed, quartered lengthwise, seeded, and thinly sliced**

9 **scallions, rinsed, trimmed, and finely chopped**

¾ cup **chopped fresh cilantro**

> Serves: 6
> **Active time:** 15 minutes
> **Start to finish:** 15 minutes
> **Each serving contains:**
> 427 calories
> 212 calories from fat
> 24 g fat
> 4 g saturated fat
> 40 g protein
> 15 g carbohydrates

1. Combine soy sauce, rice vinegar, vegetable oil, sesame oil, Dijon mustard, ginger, and hot red pepper flakes in a jar with a tight-fitting lid. Shake well and set aside.

2. Combine chicken, Napa cabbage, cucumbers, scallions, and cilantro in a large mixing bowl. Toss salad with dressing, and serve immediately.

Variation: Try shredded cooked beef or pork instead of chicken for something different.

⏱ **Speedy Solutions** _____

Many a cook has suffered a scraped knuckle when grating fresh ginger. To avoid this, peel only a small portion of the rhizome and then hold on to the unpeeled portion as a handle.

Jambalaya Salad

Like a traditional Louisiana jambalaya, this salad contains tomato-flavored rice, shrimp, ham, and chicken.

Serves: 6

Active time: 30 minutes

Start to finish: 50 minutes, including 20 minutes for chilling

Each serving contains:

434 calories

119 calories from fat

13 g fat

2.5 g saturated fat

40 g protein

37 g carbohydrates

2 cups Bloody Mary mix

1 TB. fresh thyme or 1 tsp. dried

1 cup long-grain rice

1½ cups fresh green peas or 1 (10-oz.) pkg. frozen peas, thawed

1 lb. cooked chicken, cut into ½-inch dice

½ lb. cooked shrimp, peeled, deveined, and cut in half lengthwise

¼ lb. baked ham, cut into ½-inch dice

6 scallions, rinsed, trimmed, and thinly sliced

2 celery ribs, rinsed, trimmed, and thinly sliced

½ red bell pepper, seeds and ribs removed, and chopped

¼ cup freshly squeezed lemon juice

3 garlic cloves, peeled and minced

Salt and cayenne to taste

¼ cup olive oil

6 to 8 large Boston lettuce leaves, rinsed and dried

1. Bring Bloody Mary mix and thyme to a boil in a saucepan over high heat. Add rice, reduce heat to low, and cook, covered, for 15 to 20 minutes or until rice is soft. Spread hot rice on a baking sheet, and chill for at least 20 minutes.

2. While rice is cooking, cook peas in boiling salted water for 5 minutes. Drain and plunge peas into ice water to stop the cooking action. Drain and chill well.

3. Place rice and peas in a large bowl and add chicken, shrimp, ham, scallions, celery, and red bell pepper.

4. Combine lemon juice, garlic, salt, and cayenne in a jar with a tight-fitting lid. Shake well, add olive oil, and shake well again.

5. Toss dressing with salad, and serve chilled, mounded on lettuce leaves. (Salad and dressing can be prepared 1 day in advance and refrigerated, tightly covered. Do not toss salad with dressing until ready to serve.)

 Speedy Solutions _____

Cooking rice in flavored liquid rather than water is an easy way to give it flavor without any fuss. Cooking in stock is common and the way to turn rice into pilaf, but let your imagination run wild.

Pork, Peach, and Orange Salad

Lean pork tenderloin is the perfect foil for fruit with an herbed dressing made with sweet raspberry vinegar.

1½ lb. pork tenderloin	2 TB. snipped fresh chives
1 tsp. ground ginger	1 TB. chopped fresh rosemary or 1 tsp. dried
1 tsp. dry mustard	
1 tsp. ground coriander	Salt and freshly ground black pepper to taste
Salt and cayenne to taste	
3 ripe peaches	⅓ cup olive oil
3 navel oranges	½ lb. baby spinach, rinsed and dried
¼ cup raspberry vinegar	
2 TB. chopped fresh cilantro	1 medium cucumber, rinsed and sliced

Serves: 6
Active time: 20 minutes
Start to finish: 40 minutes
Each serving contains:
334 calories
166 calories from fat
18.5 g fat
4 g saturated fat
27 g protein
16 g carbohydrates

1. Preheat the oven to 450°F, and line a baking pan with heavy-duty aluminum foil.

2. Rinse pork and pat dry with paper towels. Scrape off all fat and iridescent silverskin with a sharp paring knife.

3. Combine ginger, mustard, coriander, salt, and cayenne in a small bowl. Rub mixture onto all sides of pork.

4. Roast pork for 20 minutes or until an instant-read thermometer inserted into the center registers 140°F. Remove pork from the

Speedy Solutions

Plunging peaches or tomatoes into boiling water for 30 seconds is the fastest way to peel them. And it makes sense if you're going to be using a number of either fruit within a few days to peel them at one time and then refrigerate the peeled fruit.

oven, and allow it to rest for 15 minutes. (Pork can be roasted up to 4 hours in advance and kept at room temperature.)

5. While pork is roasting, bring a medium saucepan of water to a boil. Add whole peaches and allow them to boil for 30 seconds. Remove peaches with a slotted spoon and place under cold running water. The peel should then slide right off. Discard stones, and slice peach thinly.

6. Cut all rind and white pith off oranges, and slice thinly.

7. Combine vinegar, cilantro, chives, rosemary, salt, and pepper in a jar with a tight-fitting lid. Shake well, add oil, and shake well again.

8. Slice pork thinly.

9. To serve, arrange spinach and cucumber on individual plates or a large platter. Arrange pork, peaches, and oranges on top, and drizzle with dressing. Serve immediately.

Vietnamese Beef Salad

Using precooked roast beef from the deli department means this salad tossed with lime dressing is on the table in minutes.

Serves: 6
Active time: 20 minutes
Start to finish: 20 minutes

Each serving contains:
449 calories
287 calories from fat
32 g fat
7 g saturated fat
34 g protein
7 g carbohydrates

1½ lb. thinly sliced cooked roast beef

1 head romaine, rinsed, dried, and thinly sliced

12 scallions, rinsed, trimmed, and thinly sliced

12 radishes, rinsed, trimmed, and thinly sliced

⅓ cup freshly squeezed lime juice

¼ cup fish sauce (*nam pla*)

1 TB. grated lime *zest*

Salt and freshly ground black pepper to taste

⅓ cup Asian sesame oil

¼ cup vegetable oil

1. Trim roast beef of all visible fat and cut it into ½-inch strips. Place beef in a large mixing bowl, and add romaine, scallions, and radishes.

2. Combine lime juice, fish sauce, lime zest, salt, and pepper in a jar with a tight-fitting lid. Shake well, add sesame oil and vegetable oil, and shake well again.

3. Toss salad with dressing, and serve immediately.

Variation: Not in the mood for beef? Try turkey, chicken, or roast pork instead.

Fast Talk

Zest is the thin, colored outer portion of the citrus skin that contains all the aromatic oils. Remove the zest using a zester, a vegetable peeler, a paring knife, or the fine holes of a box grater. Be careful to get just the colored portion; the white pith underneath is very bitter.

Warm Lamb Salad

Rosy rich lamb is frequently paired with sharp Dijon mustard, and that's true for this salad.

1½ lb. boneless leg of lamb, rinsed and patted dry with paper towels

9 garlic cloves, peeled and minced

½ cup Dijon mustard

2 TB. chopped fresh rosemary or 2 tsp. dried

1 TB. fresh thyme or 1 tsp. dried

Salt and freshly ground black pepper to taste

⅓ cup red wine vinegar

¾ cup extra-virgin olive oil

3 bunches arugula, rinsed and dried

3 cups sliced romaine, rinsed and dried

½ cup sun-dried tomatoes packed in oil, drained and finely chopped

¾ cup freshly grated Parmesan cheese

Serves: 6
Active time: 20 minutes
Start to finish: 45 minutes
Each serving contains:
597 calories
465 calories from fat
52 g fat
14 g saturated fat
29 g protein
9 g carbohydrates

1. Preheat oven to 450°F. Cover a baking sheet with heavy-duty aluminum foil, and place lamb in the center.

2. Combine 6 garlic cloves, 5 tablespoons Dijon mustard, rosemary, thyme, salt, and pepper in small bowl. Rub mixture on all sides of lamb. Bake lamb for 15 to 20 minutes or until an instant-read thermometer registers 135°F for medium-rare. Remove lamb from oven and allow it to rest for 10 minutes.

Fresh Ways

Save the oil you've drained from the sun-dried tomatoes. It's a great addition to salad dressings or drizzled over foods.

3. While lamb is roasting, combine remaining garlic, remaining Dijon mustard, and red wine vinegar in a jar with a tight-fitting lid. Season to taste with salt and pepper, and shake well. Add olive oil, and shake well again.

4. Combine arugula, romaine, sun-dried tomatoes, and Parmesan in salad bowl. Drizzle with half dressing, toss well, and divide salad onto individual plates.

5. Carve lamb against the grain into thin slices, and arrange lamb on top of salad. Drizzle with additional dressing, and serve immediately.

Part 5

Redefining Fast Food

You'll be taking an around-the-world tour while cooking the recipes in Part 5—most of which are ready in less time than it would take to have a pizza delivered!

Stir-fried dishes and sautéed foods are healthful, low-fat cooking methods. We associate stir-fries with Asian food, but any food cut into small pieces qualifies regardless of seasoning. Dishes that qualify as sautés are in larger pieces, but the same quick cooking takes place.

The chapters are divided by the type of food being starred so it's easy to locate the perfect dish for a meal. Some cuts of meat like lean pork tenderloin or rosy rack of lamb roast in a very short amount of time. You'll find recipes for them, too.

14

Sensational Seafood

In This Chapter

◆ Asian fish dishes

◆ Saucy seafood delights

◆ Easy stove-top recipes

It's a chicken-and-egg situation: are we eating more fresh fish because it's more widely available, or is the fish department growing because we're eating more fish?

Regardless of the reason, more countries border on an ocean or major lake than are land-locked, so the majority of the world's cuisines include great fish dishes. Those are the recipes you'll find in this chapter. In addition to recipes for fin fish you'll find international options for preparing shrimp—the favorite crustacean of many people.

Choosing the Choicest

When making your fish selection, keep a few simple guidelines in mind: above all, do not buy any fish that actually smells fishy, indicating that it is no longer fresh or hasn't been cut or stored properly. Fresh fish has the mild, clean scent of the sea—nothing more.

Fresh Ways

If possible, select a whole fish and then have it cut to your specifications, such as fillets or steaks, because there are more signs to judge the freshness of a whole fish than any of the parts comprising it.

Look for bright, shiny colors in the fish scales, because as a fish sits, its skin becomes more pale and dull looking. Then peer into the eyes; they should be black and beady. If they're milky or sunken, the fish has been dead too long. And if the fish isn't behind glass, gently poke its flesh. If the indentation remains, the fish is old.

Fish fillets or steaks should look bright, lustrous, and moist, with no signs of discoloration or drying.

Fish Families

Although the recipes in this chapter call for specific fish, it's more important to use the freshest fish in the market rather than the particular species. All fin fish fall into three basic families, and you can easily substitute one species for another. Use the following table to make life at the fish counter easier.

A Guide to Fish

Description	Species	Characteristics
Firm, lean	black sea bass, cod family, flat fish (flounder, sole, halibut), grouper, lingcod, ocean perch, perch, pike, porgy, red snapper, smelt, striped bass, turbot, salmon, trout, drum family, tilefish	low-fat, mild to delicate flavor, firm flesh, flakes when cooked
Meaty	catfish, carp, eel, monkfish (anglerfish), orange roughy, pike, salmon, shark, sturgeon, swordfish, some tuna varieties, mahi-mahi (dolphinfish), whitefish, pompano, yellowtail	low to high fat, diverse flavors and textures, usually thick steaks or fillets
Fatty or strong-flavored	bluefish, mackerel, some tuna varieties	high fat, pronounced flavor

Shrimp: Sizing Up the Situation

Shrimp are sorted by "count," which means their size and the number that comprises 1 pound, and the smaller the number of shrimp in a pound, the higher the price. Here are the general size categories into which shrimp fall:

Colossal (less than 10 per pound)   These are sometimes referred to as U8s as well.

Jumbo (11 to 15 per pound)   These yield the highest proportion of meat to shell.

Extra large (16 to 20 per pound)   These are frequently called "cocktail shrimp."

Large (21 to 30 shrimp per pound)   This is the most common size for shrimp found in the supermarket, both cooked and raw.

Small (36 to 45 per pound) and *miniature* (more than 45 per pound)   These are usually sold as "salad shrimp." Unless they're cooked and peeled, stay away, because the labor involved in preparing them for cooking or eating is monumental.

Regardless of the color of the shell, raw shrimp are termed "green shrimp." Raw shrimp should smell of the sea with no hint of ammonia. Cooked, shelled shrimp should look plump and succulent.

Fresh Ways

If you're a fan of shrimp, it makes good sense to keep a bag of raw large shrimp in the freezer. Cooked shrimp are a great snack but are not as useful for cooking.

Asian Shrimp and Stir-Fried Vegetables

Both fresh and dried mushrooms are used in this classic Chinese preparation.

Serves: 6

Active time: 25 minutes

Start to finish: 30 minutes

Each serving contains:

268 calories

90 calories from fat

10 g fat

1.5 g saturated fat

27 g protein

14 g carbohydrates

1½ lb. extra large (16 to 20 per lb.) shrimp

¼ lb. fresh shiitake mushrooms

12 dried shiitake mushrooms

1 cup boiling water

½ cup dry sherry

3 TB. soy sauce

3 TB. freshly squeezed lime juice

2 tsp. granulated sugar

2 TB. cold water

1 TB. cornstarch

2 TB. Asian sesame oil

1 TB. vegetable oil

2 TB. grated fresh ginger

4 garlic cloves, peeled and minced

4 scallions, rinsed, trimmed, and cut into 1-in. lengths

2 celery ribs, rinsed, trimmed, and sliced

1 red bell pepper, seeds and ribs removed, cut into julienne

⅓ lb. snow peas, rinsed and stringed

Salt and freshly ground black pepper to taste

 **Fresh Ways**

An easy way to rehydrate mushrooms (or any dry ingredient), is in a French press pot coffee maker. Place the ingredients and liquid in the pot and lower the top to keep the ingredients submerged. If you're saving the soaking liquid for any reason, the mesh on the top will also serve as a strainer.

1. Peel and devein shrimp. Rinse shrimp and pat dry with paper towels.

2. Wipe fresh shiitake mushrooms with a damp paper towel. Discard stems and slice mushrooms. Set aside.

3. Soak dried shiitake mushrooms in boiling water, pushing them down with the back of a spoon, for 10 minutes. Drain mushrooms, squeezing to remove excess water. Stem mushrooms and chop coarsely. Set aside.

4. Combine sherry, soy sauce, lime juice, and sugar in a small bowl. Stir well, and set aside.

5. Combine cold water and cornstarch in a small bowl. Stir well, and set aside.

6. Heat sesame oil and vegetable oil in a heavy wok or skillet over high heat. Add ginger and garlic, and stir-fry, stirring constantly, for 30 seconds or until fragrant. Add shrimp and

cook for 1 minute. Remove shrimp from the pan with a slotted spoon, and add scallions, celery, red bell pepper, and fresh and dried shiitake mushrooms.

7. Stir-fry vegetables for 2 minutes, stirring constantly, and return shrimp to the pan. Add snow peas and sauce mixture. Bring to a boil, and simmer for 2 minutes. Stir in cornstarch mixture. Simmer 1 minute or until lightly thickened. Serve immediately.

Variation: Instead of shrimp, try substituting bay scallops or ¾-inch cubes of firm-fleshed whitefish such as grouper or swordfish.

Prawns in Garlic Sauce with Fettuccine

By the time the pasta is cooked the creamy tomato and garlic-sauced shrimp are ready to top it!

1½ lb. prawns or jumbo (11 to 15 per lb.) shrimp

½ cup olive oil

4 garlic cloves, peeled and minced

1 cup dry white wine

2 ripe tomatoes, rinsed, cored, seeded, and diced

2 TB. chopped fresh basil or 1½ tsp. dried

1½ cups light cream

Salt and freshly ground black pepper to taste

1½ lb. fresh fettuccine, cooked al dente

6 TB. freshly grated Romano cheese

6 sprigs fresh basil for garnish (optional)

Serves: 6
Active time: 20 minutes
Start to finish: 25 minutes
Each serving contains:
649 calories
353 calories from fat
39 g fat
15 g saturated fat
37 g protein
29 g carbohydrates

1. Peel and devein prawns. Rinse prawns and pat dry with paper towels. Heat olive oil in a large skillet over medium-high heat. Add prawns and garlic, and cook, stirring constantly, for 1 minute or until prawns begin to turn pink.

2. Add wine, tomatoes, basil, and cream and bring to a boil. Cook over medium heat for 3 minutes or until prawns are cooked through. Remove prawns from the pan with a slotted spoon, and *reduce* sauce over medium heat for 3 minutes or until it coats the back of a spoon. Season to taste with salt and pepper.

3. Toss pasta and prawns with sauce to heat through. Garnish each serving with 1 tablespoon cheese and 1 sprig basil (if using).

Fast Talk _____

To **reduce** in cooking is to make something thicker. The term means to boil a liquid until the volume is decreased through evaporation, thereby intensifying the flavor. The resulting liquid is called a *reduction*.

Scallops with Pine Nuts

Succulent and sweet scallops are glorified with a simple butter sauce and pine nuts add a crunchy accent to this dish.

Serves: 6

Active time: 20 minutes

Start to finish: 20 minutes

Each serving contains:

382 calories

249 calories from fat

28 g fat

9 g saturated fat

21 g protein

7 g carbohydrates

1½ lb. fresh bay scallops or sea scallops cut into quarters

3 TB. olive oil

½ cup *pine nuts*

2 garlic cloves, peeled and minced

2 large shallots, peeled and minced

1 cup dry white wine

¼ cup freshly squeezed lemon juice

6 TB. unsalted butter, cut into thin slices

Salt and freshly ground black pepper to taste

1. Rinse scallops, pat dry on paper towels, and set aside.

2. Heat olive oil in a heavy 12-inch skillet over high heat. Add scallops and pine nuts, and cook, stirring constantly, for 1 minute or until pine nuts are golden.

3. Remove scallops and nuts from the pan with a slotted spoon and reserve. Add garlic and shallots to the pan, and cook for 30 seconds. Add wine and lemon juice, and continue cooking until liquid is reduced to ¼ cup. Add any juice rendered from scallops.

4. Reduce heat to low. Add bits of butter to the pan, whisking constantly, allowing bits to melt but not letting sauce come to

a boil or it will separate and thin out. Return scallops and pine nuts to the pan to reheat briefly. Season to taste with salt and pepper, and serve immediately.

Fast Talk _____

Pine nuts, also called *piñon* in the American Southwest or *pingnoli* in Italy, don't actually fall from pine trees. They are found inside pinecones, and the cones have to be heated to release them. This labor-intensive process is the reason behind their high cost.

Pan-Fried Flounder with Black Walnut Butter

The slightly bitter flavor of all-American black walnuts is a great match for the delicate fish.

6 (6- to 8-oz.) flounder fillets

4 cups black walnut pieces

1½ cups yellow cornmeal

½ cup all-purpose flour

Salt and freshly ground black pepper to taste

¾ cup whole milk

2 large eggs

½ tsp. hot red pepper sauce

½ cup vegetable oil

¼ lb. (1 stick or ½ cup) unsalted butter, sliced into thin slices

⅓ cup freshly squeezed lemon juice

1 cup chopped fresh parsley

Serves: 6

Active time: 25 minutes

Start to finish: 25 minutes

Each serving contains:

1251 calories

857 calories from fat

95 g fat

17.5 g saturated fat

60 g protein

56 g carbohydrates

1. Rinse flounder fillets and pat dry with paper towels.

2. Place 2 cups black walnut pieces in a food processor fitted with a steel blade. Chop finely using on-and-off pulsing.

3. Combine chopped nuts, cornmeal, flour, salt, and pepper in a shallow dish and mix well.

4. Combine milk, eggs, and red pepper sauce in a mixing bowl and whisk well.

Fast Talk

To **dredge**
means to completely
coat a food with
some sort of dry mix-
ture before cooking
it. It can be as simple
as seasoned flour
for cubes of meat to
be browned before
braising, or it can
be a flavorful mixture
such as this one.

5. Heat vegetable oil in a large skillet over medium-high heat. Dip fillets in milk mixture and then *dredge* fillets in black walnut flour, coating them evenly. Add fillets to the skillet, and cook for 2 to 3 minutes per side or until browned, turning fillets gently with a slotted spatula. Remove fillets from the skillet and pat with paper towels. Keep warm.

6. Pour grease out of the skillet, and wipe the skillet clean with paper towels. Return the skillet to the stove over medium heat. Add butter and remaining 2 cups black walnut pieces, and cook, stirring frequently, for 2 minutes or until black walnuts are browned. Add lemon juice and parsley, and cook for 1 minute. Season sauce to taste with salt and pepper.

7. To serve, place flounder fillets on six plates, and spoon sauce across center of each fillet. Serve immediately.

Scrod with Red Onion Marmalade

Red wine and red currant jelly create a sweet and sour flavor for the onion garnish in this easy fish entrée.

Serves: 6

Active time: 20 minutes

Start to finish: 30 minutes

Each serving contains:

339 calories

162 calories from fat

18 g fat

8 g saturated fat

31 g protein

7 g carbohydrates

6 (6- to 8-oz.) scrod fillets

Salt and freshly ground black pepper to taste

5 TB. unsalted butter

5 medium red onions, peeled and thinly sliced

¾ cup dry red wine

1 tsp. grated orange zest

2 TB. beach plum or red currant jelly

3 TB. olive oil

1. Rinse scrod fillets and pat dry with paper towels. Season fillets to taste with salt and pepper, and set aside.

2. Melt 3 tablespoons butter in a large skillet over medium heat. Add onions, toss to coat, cover the pan, and cook over low heat for 10 minutes. Uncover the pan and cook onions over medium heat until soft, about 15 minutes, stirring frequently. Add wine, orange zest, and jelly, and boil over medium-high heat until liquid has almost evaporated. Season to taste with salt and pepper, and keep warm. (You can do this up to 2 days in advance and refrigerate, tightly covered. Reheat over low heat, stirring occasionally, until hot.)

3. Heat oil and remaining 2 tablespoons butter in a large skillet over medium-high heat. When butter foam begins to subside, add fillets. Cook fillets for 2 to 3 minutes on a side, turning gently with a slotted spatula.

4. To serve, divide onion mixture among 6 plates, and place a fish fillet on top.

Variation: Fillets of halibut or any firm-fleshed whitefish or salmon fillets can be substituted for the flounder in this recipe without changing the cooking time.

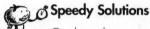

Speedy Solutions

Cooking the onions takes the most time in this recipe, so it makes sense to spend a few more minutes cooking a double or triple batch and freezing the remainder for future use.

Roast Monkfish in Plum Wine Sauce

A host of Asian flavors from fruity plum wine to ginger create the sauce for this treatment of the fish dubbed "poor man's lobster."

2 lb. thick monkfish fillets

3 TB. sliced fresh ginger

3 garlic cloves, peeled and minced

1 cup plum wine

¾ cup dry sherry

½ cup rice wine vinegar

¼ cup freshly squeezed lemon juice

2 tsp. grated lemon zest

2 TB. soy sauce

3 dried Chinese chilies

1 TB. coriander seed

2 TB. chopped fresh cilantro or parsley

½ tsp. cayenne pepper

½ cup dried shiitake mushrooms

2 celery ribs, rinsed, trimmed, and thinly sliced

2 carrots, peeled and thinly sliced

1 cup fresh bean sprouts, rinsed

8 scallions, rinsed, trimmed, and thinly sliced

Serves: 6

Active time: 20 minutes

Start to finish: 1 hour, including 30 minutes for marinating

Each serving contains:

212 calories

24 calories from fat

3 g fat

1 g saturated fat

24 g protein

13 g carbohydrates

1. If monkfish fillets are not trimmed, use a sharp paring knife and remove the shiny membrane covering fillets. Trim to an even thickness, rinse, and pat dry with paper towels. Cut monkfish into 6 equal serving pieces.

2. Combine ginger, garlic, plum wine, sherry, rice wine vinegar, lemon juice, lemon zest, soy sauce, Chinese chilies, coriander seed, cilantro, and cayenne in a heavy resealable plastic bag (or a glass or stainless-steel mixing bowl). Add monkfish and marinate at room temperature for 30 minutes, turning the bag occasionally.

3. Soak dried shiitake mushrooms in boiling water to cover for 10 minutes, pushing them down with the back of a spoon to absorb water. Drain, stem, and slice.

4. Preheat the oven to 450°F. Remove monkfish from marinade, reserving marinade. Place monkfish in a 9×13-inch baking dish, and bake for 10 to 12 minutes or until flesh springs back to the touch. Remove and keep warm.

5. While monkfish is roasting, boil down marinade in a small saucepan until reduced by half. Strain sauce, and return it to the pan. Add shiitake, celery, and carrots and simmer for 5 minutes. Add bean sprouts, and simmer 2 minutes.

6. To serve, place a monkfish fillet on each plate and top with vegetables and sauce. Scatter chopped scallions over fillets.

Fish Steamed in Napa Cabbage with Red Pepper Sauce

This dish is stunning when it comes to the table with a combination of salmon and sole in vivid red sauce.

Serves: 6
Active time: 40 minutes
Start to finish: 45 minutes

Each serving contains:
305 calories
129 calories from fat
14 g fat
3 g saturated fat
33 g protein
13 g carbohydrates

2 red bell peppers or 2 jarred roasted red peppers, rinsed

12 leaves Napa or savoy cabbage

1 lb. salmon fillets, skinned

1 lb. sole fillets

1 TB. vegetable oil

1 TB. Asian sesame oil

3 scallions, rinsed, white part only, finely minced

1 TB. plus 1½ tsp. freshly squeezed lemon juice

1 TB. soy sauce

1½ cups fish stock

1 TB. grated fresh ginger

Salt and freshly ground black pepper to taste

1. Preheat an oven broiler. Place red bell peppers on the rack of a broiler pan and broil 4 inches from the broiler element until skin is charred and black. Turn peppers with tongs to char all sides. Plunge peppers into ice water, and when cool enough to handle, remove and discard cap, skin, and seeds.

2. Bring a large pot of water to a boil. Add cabbage leaves and cook for 2 minutes or until leaves are pliable. Drain and set aside.

3. Rinse salmon and sole fillets, and pat dry with paper towels. Cut salmon and sole into ½-inch cubes and set aside.

4. Heat vegetable oil and sesame oil in a small skillet over medium heat. Add scallions and cook, stirring frequently, for 3 minutes or until scallions are translucent. Add to fish along with 1 tablespoon lemon juice and soy sauce.

5. Lay out 2 cabbage leaves so they overlap slightly, and divide fish mixture in the center of leaves. Roll cabbage, tucking in the sides to enclose filling, and secure rolls with toothpicks. Place rolls in a bamboo steamer, and steam over boiling water for 10 minutes.

6. While rolls are steaming, purée stock, peppers, remaining 1½ teaspoons lemon juice, ginger, salt, and pepper in a blender or food processor fitted with the steel blade. Pour into a small saucepan, and bring to boil over medium heat. Reduce by half, stirring frequently.

7. To serve, place a pool of sauce on the plate and top with a cabbage roll.

Speedy Solutions

Skinning fish is an easy task. Using an 8-inch chef's knife, start at one end of the fillet by pulling the skin away from the fillet with your fingers. Then hold on to the skin and push the knife away from you. It will scrape the fish away from the skin so you can then discard the skin.

Creole Swordfish

The "Creole Trinity" of celery, onion, and green bell pepper is joined with herbs in this dynamically flavored dish.

Serves: 6

Active time: 25 minutes

Start to finish: 30 minutes

Each serving contains:

283 calories

82 calories from fat

9 g fat

2 g saturated fat

33 g protein

14 g carbohydrates

2 lb. swordfish steaks, approximately 1 in. thick, cut into 6 equal serving pieces

1 TB. olive oil

1 large onion, peeled and finely chopped

2 celery ribs, rinsed, trimmed, and finely chopped

3 garlic cloves, peeled and minced

1 green bell pepper, seeds and ribs removed, finely chopped

½ cup seafood stock

½ cup dry white wine

2 lb. ripe plum tomatoes, rinsed, cored, and finely chopped

1 (8-oz.) can tomato sauce

½ to 1 tsp. hot red pepper sauce

¼ cup chopped fresh parsley

2 tsp. chopped fresh thyme or ½ tsp. dried

Salt and freshly ground black pepper to taste

1. Rinse swordfish steaks and pat dry with paper towels. Set aside.

2. Heat oil in a large skillet over medium-high heat. Add onion, celery, garlic, and green bell pepper. Cook, stirring frequently, for 3 minutes or until onion is translucent.

3. Add swordfish steaks, stock, wine, tomatoes, tomato sauce, hot red pepper sauce, parsley, and thyme. Bring to a boil over medium heat. *Poach* swordfish, partially covered, for 5 to 7 minutes, depending on thickness. Turn swordfish gently with a slotted spatula, and poach an additional 5 to 7 minutes or until cooked through.

4. Remove swordfish from the pan with a slotted spatula and keep warm. Raise the heat to high, and reduce sauce by ⅓, stirring frequently. Season sauce to taste with salt and pepper. To serve, spoon sauce over swordfish steaks. (Swordfish can be served either hot or at room temperature.)

Variation: Thick fillets of halibut or salmon can be substituted for the swordfish without changing the cooking time; however, if you're using flounder, tilapia, or sole, reduce the cooking time to no more than a total of 5 minutes.

Fast Talk

To **poach** is to cook food gently in liquid that's just at the boiling point and barely simmering. This way of cooking preserves the tenderness of what's being cooked, be it an egg or a fish steak.

Salmon with Basil Cream Sauce

Delicate pink salmon is paired with an equally delicate cream sauce for this elegant dinner option.

6 (6- to 8-oz.) salmon fillets	**¼ cup chopped fresh parsley**
2 TB. unsalted butter	**¾ cup dry white wine**
3 shallots, peeled and minced	**⅔ cup light cream**
1 garlic clove, peeled and minced	**1 TB. freshly squeezed lemon juice**
1½ cups firmly packed chopped fresh basil	**Salt and freshly ground black pepper to taste**

Serves: 6

Active time: 20 minutes

Start to finish: 30 minutes

Each serving contains:

459 calories

278 calories from fat

31 g fat

11.5 g saturated fat

35 g protein

3 g carbohydrates

1. Skin salmon (if necessary), rinse, and pat dry on paper towels.

2. Melt butter in a large skillet over medium-high heat. Sear salmon on both sides for about 2 to 3 minutes, keeping the center slightly rare. Remove fish from the pan with a slotted spatula and keep warm. Reduce heat to low, and add shallots and garlic to the pan. Cook, stirring frequently, for 3 minutes or until shallots are translucent.

3. Add basil, parsley, wine, cream, and lemon juice to the pan and cook over medium heat, stirring frequently, until mixture is reduced by ½. Return fish to the skillet and cook for 2 minutes. Season sauce to taste with salt and pepper. Serve immediately.

Variation: You could use thick fillets of halibut or swordfish instead of salmon without changing the cooking time. If you're using flounder, tilapia, or sole, reduce the cooking time to no more than a total of 5 minutes.

Fresh Ways

Certain ingredients are always packed firmly into mixing cups for accurate measurement. Brown sugar is one because it ranges from dense to fluffy depending on the brand. Herbs such as basil and vegetables such as lettuce or watercress are other foods that should always be packed down.

Halibut in White Wine with Pearl Onions and Oranges

This is a fabulous dish to serve guests who shy away from assertive seasoning. It's delicate but also colorful and flavorful.

Serves: 6

Active time: 17 minutes

Start to finish: 30 minutes

Each serving contains:

323 calories

75 calories from fat

8 g fat

1 g saturated fat

30 g protein

30 g carbohydrates

3 scallions

2 TB. olive oil

1 celery rib, trimmed and sliced

3 garlic cloves, peeled and minced

1 (16-oz.) pkg. frozen pearl onions, thawed

2 lb. ripe plum tomatoes, rinsed, cored, seeded, and chopped, or 1 (14.5-oz.) can diced tomatoes, drained

¼ cup chopped fresh parsley

1½ cups fish or chicken stock

½ cup dry white wine

1 cup freshly squeezed orange juice

1 bay leaf

Salt and freshly ground black pepper to taste

1½ to 2 lb. halibut fillets, cut into 6 pieces, rinsed

2 navel oranges, rind and white pith removed, and cut into ½-inch cubes

¾ lb. sugar snap peas, rinsed and stemmed

Speedy Solutions

One of the worst jobs in the kitchen is peeling tiny pearl onions. There's really no reason to use fresh ones, though. They're always cooked in recipes, and frozen pearl onions are even a better thing than sliced bread.

1. Rinse and trim scallions. Discard all but 2 inches of green tops, and slice scallions thinly.

2. Heat olive oil in a large skillet over medium heat. Add scallions, celery, and garlic, and cook, stirring frequently, for 3 minutes. Add pearl onions, tomatoes, parsley, fish stock, white wine, orange juice, and bay leaf. Season to taste with salt and pepper. Bring to a boil, and simmer, uncovered, for 3 minutes.

3. Add halibut and orange pieces to the skillet. Cover, bring to a boil, reduce heat to low, and cook for 5 minutes. Turn halibut gently with a slotted spatula, add sugar snap peas, and cook for an additional 5 minutes.

4. To serve, place halibut on plates and surround each portion with vegetables. Serve immediately.

Variation: Also try thick fillets of salmon or swordfish instead of the halibut without changing the cooking time. If you're using flounder, tilapia, or sole, reduce the cooking time to no more than a total of 5 minutes.

Tuna Steaks with Tomato Relish

Baking tuna is a way to avoid the pitfall of overcooking, and the fresh vegetable relish contrasts with the meatiness of the fish.

3 TB. olive oil

6 (6- to 8-oz.) tuna steaks, about ¾-inch thick

Salt and freshly ground black pepper to taste

2 garlic cloves, peeled and minced

2 large ripe beefsteak tomatoes, rinsed, cored, seeded, and chopped

4 scallions, rinsed, trimmed, and sliced

3 TB. chopped fresh chives

½ cup refrigerated salsa

3 TB. freshly squeezed lime juice

Serves: 6
Active time: 15 minutes
Start to finish: 25 minutes
Each serving contains:
262 calories
77 calories from fat
9 g fat
1 g saturated fat
41 g protein
4 g carbohydrates

1. Preheat the oven to 350°F. Line a baking sheet with heavy-duty aluminum foil, and spread 1 tablespoon olive oil on the foil.

2. Rinse tuna and pat dry with paper towels. Sprinkle on both sides with salt and pepper, and rub with garlic.

3. Heat remaining 2 tablespoons olive oil in a large skillet over high heat. Add tuna, and *sear* for 1 minute per side. Remove tuna from the skillet and arrange on the baking sheet. Bake tuna for 10 to 12 minutes or until still rare in the center when probed with the tip of a paring knife.

4. While tuna is baking, combine tomatoes, scallions, chives, salsa, lime juice, and remaining 1 tablespoon olive oil in a mixing bowl. Stir well, and season to taste with salt and pepper.

5. Remove tuna steaks from the oven, and spoon sauce over. Serve immediately.

Variation: You can also use thick fillets of salmon, swordfish, or halibut instead of tuna. Increase the baking time to 15 to 17 minutes unless you want the fish as rare as tuna.

 Fast Talk

To **sear** is to cook food over high heat to brown the exterior and seal in the juices. Searing meat prior to braising it produces a richness in the sauce, while moisture retention is the goal of searing fish.

Chapter 15

Poultry Pals

In This Chapter

- ◆ Asian stir-fries
- ◆ European flavors
- ◆ Homey turkey treats

The versatility of the boneless, skinless chicken breast knows no bounds. There's hardly a cuisine in the world that doesn't have a way to treat these quick-cooking, lean chicken parts, as you'll see by the recipes in this chapter. Chicken breasts take to every sort of seasoning. In addition, when crunchy, vibrantly colored vegetables are added to the mix, the dishes are as visually pleasing as they are delicious.

This chapter ends with two homey recipes that utilize ground turkey, although you can substitute turkey cutlets or ground turkey for chicken in the other recipes, too. These two birds are interchangeable at all times. Chicken has a more delicate flavor, but to some people that's a negative rather than a positive quality. The two foods also cook in the same amount of time, so it's personal preference.

Stir-Fry Strategy

Advance planning, speed, and control are the keys to a successful stir-fry. But stir-frying isn't just for Asian dishes anymore; many other recipes are now utilizing the technique. It's quick, requires little fat, and leaves food with a lovely crisp-tender texture.

Because the final cooking is a quick process, the prepared ingredients must be ready and waiting in bowls or dishes within arm's reach. Cut all pieces of the same ingredient the same size, have your seasonings at hand, and be sure any vegetables requiring partial cooking—such as blanching broccoli—have gotten it.

 **Stale Stuff** _____

Never place too much food in the wok or skillet at one time. The food must be able to be seared on all sides, without steaming from being buried under a layer of food.

The best pan to use for a stir-fry is an Asian wok because the rounded bottom facilitates keeping the food moving constantly. But if all you have is a large skillet, you can use that, too.

To cook, place the wok or skillet over a high flame and heat it to very hot. Listen for the sound of sizzles; if a few drops of water evaporate immediately, the pan is ready to cook in. Add the required amount of oil to the pan, and swirl it around gently to coat all sides.

Mock Mu Shu Chicken

Easy-to-find flour tortillas take the place of Chinese pancakes for these roll-ups.

8 large dried shiitake mushrooms

1 oz. dried *wood ear mushrooms*

1 cup boiling water

¼ cup soy sauce

1 TB. dry sherry

2 TB. cornstarch

1 lb. boneless, skinless chicken breast

2 TB. vegetable oil

6 scallions, rinsed, trimmed, and sliced

3 garlic cloves, peeled and minced

5 large eggs, lightly beaten

Salt and freshly ground black pepper to taste

½ cup plum sauce

12 (6-in.) flour tortillas

Serves: 6
Active time: 25 minutes
Start to finish: 25 minutes
Each serving contains:
486 calories
136 calories from fat
15 g fat
3.5 g saturated fat
30 g protein
56 g carbohydrates

1. Place dried shiitake mushrooms and wood ear mushrooms in a small mixing bowl. Pour boiling water over mushrooms, pressing them into water with the back of a spoon. Soak mushrooms for 10 minutes and then drain, squeezing out as much liquid as possible. Discard stems, and slice mushrooms thinly. Set aside.

2. Rinse chicken and pat dry with paper towels. Trim chicken of all visible fat, and cut chicken into thin slivers by cutting into thin slices and then cutting slices lengthwise.

3. Combine soy sauce, sherry, and cornstarch in a mixing bowl. Stir well, and add chicken. Toss to coat chicken evenly.

4. Heat oil in a heavy wok or large skillet over medium-high heat. Add scallions and garlic, and stir-fry for 30 seconds, stirring constantly. Add chicken mixture and stir-fry for 2 minutes or until chicken is cooked through and no longer pink. Add mushrooms and eggs to the pan and stir. Cook for 1 minute and then scrape the bottom of the pan to dislodge cooked egg. Cook for an additional 1 or 2 minutes or until eggs are just set. Season to taste with salt and pepper.

5. To serve, spread plum sauce on the surface of each tortilla. Place a portion of filling in the center. Tuck one edge over filling, and roll tortillas firmly to enclose filling. Serve immediately.

Variation: No chicken? Try this with pork tenderloin.

 **Fast Talk**

Wood ear mushrooms, also called *cloud ear mushrooms*, are a form of Asian dried mushroom with a slightly crunchy texture and very delicate flavor. They're almost brownish black and expand to five times their size when rehydrated.

Chicken with Plum Sauce

This easy stir-fry has the popular sweet and sour flavor, and the vegetables make it colorful.

Serves: 6
Active time: 25 minutes
Start to finish: 25 minutes
Each serving contains:
279 calories
101 calories from fat
11 g fat
2 g saturated fat
28 g protein
15 g carbohydrates

1½ lb. boneless, skinless chicken breast halves

2 TB. cornstarch

2 TB. dry sherry

2 TB. soy sauce

1 TB. rice wine vinegar

6 scallions

1 cup chicken stock

⅓ cup plum sauce

1 tsp. *Chinese five-spice powder*

¼ cup vegetable oil

4 garlic cloves, peeled and minced

2 TB. grated fresh ginger

2 celery ribs, rinsed, trimmed, and thinly sliced on the diagonal

1 red bell pepper, seeds and ribs removed, and thinly sliced

Salt and freshly ground black pepper to taste

Fast Talk

Chinese five-spice powder is perhaps the oldest blend of spices around. Used in traditional Chinese cooking for centuries, it's made up of equal parts cinnamon, cloves, fennel seed, star anise, and Szechwan peppercorns. It's available in most supermarkets, found either with spices or with Asian food.

1. Rinse chicken and pat dry with paper towels. Trim chicken of all visible fat, and cut chicken into ½-inch cubes. Place chicken in a mixing bowl, and sprinkle with cornstarch. Toss to coat evenly, and add sherry, soy sauce, and rice wine vinegar, tossing again to coat evenly.

2. Rinse and trim scallions. Cut into 1-inch lengths and then slice lengthwise into thin strips. Set aside.

3. Combine chicken stock, plum sauce, and Chinese five-spice powder in a small bowl. Stir well, and set aside.

4. Heat vegetable oil in a heavy wok or large skillet over high heat, swirling to coat the pan. Add scallions, garlic, and ginger, and stir-fry for 30 seconds or until fragrant, stirring constantly. Add chicken and cook for 1 minute, stirring constantly. Add celery and red bell pepper, and stir-fry vegetables for 2 minutes more, stirring constantly.

5. Add sauce mixture and cook, stirring constantly, for 2 minutes or until chicken is cooked through and no longer pink and sauce is slightly thickened. Season to taste with salt and pepper, and serve immediately.

Variation: Instead of chicken, try this with boneless pork chops, trimmed of all fat and cut into ½-inch cubes.

Chicken Fajitas

Colorful red bell pepper, sweet red onion, and fiery jalapeño are cooked along with the chicken in this colorful Mexican favorite.

1½ lb. boneless, skinless chicken breast halves

¼ cup olive oil

1 large red onion, peeled and thinly sliced

1 large red bell pepper, seeds and ribs removed, and thinly sliced

2 jalapeño chilies, seeds and ribs removed, and finely chopped

4 garlic cloves, peeled and minced

2 medium ripe tomatoes, rinsed, cored, seeded, and diced

¼ cup freshly squeezed lime juice

2 tsp. ground *cumin*

¼ cup chopped fresh cilantro

Salt and freshly ground black pepper to taste

8 (6-in.) flour tortillas

Sour cream (optional)

Salsa (optional)

Guacamole (recipe in Chapter 3; optional)

Serves: 4

Active time: 25 minutes

Start to finish: 25 minutes

Each serving contains:

555 calories

191 calories from fat

21 g fat

4 g saturated fat

46 g protein

44 g carbohydrates

---

1. Rinse chicken and pat dry with paper towels. Trim chicken of all visible fat. Place chicken between 2 sheets of plastic wrap, and pound to an even ½-inch thickness. Cut chicken into strips 2 inches long and ¾ inch wide.

2. Heat 2 tablespoons olive oil in a heavy 12-inch skillet over medium-high heat. Add chicken and cook, stirring frequently, for 4 or 5 minutes or until chicken is cooked through and no longer pink. Remove chicken from the skillet with a slotted spoon and set aside.

3. Add remaining olive oil to the skillet, and heat over medium-high heat. Add onion, red bell pepper, jalapeño, and garlic. Cook, stirring frequently, for 4 to 6 minutes, or until onion is soft. Add tomatoes, and cook for 1 minute. Add lime juice, cumin, cilantro, and chicken. Cook for 2 minutes, stirring frequently. Season to taste with salt and pepper.

4. Roll up filling in tortillas, and serve with small bowls of sour cream, salsa, and guacamole (if using) for garnish. Serve immediately.

Variation: You could use flank steak or pork loin cut to the same size as the chicken strips. Cook beef to the desired doneness, and cook pork for the same amount of time as the chicken.

 **Fast Talk**

Cumin
(*KOO-men*) is frequently found in markets under its Spanish name, *comino*. The seeds from which it's ground are the dried fruit from a very aromatic plant in the parsley family. Cumin is one of the major ingredients in commercial chili powder, so you can always substitute chili powder if necessary.

Chicken with Garlic and Parsley

This Italian dish balances pungent garlic with fragrant parsley, and it's great on top of pasta.

Serves: 4

Active time: 20 minutes

Start to finish: 20 minutes

Each serving contains:

442 calories

251 calories from fat

28 g fat

10 g saturated fat

40 g protein

6 g carbohydrates

1½ lb. boneless, skinless chicken breast halves

3 TB. all-purpose flour

Salt and freshly ground black pepper to taste

¼ cup olive oil

4 garlic cloves, peeled and minced

¼ cup chopped fresh parsley

4 TB. unsalted butter

3 TB. freshly squeezed lemon juice

1. Rinse chicken and pat dry with paper towels. Trim chicken of all visible fat, and cut chicken into ½-inch cubes. Toss chicken with flour, salt, and pepper in a bowl.

2. Heat oil in a 12-inch skillet over high heat, add chicken cubes, and cook, stirring frequently, for 3½ minutes or until chicken is cooked through and no longer pink.

3. Add garlic, parsley, and butter to the skillet and cook for 1 minute, shaking the skillet occasionally to coat the chicken. Add lemon juice, and season to taste with salt and pepper. Serve immediately.

Variation: For a seafood slant, use extra-large (16 to 20 per pound) raw shrimp, peeled and deveined, or 1-inch cubes of a firm-fleshed whitefish like cod or halibut instead of the chicken.

Speedy Solutions

Especially if you're cutting chicken into small cubes for a crowd, an alternative method is to pound the breasts to an even ½-inch thickness and then dice.

Poached Chicken with Balsamic Vinegar

Zesty dried currants and orange juice add fruity sweetness to the sauce on this lean dish.

4 (6-oz.) boneless, skinless chicken breasts

1 cup dry white wine

½ cup freshly squeezed orange juice

½ cup balsamic vinegar

½ cup golden raisins

½ cup dried currants

2 TB. extra-virgin olive oil

1 TB. grated lemon zest

2 TB. grated orange zest

2 tsp. chopped fresh tarragon or ½ tsp. dried

Salt and freshly ground black pepper to taste

Serves: 4
Active time: 15 minutes
Start to finish: 20 minutes
Each serving contains:
448 calories
84 calories from fat
9 g fat
2 g saturated fat
41 g protein
40 g carbohydrates

1. Rinse chicken and pat dry with paper towels. Trim chicken of all visible fat. Place chicken between 2 sheets of plastic wrap, and pound to a uniform ½-inch thickness. Set aside.

2. Pour wine into a large skillet, and bring to a boil over medium-high heat. Add chicken, reduce heat to a simmer, and poach chicken for 5 to 7 minutes or until chicken is cooked through and no longer pink. Remove chicken from the skillet with a slotted spoon, and set aside.

3. While wine is heating, bring orange juice and vinegar to a boil in a small saucepan. Remove the pan from the heat and add raisins and currants. *Plump* fruit for 10 minutes.

4. Add reserved wine, olive oil, lemon zest, orange zest, and tarragon to the saucepan. Bring to a boil over high heat. Reduce the heat to medium-high, and boil sauce for 5 to 10 minutes or until the mixture is reduced by ½.

5. Cut chicken into ½-inch slices. Pour sauce over chicken, and serve immediately.

Fast Talk

To **plump** is to rehydrate dried food, especially dried fruit, so it softens. Foods are plumped in hot liquid, which speeds up the process.

Tarragon Chicken with Spring Vegetables

While it can still be classified as "comfort food," the creamy wine sauce is lighter than ones for red meats.

Serves: 4

Active time: 15 minutes

Start to finish: 25 minutes

Each serving contains:

562 calories

270 calories from fat

30 g fat

18 g saturated fat

46 g protein

20 g carbohydrates

 Fresh Ways

While the green tops of leeks are not used very often in cooking, save them if you're making a stock and use them in place of onion. They give stocks a rich color as well as an improved flavor.

4 (6-oz.) boneless, skinless chicken breast halves

Salt and freshly ground black pepper to taste

½ lb. fresh asparagus spears

2 large leeks, white part only

4 TB. unsalted butter

2 garlic cloves, peeled and minced

1 cup chicken stock

⅔ cup dry white wine

⅔ cup heavy cream

¼ cup chopped fresh tarragon or 2 tsp. dried

2 medium carrots, peeled and thinly sliced

2 small zucchini, rinsed, trimmed, and sliced

⅔ cup green peas

1. Rinse chicken and pat dry with paper towels. Trim chicken of all visible fat, and cut chicken into 1-inch cubes. Sprinkle chicken with salt and pepper to taste.

2. Rinse asparagus and discard woody stems. Cut asparagus into 1-inch lengths. Set aside.

3. Trim leeks, cut in half lengthwise, slice thinly, and rinse slices well in a colander. Set aside.

4. Heat butter in a heavy 12-inch skillet over medium heat. Add chicken cubes, and cook for 3 minutes or until chicken is opaque. Add leeks and garlic, and cook, stirring occasionally, for 3 minutes or until leek is translucent.

5. Stir chicken stock, wine, cream, tarragon, and carrots into the skillet. Bring to a boil, reduce the heat to medium-low, and simmer for 5 minutes. Add zucchini, asparagus, and peas, and simmer for an additional 5 minutes or until chicken is cooked through and no longer pink. Season to taste with salt and pepper. Serve immediately.

Chicken Marsala with Mushrooms and Sage

Woodsy sage adds a more complex flavor to this classic Italian dish.

1½ lb. boneless, skinless chicken breast halves

¼ cup all-purpose flour

Salt and freshly ground black pepper to taste

½ lb. white mushrooms

⅓ cup olive oil

1 small onion, peeled and diced

5 garlic cloves, peeled and minced

1 cup dry marsala wine

1 cup chicken stock

¼ cup chopped fresh parsley

2 TB. chopped fresh sage or 2 tsp. dried

Serves: 4
Active time: 15 minutes
Start to finish: 25 minutes
Each serving contains:
454 calories
191 calories from fat
21 g fat
3 g saturated fat
43 g protein
13 g carbohydrates

1. Rinse chicken and pat dry with paper towels. Trim chicken of all visible fat, and cut chicken into 1-inch cubes. Season flour to taste with salt and pepper. Dust chicken with seasoned flour, shaking off any excess.

2. Wipe mushrooms with a damp paper towel. Discard stems, and thinly slice mushrooms.

3. Heat olive oil in a heavy 12-inch skillet over medium high heat. Add chicken pieces, and cook, stirring frequently, for 3 minutes or until chicken is opaque. Remove chicken from the pan with a slotted spoon, and set aside.

4. Add onion, garlic, and mushrooms to the skillet. Cook, stirring frequently, for 3 minutes or until onion is translucent. Return chicken to the skillet, and add marsala, chicken stock, parsley, and sage. Bring to a boil, stirring occasionally.

5. Reduce heat to medium, and simmer mixture, uncovered, for 10 minutes or until chicken is cooked through and no longer pink. Season to taste with salt and pepper. Serve immediately.

Variation: Instead of chicken, you can use veal scallops pounded to an even ½-inch thickness. The cooking time does not change.

Speedy Solutions

If you have leftover stock and don't think you'll use it within a few days, freeze it in ice cube trays. Measure the capacity of your ice cube tray with a measuring tablespoon, and when the cubes are frozen, transfer them to a resealable plastic bag. If you need a few tablespoons of stock later, you're all set.

Italian Chicken with Lemon and Capers (*Pollo Piccata*)

The light lemon sauce on this chicken is punctuated by piquant capers.

Serves: 4

Active time: 10 minutes

Start to finish: 20 minutes

Each serving contains:

394 calories

181 calories from fat

20 g fat

3 g saturated fat

42 g protein

11 g carbohydrates

4 (6-oz.) boneless, skinless chicken breast halves

⅓ cup all-purpose flour

Salt and freshly ground black pepper to taste

⅓ cup olive oil

1½ cups chicken stock

½ cup freshly squeezed lemon juice

⅓ cup chopped fresh parsley

¼ cup *capers*, drained and rinsed

1. Rinse chicken and pat dry with paper towels. Trim chicken of all visible fat. Place chicken between two sheets of plastic wrap, and pound to an even ½-inch thickness.

2. Season flour to taste with salt and pepper. Dust chicken with seasoned flour, shaking off any excess.

3. Heat olive oil in a heavy 12-inch skillet over medium high heat. Add chicken and cook for 2 minutes per side, turning with a slotted spatula.

4. Add chicken stock, lemon juice, parsley, and capers to the skillet. Bring to a boil, reduce the heat to low, cover the pan, and simmer chicken for 5 minutes. Turn chicken over and simmer for an additional 5 minutes or until chicken is cooked through and no longer pink. Season to taste with salt and pepper. Serve immediately.

Variation: Instead of chicken, you can substitute veal scallops pounded to an even ¼-inch thickness. Cook the veal for 2 minutes per side.

Fast Talk

Capers are the flower bud of a low bush native to the Mediterranean. After harvest, they're sun-dried and pickled in vinegar. The best capers are the tiny ones from France, and while they are customarily packed in brine, they are also sometimes packed in coarse salt. However, you buy them, rinse them well before using.

Turkey Chili

Ground turkey is lighter than hearty beef, but there's still a lot of flavor in this traditionally seasoned dish.

3 lb. ripe plum tomatoes, or 2 (14.5-oz.) cans diced tomatoes, drained

¼ cup vegetable oil

1 large onion, peeled and chopped

3 garlic cloves, peeled and minced

1 red bell pepper, seeds and ribs removed, and chopped

1 green bell pepper, seeds and ribs removed, and chopped

1½ lb. ground turkey

2 TB. all-purpose flour

3 TB. chili powder

2 TB. ground cumin

2 tsp. powdered cocoa

Salt and cayenne to taste

2 (15-oz.) cans kidney beans, drained and rinsed

Serves: 6
Active time: 20 minutes
Start to finish: 55 minutes
Each serving contains:
469 calories
190 calories from fat
21 g fat
4 g saturated fat
31 g protein
42 g carbohydrates

1. Rinse, core, and seed tomatoes. Chop tomatoes finely, and set aside.

2. Heat oil in a Dutch oven over medium-high heat. Add onion, garlic, red bell pepper, and green bell pepper. Cook, stirring frequently, for 3 minutes or until onion is translucent. Add turkey and cook, stirring constantly, for 5 minutes, breaking up lumps with a fork.

3. Stir in flour, chili powder, cumin, cocoa, salt, and cayenne. Cook over low heat, stirring frequently, for 3 minutes. Add tomatoes and bring to a boil over medium heat. Simmer chili, stirring occasionally, for 30 to 40 minutes or until thick. Add beans and cook for an additional 5 minutes.

Variation: No turkey? Use ground beef or ground pork instead.

Fresh Ways

You cook the flour and spices before adding other ingredients so the flour cooks in the accumulated fat and the dish doesn't get a "floury" taste.

Turkey Meatloaf

Crushed corn flakes create a crispy topping for this loaf that incorporates cheese and well as vegetables.

Serves: 6

Active time: 15 minutes

Start to finish: 55 minutes

Each serving contains:

413 calories

191 calories from fat

21 g fat

5 g saturated fat

24 g protein

31 g carbohydrates

¼ cup olive oil

1 medium onion, peeled and chopped

3 garlic cloves, peeled and minced

2 medium carrots, peeled and grated

1¼ lb. ground turkey

2 large eggs, lightly beaten

½ cup grated mozzarella cheese

½ cup Italian breadcrumbs

5 TB. whole milk

½ cup *chili sauce* or ketchup

1 TB. Worcestershire sauce

1 TB. fresh thyme or 1 tsp. dried

Salt and freshly ground black pepper to taste

3 cups cornflakes

1. Preheat the oven to 375°F, and line a baking sheet with heavy-duty aluminum foil.

2. Heat olive oil in a medium skillet over medium-high heat. Add onion, garlic, and carrots. Cook, stirring frequently, for 3 minutes or until onion is translucent. Scrape mixture into a mixing bowl.

3. Add ground turkey, eggs, mozzarella, breadcrumbs, milk, ¼ cup chili sauce, Worcestershire sauce, thyme, salt, and pepper to the mixing bowl. Mix well. (Mixture can be made up to 1 day in advance and refrigerated, tightly covered.)

4. Form meat into a log 10 inches long and 3 inches wide on a baking sheet. Spread top with remaining chili sauce.

5. Place cornflakes in a heavy resealable plastic bag. Crush into coarse crumbs with the flat side of a meat mallet or the bottom of a skillet. Press crumbs into top and sides of meatloaf. Bake for 40 minutes or until an instant-read thermometer inserted into the center of loaf registers 180°F. Serve immediately.

Variation: Instead of turkey, try ground beef or a combination of pork and beef.

Fast Talk

Contrary to its name, **chili sauce** is closer to a chunky ketchup than a fiery sauce. This tomato-based condiment contains onions, green peppers, vinegar, sugar, and spices.

Chapter 16

Grazing Greats

In This Chapter

- ◆ Quick-cooking pork and veal
- ◆ Sautéed beef
- ◆ Luscious lamb

You probably know that it's fast to grill a steak—after the grill heats, that is—but you might not know that you can fulfill your carnivore cravings in the same short amount of time at the stove or in the oven. Those are the recipes you'll find in this chapter.

In these pages you'll find delicious recipes for beef stir-fried with Asian flair or sautéed with European style. And then there are other recipes for cuts of meat like lean pork tenderloins and rich and rosy rack of lamb that bake to perfection within minutes.

Sauté Savvy

Sauté is another cooking term we've adopted from the French; it means literally "to jump." What this means for the dishes in this chapter is quick cooking with just a little fat over moderate to high heat.

Fresh Ways _____

> Stir-frying and sautéing are first cousins. The main difference is that foods to be stir-fried are cut into small pieces and stirred continually to keep them moving, while sautéed food can be larger and is left alone for longer periods of time. And like a stir-fry, these dishes produce a meal in very little time and in one pan. (To learn more about stir-frying, see Chapter 15.)

Like broiling, sautéing is reserved for relatively thin and tender pieces of protein. It's not for "stewing meat" that needs both time and moisture to get tender. Nor is it suited to large pieces, because the outer portions would become dry—and possibly burnt—before the interior cooked properly.

Subbing with Success

I list variations for many recipes in this chapter. But you can also improvise on your own. To help with that, here's a chart of what cuts of different meats can be sautéed successfully.

Meat Choices for Sautéing

Meat	Thickness
Beef: Rib-eye or Delmonico steak, filet mignon, flank steak, New York strip, round steak, boneless sirloin	1 to 1½ inches
Lamb: Boneless rib chops, boneless loin chops or saddle	1 to 1½ inches
Pork: Pounded tenderloin, boneless loin chops, ham steaks, butterflied chops	½ inch
Veal: Scallops or cutlets from the leg, tenderloin or round steak	⅛ to ¼ inch

Pork Scaloppine

Pork is incredibly tender when quickly cooked after coating with breadcrumbs, and fresh mushrooms complete the dish.

1 lb. white mushrooms

2 (12- to 16-oz.) pork tender-loins

Salt and freshly ground black pepper to taste

2 large eggs

2 cups Italian breadcrumbs

⅓ cup freshly grated Parmesan cheese

2 tsp. Italian seasoning

⅓ cup olive oil

3 TB. unsalted butter

2 shallots, peeled and chopped

⅓ cup freshly squeezed lemon juice

2 TB. chopped fresh parsley

Serves: 4
Active time: 25 minutes
Start to finish: 25 minutes
Each serving contains:
804 calories
409 calories from fat
45 g fat
13.5 g saturated fat
55 g protein
46 g carbohydrates

1. Preheat the oven to 150°F.

2. Wipe mushrooms with a damp paper towel. Discard stems, and slice mushrooms. Set aside.

3. Rinse tenderloins and pat dry with paper towels. Trim each tenderloin by cutting off all visible fat and then scrape off the iridescent silverskin. Cut each tenderloin crosswise into 6 slices. Pound slices between two sheets of plastic wrap to an even ¼-inch thickness, and sprinkle with salt and pepper.

4. Beat eggs with a fork in a shallow bowl. Combine bread-crumbs, cheese, and Italian seasoning in another shallow bowl. Dip meat slices into egg, letting any excess drip off, and then dip meat into crumb mixture, pressing crumbs into meat on both sides.

5. Heat ¼ cup olive oil in a large, heavy skillet over medium-high heat. Cook pork for 1½ minutes or until nicely browned. Turn gently with tongs, and cook the second side for 1½ minutes. Transfer pork to a baking sheet, and place it in the oven to keep warm.

6. Wipe the skillet with paper towels. Heat remaining olive oil and butter over medium-high heat. Add shallots and cook, stir-ring frequently, for 3 minutes or until shallots are translucent. Add mushrooms and cook for 3 to 5 minutes, stirring fre-quently, or until mushrooms are lightly browned and most of their liquid has evaporated. Stir in lemon juice and parsley, and season to taste with salt and pepper.

 Fast Talk

Silverskin
is the iridescent membrane covering tenderloins of any animal. It should be removed before cooking because it becomes tough gristle when the meat is cooked.

7. Remove pork from the oven. Spoon mushrooms over pork, and serve immediately.

Variation: Instead of pork, you can use chicken breasts pounded to the same ¼-inch thickness. Cook the chicken for 2 minutes per side or until cooked through and no longer pink.

Pork with Prosciutto, Mozzarella, and Sage (*Porchetta Saltimbocca*)

This dish is cooked in two steps so the pork remains moist after being layered with the cheese, ham, and herbs.

Serves: 4

Active time: 15 minutes

Start to finish: 30 minutes

Each serving contains:

453 calories

210 calories from fat

23 g fat

11 g saturated fat

55 g protein

3 g carbohydrates

2 (12- to 16-oz.) pork tender- loins

Salt and freshly ground black pepper to taste

4 garlic cloves, peeled and minced

1 tsp. Italian seasoning

16 to 20 fresh sage leaves

8 slices imported prosciutto, trimmed of visible fat

½ lb. whole milk mozzarella cheese, thinly sliced

1. Preheat the oven to 450°F, and line a 10×14-inch baking pan with heavy-duty aluminum foil.

2. Rinse pork and pat dry with paper towels. Trim off all visible fat and iridescent silverskin. Sprinkle pork with salt and pepper, and rub with garlic and Italian seasoning. Tuck thin tail under pork to form an even-size roll, and tie tail section with kitchen string or pin it with wooden toothpicks.

3. Place pork in the baking pan and bake for 10 minutes. Remove pork from the oven, and discard string or toothpicks. Allow pork to rest 5 minutes. Slice pork into ½-inch slices. Pork will still be rare.

4. Arrange pork slices in the baking pan in 4 columns, slightly overlapping slices. Top each with ¼ sage leaves, 2 slices prosciutto, and ¼ cheese slices. Bake for 5 to 7 minutes or until cheese is melted and bubbly. Serve immediately.

Fresh Ways

For small quantities of foods, like a few slices of prosciutto, it's best to visit your supermarket's deli department. Even the smallest package of prepackaged meats are 4 to 6 ounces—more than you probably need.

Herb-Crusted Pork Tenderloin

Rather than stuffing the pork on the inside, crumbled herbed corn muffins become the basis for a coating patted on the outside of the tenderloins.

2 (12- to 16-oz.) pork tenderloins

Salt and freshly ground black pepper to taste

2 TB. olive oil

2 TB. unsalted butter

3 garlic cloves, peeled and minced

2 large corn muffins, crumbled (2 cups crumbs)

2 TB. chopped fresh parsley

1 TB. fresh thyme or 1 tsp. dried

1 TB. chopped fresh rosemary or 1 tsp. dried

2 tsp. chopped fresh sage or ½ tsp. dried

¼ cup Dijon mustard

Serves: 4
Active time: 20 minutes
Start to finish: 30 minutes
Each serving contains:
455 calories
220 calories from fat
24 g fat
9 g saturated fat
42 g protein
17 g carbohydrates

1. Preheat the oven to 425°F, and line a 10×14-inch baking pan with heavy-duty aluminum foil.

2. Rinse pork and pat dry with paper towels. Trim off all visible fat and iridescent silverskin. Sprinkle pork with salt and pepper. Tuck thin tail under pork form an even-size roll , and tie tail section with kitchen string or pin it with wooden toothpicks.

3. Heat oil in a large, heavy skillet over high heat. Sear pork on all sides, turning gently with tongs, for 3 minutes or until browned. Remove pork from the pan, and transfer to the baking pan. Discard string or toothpicks.

4. Reduce the heat to low, and add butter to the skillet. Add garlic and cook, stirring constantly, for 30 seconds or until fragrant. Remove the pan from the heat and stir in corn muffin crumbs, thyme, rosemary, and sage. Season to taste with salt and pepper.

5. Spread mustard over pork and pat seasoned crumbs onto mustard. Roast pork for 10 to 15 minutes or until an instant-read thermometer inserted into the center registers 150°F. Allow pork to rest for 5 minutes, slice, and serve immediately.

 Fresh Ways

Let roasted and sometimes grilled food rest to allow the juices to be reabsorbed into the fiber of the meat, thus making it juicier when sliced. During this resting period, the internal temperature continues to rise and finish the cooking process.

Japanese Sautéed Beef with Scallions (Negimaki)

This dish is stunning on a plate, with a core of bright green scallions surrounded by succulent tender beef.

Serves: 6
Active time: 25 minutes
Start to finish: 40 minutes

Each serving contains:
358 calories
182 calories from fat
20 g fat
5 g saturated fat
37 g protein
7 g carbohydrates

1 (2-lb.) beef tenderloin, well trimmed

18 to 24 scallions, rinsed, trimmed, with all but 2 inches of green tops discarded

½ cup soy sauce

1 TB. grated fresh ginger

2 garlic cloves, peeled and minced

¼ tsp. Chinese five-spice powder

2 TB. Asian sesame oil

1 cup beef stock

2 TB. vegetable oil

1 small piece *star anise*

Salt and freshly ground black pepper to taste

1. Rinse beef and pat dry with paper towels. Trim off all visible fat and iridescent silverskin. Slice into 12 (½-inch-thick) slices, and place them well apart between 2 sheets of plastic wrap. Pound into ¼-inch-thick ovals.

2. Place 1½ to 2 scallions along the edge of each beef slice, and roll tightly. Secure rolls with toothpicks, or tie with string.

3. Mix soy sauce, ginger, garlic, Chinese five-spice powder, and Asian sesame oil in a small bowl and set aside.

4. Bring beef stock to a boil in a small saucepan over high heat. Boil for 5 minutes or until reduced by ½. Set aside.

5. Heat vegetable oil over high heat in a heavy 12-inch skillet. Brush beef rolls with soy mixture and sear, turning with tongs, until brown on all sides. Lower the heat to medium, and continue to cook and turn beef rolls for 5 minutes. Remove and repeat with remaining beef. Place cooked rolls on a heated platter to keep warm.

6. Add reduced stock, star anise, and remaining brushing sauce to the pan. Deglaze the pan by stirring to loosen brown bits. Season to taste with salt and pepper.

7. Slice beef rolls into medallions on the diagonal and arrange them in a circle on a platter or on individual plates. Spoon sauce over medallions, and serve immediately.

Fast Talk

Star anise is a spice native to China that has a more distinct licorice flavor than European anise seed. It's one of the ingredients used in Chinese five-spice powder.

Variation: Try chicken breasts instead of the beef. Cook chicken to a temperature of 160°F on an instant-read thermometer or until cooked through and no longer pink.

Pan-Seared Filet Mignon with Red Wine Sauce

Deglazing a pan with red wine to create a sauce—as done in this dish—is a classic of French cooking, and it's always delicious.

4 (6-oz.) filet mignons

Salt and freshly ground black pepper to taste

3 TB. olive oil

3 TB. unsalted butter

3 large shallots, peeled and chopped

3 garlic cloves, peeled and minced

1½ cups dry red wine

⅔ cup beef stock

3 TB. chopped fresh parsley

1 TB. fresh thyme or 1 tsp. dried

Serves: 4
Active time: 15 minutes
Start to finish: 25 minutes
Each serving contains:
460 calories
206 calories from fat
23 g fat
8 g saturated fat
41 g protein
5 g carbohydrates

1. Preheat the oven to 150°F.

2. Rinse steaks and pat dry with paper towels. Trim to remove any excess fat, season to taste with salt and pepper, and set aside.

3. Heat oil in a heavy 12-inch skillet over high heat. Add steaks and sear on each side for 1 minute. Reduce the heat to medium-high and cook steaks for 2 to 3 minutes on a side for rare or to desired doneness. Remove steaks from the pan with tongs and place them on a serving platter. Place steaks in the oven to keep warm.

4. Pour oil out of the pan, and place the pan over medium heat. Heat butter, and add shallots and garlic. Cook, stirring frequently, for 3 minutes, or until shallots are translucent.

5. Raise the heat to medium-high, and add red wine, beef stock, parsley, and thyme. Cook, stirring occasionally, until sauce is reduced by ½. Season to taste with salt and pepper, and pour sauce over steaks. Serve immediately.

 Fresh Ways

Meat is rare and ready to turn when the meat begins to feel soft and spongy. It's medium when drops of juice begin to appear and the meat resists when pressed. When it's well done, the meat is firm when pressed.

Beef Stroganoff

Slices of tender beef are cooked with mushrooms and then served in a sauce finished with tangy sour cream in this comfort food dish.

Serves: 4

Active time: 25 minutes

Start to finish: 25 minutes

Each serving contains:

635 calories

436 calories from fat

49 g fat

18 g saturated fat

37 g protein

12 g carbohydrates

Stale Stuff

Sour cream adds a luscious richness and tangy flavor to sauces, but it curdles if boils and then your sauce is ruined, so watch it carefully. You can substitute crème fraîche, which does not curdle.

1 (1¼ lb.) beef tenderloin

Salt and freshly ground black pepper to taste

4 TB. unsalted butter

2 TB. all-purpose flour

1½ cups beef stock

2 TB. tomato paste

4 TB. olive oil

3 large shallots, peeled and thinly sliced

1 lb. crimini mushrooms, wiped with a damp paper towel, stemmed, and sliced

⅓ cup sour cream

2 tsp. Dijon mustard

2 TB. chopped fresh parsley

1. Rinse tenderloin and pat dry with paper towels. Trim off all visible fat, and scrape off iridescent silverskin. Cut tenderloin into ½-inch-thick slices. Pound between two sheets of plastic wrap to an even thickness of ¼ inch. Season to taste with salt and pepper, and set aside.

2. Melt 2 tablespoons butter in a heavy 1-quart saucepan over medium heat. Stir in flour, and cook, stirring constantly, for 1 minute. Add beef stock in a slow stream, whisking constantly, and bring to a boil. Whisk in tomato paste. Reduce the heat and simmer, whisking occasionally, for 3 minutes. Remove the pan from the heat, and cover to keep warm.

3. While sauce is simmering, heat 2 tablespoons olive oil in a heavy 12-inch skillet over medium-high heat. Add beef and cook, turning gently with tongs, until browned on both sides but still pink inside, about 1 minute total time. Remove meat from the skillet.

4. Add remaining butter and olive oil to the skillet and heat over medium high heat. Add shallots and cook, stirring frequently, for 3 minutes or until shallots are translucent. Add mushrooms and cook, stirring occasionally, for 5 to 7 minutes or until liquid mushrooms give off has evaporated.

5. Return meat to the skillet, along with any juices that accumulated. Add sauce and whisk in sour cream, Dijon mustard, and parsley. Do not let sauce boil. Season to taste with salt and pepper, and serve immediately.

Mustard-Crusted Rack of Lamb

This is one of the most elegant entrées you can serve, with its dramatic and flavorful topping over a rack of rosy lamb.

2 (1½-lb.) racks of lamb, trimmed	6 garlic cloves, peeled and minced
Salt and freshly ground black pepper to taste	½ cup Italian breadcrumbs
2 TB. vegetable oil	¼ cup freshly grated Parmesan cheese
4 TB. Dijon mustard	2 TB. chopped fresh rosemary

> Serves: 4
> **Active time:** 12 minutes
> **Start to finish:** 30 minutes
> **Each serving contains:**
> 986 calories
> 655 calories from fat
> 73 g fat
> 30 g saturated fat
> 67 g protein
> 15 g carbohydrates

1. Preheat the oven to 450°F, and line a 10×14-inch baking pan with heavy-duty aluminum foil.

2. Season racks of lamb well on all sides with salt and pepper. Heat oil in a large skillet over high heat. Add 1 rack of lamb and brown well on all sides. Transfer lamb to the baking pan. Repeat with second rack of lamb.

3. Spread Dijon mustard evenly over all sides of lamb racks. Combine garlic, breadcrumbs, Parmesan cheese, and rosemary in a small bowl. Press mixture onto the top of lamb with your hands.

4. Bake lamb for 13 to 15 minutes for medium rare or until it registers 130°F on an instant-read thermometer. Allow lamb to rest for 5 minutes and then carve into individual chops. Serve immediately.

Stale Stuff

Most racks of lamb are trimmed when you buy them, but if yours isn't, here's how you do it. Cut between the rib bones and scrape off the meat, exposing the bottom few inches of bone. Be sure the rack is cut through at the thick end so the individual chops can be carved off.

Veal Scaloppine with Fresh Shiitake Mushrooms

Tender veal sautéed with a variety of woodsy mushrooms is napped with a simple sauce for this delicate dish.

Serves: 4

Active time: 25 minutes

Start to finish: 25 minutes

Each serving contains:

349 calories

177 calories from fat

20 g fat

6 g saturated fat

38 g protein

6 g carbohydrates

1½ lb. veal scallops

¼ lb. fresh shittake mushrooms

¼ lb. white mushrooms

2 TB. walnut oil

2 TB. unsalted butter

4 shallots, peeled and chopped

2 garlic cloves, peeled and minced

2 cups veal or chicken stock

2 tsp. chopped fresh thyme or ½ tsp. dried

Salt and freshly ground black pepper to taste

2 tsp. cornstarch

1 TB. cold water

1. Rinse veal and pat dry with paper towels. Place veal between two sheets of plastic wrap and pound to an even ⅛-inch thickness.

2. Wipe fresh shiitake and white mushrooms with a damp paper towel. Discard stems, and slice mushrooms. Set aside.

3. Heat walnut oil in a 12-inch skillet over medium-high heat. Sear veal on both sides, turning quickly. Remove veal with a slotted spatula to a platter and repeat until all veal is seared.

4. Add butter to the pan, and add shiitake mushrooms, white mushrooms, shallots, and garlic. Cook, stirring frequently, for 5 minutes or until shallots and mushrooms are soft.

5. Add veal stock and thyme, and bring to a boil over medium heat. Simmer until stock is reduced by ½ and season to taste with salt and pepper.

6. Combine cornstarch and water in a small bowl and stir well. Stir mixture into sauce, and simmer for an additional minute or until slightly thickened.

7. Return veal to the pan, and bring back to a boil to heat veal through. Do not let veal cook further, or it will toughen. Serve immediately.

Variation: Thin slices of filet mignon can be substituted for the veal.

Stale Stuff

Never season a sauce that's going to reduce with salt and pepper prior to the reduction, or the sauce could be too salty. When the water evaporates during reduction, it intensifies flavors, including that of salt.

Part 6 Great Grills

Everything tastes better when it's cooked outdoors, and those are the recipes in Part 6. Perhaps you grill year-round, or maybe you save this quick-cooking method for bucolic summer evenings. Regardless, you'll find recipes that are ready in minutes.

One chapter contains dishes that get grilled as soon as the grill is heated up. Those recipes are then dressed up with toppings and sauces you make while the food cooks. Then I give you a chapter devoted to all manner of burgers, extending far beyond traditional beef burgers.

Part 6 ends with a chapter on marinated foods. They do need a few hours to absorb flavor from the marinade, but that's all time you're doing something else.

Ready, Set, Grill!

In This Chapter

- ◆ Seafood with relishes
- ◆ Poultry with stuffings
- ◆ Meats with sauces

Ahhh, the grill. Nothing says summer like grilling out, and in the winter, having a grilled dinner is a special treat (well, except maybe for the cook, who has to stand outside in the cold). Whether the grill is Dad's bastion or Mom takes a turn manning the coals (or gas), whoever holds the title of "Grill Master" will enjoy the recipes in this chapter.

All these dishes have been formulated to be ready to grill by the time the grill is hot. There's no marinating involved. You will find some flavorful herb and spice rubs as well as sauces to top the food after it's whisked from the grill. Yum!

Gas vs. Charcoal

I'm sure there's a debate among grillers about which is better, charcoal grills or gas grills: "Charcoal gives better flavor!" "Gas is so much more convenient!" "Charcoal is messy!" "Gas kills the flavor!"

I'll not get into that debate here, and besides, chances are you already have a grill or at least an idea which is better for your needs and tastes. For our purposes, I'll assume you have a grill already and know how to use it—or know where you put the instruction manual that came with it!

Where There's Smoke

Whether you use them with gas or charcoal, wood chips made from aromatic woods like hickory, mesquite, and cherry add immeasurably to the flavor of grilled foods, as well as giving the skin of poultry a rich mahogany color.

For charcoal grills, the secret is to cover the chips in water to soak for at least 30 minutes. When the coals just begin to form white ash but are still somewhat red, drain the chips and scatter them over the charcoal.

Fresh Ways _____

You can also soak woody herb sprigs like rosemary or grape vines, or try whole garlic cloves and pieces of citrus peel. All add flavor.

Even though it's not as pronounced a flavor, you can also use wood chips on a gas grill. Place about 2 cups dry wood chips in the center of a large (12×18-inch) piece of heavy-duty aluminum foil. Bring up the foil on all sides and roll the ends together to seal the pouch. Poke several small holes in the top of the packet. When the grill is hot, place the wood chip pouch under the grate across the burner shields. Smoke will eventually come out from the holes.

Taking Your Grill's Temperature

Ignore the thermometer sticking out of the grill's lid. All that's going to tell you is the temperature of the air in the upper part of the grill lid, and not the temperature at the grate level where the food is grilling.

The best way to judge your grill's surface temperature is with the palm of your hand. After the coals have a light coating of ash place your hand, palm side down, about 4 to 5 inches above the cooking rack. Here are your readings:

Hot grill: 2 seconds

Medium-hot grill: 3 to 4 seconds

Medium grill: 5 to 6 seconds

Medium-low grill: 7 seconds

Grilling is a high-heat cooking method, so if you can hold your hand over the coals for more than 7 seconds it means you should be adding more coals or preheating the gas burners longer.

Play It Safe

Grilling might be man's oldest cooking method, but tried-and-true doesn't necessarily mean safe. You're dealing with live flames, after all. Safety is important:

◆ There's a reason why grill tools have long handles—to keep your fingers (hands, arms, body) away from the flame and heat. Use them.

◆ Use charcoal lighter fluid only as directed, and *never* use it again once charcoal has been initially lit.

◆ Keep the grill a safe distance from the walls of the house or any deck railing. If the grill is on wood, place a layer of bricks or a metal plate underneath it.

◆ When you need to oil the grill rack so foods don't stick, *never* use vegetable oil spray on a grill rack while it's on the grill. The oil can explode. If you want to spray the rack, remove it from the grill first.

◆ Charcoal can carry residual heat for at least a day; don't remove any ashes until the day after you've grilled, and even then they shouldn't go into paper or plastic. Use a can or some other metal container instead.

◆ Don't store charcoal next to the grill or anything else that produces heat. Keep it in a cool, dry place.

◆ Do you know where your instruction manual is? Be sure to study how to change the propane tank, or ask someone experienced to show you how to do it.

◆ Overall, remember safety first. You're cooking with fire or high heat. Children and pets should be kept far from the grill at all times. You don't want to risk a little one knocking over or getting burned on a hot grill.

Note: In all the recipes in this chapter, the "Start to finish time" includes 30 minutes for the grill to heat.

Salmon with Tomatillo Sauce

Delicate salmon is topped with a bright green sauce made with Mexican green tomatoes and aromatic cilantro.

Serves: 4

Active time: 15 minutes

Start to finish: 45 minutes*

Each serving contains:

599 calories

350 calories from fat

39 g fat

10g saturated fat

47 g protein

12.5 g carbohydrates

4 (8-oz.) salmon fillets, skinned

2 TB. olive oil

Salt and freshly ground black pepper to taste

1¼ lb. *tomatillos*

2 TB. unsalted butter

2 garlic cloves, peeled and minced

1 jalapeño chili, rinsed, seeds and ribs removed, and diced

2 TB. white wine vinegar

2 TB. white wine

1 TB. granulated sugar

¼ cup firmly packed cilantro leaves

Cilantro sprigs for garnish (optional)

1. Light a charcoal or gas grill according to the manufacturer's instructions. Begin cooking when the fire is medium-hot.

2. Rinse salmon and pat dry with paper towels. Rub salmon with olive oil, sprinkle with salt and pepper, and set aside.

3. Discard papery husks from tomatillos and then rinse, core, and dice tomatillos.

4. Heat butter in a medium saucepan over medium heat. Add tomatillos, garlic, jalapeño, vinegar, wine, and sugar. Bring to a boil, and cook, stirring frequently, for 10 minutes or until tomatillos are soft.

5. Pour mixture into a food processor fitted with a steel blade or a blender. Add cilantro, and purée until smooth. Return mixture to the pan, season to taste with salt and pepper, and keep warm.

6. Grill salmon for 3 to 5 minutes per a side, turning gently with a wide spatula. Edges should be opaque, but the center should still be slightly translucent.

7. To serve, ladle some sauce onto each plate, and place salmon top. Garnish with cilantro sprigs (if using).

Variation: Instead of salmon, try swordfish, halibut, or boneless chicken breasts pounded to an even ½-inch thickness. Cook the chicken to an internal temperature of 160°F.

Fast Talk

Tomatillos (*tohm-aah-TEE-os*) are green tomatoes, popular in Mexican and Southwestern cooking. They're covered in a thin, parchmentlike husk that must be pulled off and discarded before cooking. You can use tomatillos raw in salsa, but their distinctive tangy flavor with hints of lemon and herbs is released when they're cooked.

Tuna with Ginger Vinaigrette

The Asian flavors in this easy dressing moisten tender tuna steaks seared until just rare.

4 (8-oz.) fresh tuna steaks, at least 1 in. thick

¾ cup olive oil

Salt and freshly ground black pepper to taste

¼ cup sesame seeds

½ cup rice wine vinegar

Juice of 2 limes

2 TB. soy sauce

3 shallots, peeled and chopped

2 TB. grated fresh ginger

2 TB. chopped fresh cilantro

3 TB. Asian sesame oil

Serves: 4
Active time: 15 minutes
Start to finish: 40 minutes*
Each serving contains:
775 calories
520 calories from fat
58 g fat
8 g saturated fat
56 g protein
6 g carbohydrates

1. Light a charcoal or gas grill according to the manufacturer's instructions. Begin cooking when the fire is very hot.

2. Rinse tuna and pat dry with paper towels. Rub tuna with 2 tablespoons olive oil, and sprinkle with salt and pepper. Place tuna on a sheet of plastic wrap on a platter and place in the freezer while the grill heats.

3. Place sesame seeds in a small dry skillet over medium heat. Toast seeds for 2 minutes, or until browned, shaking the pan frequently. Set aside.

4. Combine vinegar, lime juice, soy sauce, shallots, ginger, cilantro, and salt and pepper to taste in a jar with a tight-fitting lid. Shake well. Add remaining olive oil and sesame oil, and shake well again. Set aside.

Fresh Ways _____

Deep-chilling the tuna in the freezer for a short time is a way to ensure that it won't become overcooked when grilled.

5. Sear tuna for 2 minutes per side; the interior should be very rare. Remove tuna from the grill, drizzle with dressing, and sprinkle with sesame seeds. Serve immediately.

Variation: Any thick fish steak such as cod, salmon, or halibut can be substituted for the tuna, but unless you like all fish very raw, increase the cooking time to a total of 10 minutes per inch of thickness.

Sea Scallops with Mango Salsa and Chili Vinaigrette

A colorful mango salsa enlivened with chili oil tops succulent and tender grilled sea scallops in this dish.

Serves: 6
Active time: 20 minutes
Start to finish: 50 minutes*
Each serving contains:
414 calories
257 calories from fat
29 g fat
4 g saturated fat
26 g protein
13 g carbohydrates

12 bamboo or 6 metal skewers

1 red bell pepper or 1 jarred roasted red pepper

2 lb. sea scallops

1 large, ripe mango, peeled, seeded, and cut into ¼-inch dice

½ small cucumber, rinsed and finely chopped

½ small red onion, peeled and finely chopped

3 TB. chopped fresh cilantro

¾ cup olive oil

2 TB. freshly squeezed lime juice

Salt and freshly ground black pepper to taste

⅓ cup cider vinegar

¼ to ¾ tsp. Chinese chili oil or to taste

1. If using bamboo skewers, cover them in water to soak for at least 30 minutes.

2. Light a charcoal or gas grill according to the manufacturer's instructions. Begin cooking when the fire is medium-hot.

3. Place red bell pepper on the hot grill rack, and grill until skin is charred and black. Turn pepper with tongs to char all sides. Plunge pepper into ice water, and when cool enough to handle, remove and discard cap, skin, and seeds.

4. Rinse scallops and pat dry with paper towels. Thread scallops onto skewers, and refrigerate until ready to grill.

5. Combine mango, cucumber, onion, cilantro, 1 tablespoon olive oil, and lime juice in a glass or stainless-steel mixing bowl. Stir gently and season to taste with salt and pepper. Allow salsa to sit at room temperature for at least 15 minutes to blend flavors.

6. Combine roasted red pepper and vinegar in a food processor fitted with a steel blade or in a blender. With the motor running, slowly add remaining olive oil and Chinese chili oil through the feed tube to emulsify dressing. Season to taste with salt and pepper, and set aside. (Salsa and dressing can be made up to 1 day in advance and refrigerated, tightly covered. Allow both to reach room temperature before serving.)

7. Season scallops with salt and pepper, and brush with vinaigrette. Grill skewers for 1½ to 2 minutes per side. To serve, drizzle vinaigrette over skewers and place salsa next to them on the plate.

Variation: You could use extra-large (16 to 20 per pound) shrimp or cubes of firm-fleshed whitefish like cod or swordfish instead of the scallops.

Speedy Solutions

Metal skewers have a flat back so food isn't likely to spin when you turn it, but that's not the case with bamboo skewers. Try this trick: skewer food with two bamboo skewers parallel to one another. That makes food easier to turn.

Swordfish with Smoked Cheddar Sauce

The smoky nuances from the cheese and bacon in the sauce are the perfect complement for this grilled fish.

Serves: 4

Active time: 20 minutes

Start to finish: 40 minutes*

Each serving contains:

938 calories

639 calories from fat

71 g fat

34 g saturated fat

65 g protein

8 g carbohydrates

 **Stale Stuff**

Thin fish fillets such as sole or flounder should never be grilled; they fall apart. Save them for more delicate cooking methods like baking or sautéing. Be sure any fish you grill is at least ⅔ inch thick.

½ lb. bacon, cut into small pieces

3 shallots, peeled and chopped

2 garlic cloves, peeled and minced

1 cup chicken stock

1 cup heavy cream

2 tsp. cornstarch

1½ cups grated smoked cheddar cheese

1 ripe plum tomato, rinsed, cored, seeded, and finely chopped

Salt and freshly ground black pepper to taste

4 (8-oz.) swordfish steaks

4 to 6 TB. fresh tomato salsa (your favorite; optional)

1. Light a charcoal or gas grill according to the manufacturer's instructions. Begin cooking when the fire is hot.

2. Cook bacon in a heavy skillet over medium-high heat for 5 to 7 minutes or until crisp. Remove bacon from the pan with a slotted spoon and set aside.

3. Discard all but 2 tablespoons bacon fat from the pan. Add shallots and garlic, and cook over medium heat, stirring frequently, for 3 minutes or until shallots are translucent. Add ¾ cup stock and cream. Bring to a boil, and simmer for 5 minutes.

4. Mix cornstarch with remaining stock, and stir mixture into sauce. Simmer for 1 to 2 minutes or until sauce is lightly thickened. Stir in grated cheese, and stir until melted. Add tomato and bacon, and season to taste with salt and pepper. (Sauce can be prepared up to 2 days in advance and refrigerated, tightly covered. Reheat it in a saucepan over low heat, stirring frequently.)

5. Sprinkle swordfish with salt and pepper, and grill fish for 2 to 4 minutes per side, depending on thickness, or until fish is still slightly translucent in the center. To serve, ladle sauce onto the center of a plate, and top with a fish steak. Garnish with a mound of salsa (if using).

Variation: No swordfish? Try thick fillets of cod, halibut, or sea bass instead.

Ham and Cheese-Stuffed Chicken

The flavorful stuffing keeps the chicken moist as it grills and can be personalized in myriad ways.

4 (10-oz.) chicken breast halves, with skin and bones

Salt and freshly ground black pepper to taste

¼ lb. (1 cup) Gruyère cheese, grated

¼ lb. cooked ham, cut into ¼-inch dice

1 TB. fresh thyme or 1 tsp. dried

3 TB. unsalted butter, melted

2 TB. freshly squeezed lemon juice

2 TB. Worcestershire sauce

Serves: 4

Active time: 15 minutes

Start to finish: 55 minutes*

Each serving contains:

727 calories

408 calories from fat

45 g fat

19 g saturated fat

73 g protein

3 g carbohydrates

1. Light a charcoal or gas grill according to the manufacturer's instructions. Begin cooking when the fire is medium-hot.

2. Rinse chicken and pat dry with paper towels. Insert a sharp paring knife into the thicker side of chicken breasts, and cut a lengthwise pocket, being careful not to puncture the skin. Sprinkle chicken with salt and pepper, and set aside.

3. Combine cheese, ham, and thyme in a small bowl. Gently stuff mixture into chicken pocket, and secure opening with a toothpick or skewer.

4. Combine butter, lemon juice, and Worcestershire sauce in a small bowl, and set aside.

5. Grill chicken for 10 to 12 minutes per side, basting frequently with sauce. Do not baste for final 2 minutes of cooking, and discard any unused sauce. Chicken is cooked when it registers 160°F on an instant-read thermometer inserted into the thickest part. Serve immediately.

Variation: For a different taste, try cheddar cheese and cooked sausage instead of Gruyère and ham. Either stuffing can also be used for pork chops.

Stale Stuff

When you start basting a raw or partially cooked chicken with a sauce, the sauce comes into contact with the natural bacteria on the chicken and must be discarded. Cross-contamination is one of the leading causes of food illness.

Mexican Chicken with Mole Sauce

Unsweetened chocolate and peanut butter are the "secret ingredi-ents" that give this sauce its rich flavor.

Serves: 4

Active time: 25 minutes

Start to finish: 50 min-utes*

Each serving contains:

672 calories

435 calories from fat

48 g fat

10.5 g saturated fat

33 g protein

31 g carbohydrates

Fast Talk

Mole (*MOH-lay*) is an ancient Mexican spicy sauce that dates from the Aztec era. Unsweetened choco-late adds to its rich-ness, and it always includes some sort of nut or legume for thickening.

4 to 8 chicken pieces (your choice: breasts, thighs, legs), with skin and bones

5 TB. olive oil

6 garlic cloves, peeled and minced

4 TB. chili powder

Salt and cayenne to taste

2 medium onions, peeled and chopped

2 tsp. ground cumin

2 cups chicken stock

3 ripe plum tomatoes, rinsed, cored, seeded, and chopped

¼ cup peanut butter

¼ cup raisins

1 TB. granulated sugar

1 TB. unsweetened cocoa powder

1. Light a charcoal or gas grill according to the manufacturer's instructions. Begin cooking when the fire is medium-hot.

2. Rinse chicken and pat dry with paper towels.

3. Combine 3 tablespoons oil, 2 garlic cloves, and 2 tablespoons chili powder in a small bowl. Season to taste with salt and cay-enne. Mix well, and rub mixture on chicken. Set aside.

4. Heat remaining 2 tablespoons oil in a heavy saucepan over medium-high heat. Add onions and remaining garlic, and cook, stirring frequently, for 3 minutes or until onions are translu-cent. Stir in remaining chili powder and cumin, and cook, stir-ring constantly, for 1 minute.

5. Add chicken stock, tomatoes, peanut butter, raisins, sugar, and cocoa powder. Stir well, and bring to a boil over high heat. Reduce the heat to low, and simmer *mole* sauce for 15 minutes or until lightly thickened. Season to taste with salt and cay-enne.

6. Grill chicken starting with skin side down for 8 to 10 minutes per side or until white meat registers 160°F and dark meat reg-isters 180°F on an instant-read thermometer. Remove chicken from the grill, and serve immediately, passing sauce on the side.

Variation: Pork chops can be substituted for the chicken pieces.

Sweet and Hot Chicken Skewers

You can make these skewers basted with a sweet and hot Asian sauce smaller and serve them as an hors d'oeuvre, too.

12 bamboo skewers

4 (6-oz.) boneless, skinless chicken breast halves

⅓ cup unsweetened apple-sauce

¼ cup hoisin sauce

2 TB. firmly packed dark brown sugar

3 TB. ketchup

1 TB. honey

1 TB. rice wine vinegar

1 TB. soy sauce

2 tsp. Chinese chili paste with garlic or to taste, or hot red pepper sauce

Serves: 4
Active time: 15 minutes
Start to finish: 40 minutes*
Each serving contains:
288 calories
24 calories from fat
3 g fat
1 g saturated fat
40 g protein
24 g carbohydrates

1. Light a charcoal or gas grill according to the manufacturer's instructions. Begin cooking when the fire is hot.

2. Cover bamboo skewers in water to soak for 30 minutes.

3. Rinse chicken, pat dry with paper towels, and trim of all visible fat. Cut chicken into strips 2 inches long and ½ inch wide.

4. Combine applesauce, hoisin sauce, brown sugar, ketchup, honey, rice wine vinegar, soy sauce, and Chinese chili paste in a mixing bowl. Whisk until smooth, and divide sauce into two small bowls.

5. Thread chicken onto skewers. Grill chicken, basting with sauce every 2 minutes, for 3 to 5 minutes per side. Do not baste for the last 2 minutes, and discard basting sauce. Remove chicken from the grill, and serve immediately, passing extra sauce separately.

Variation: Not in the mood for chicken? Cubes of pork loin or pork tenderloin or extra-large (16 to 20 per pound) shrimp can grilled instead.

Ó Speedy Solutions

To save time when making a recipe with many liquid ingredients, measure them into the same large cup, calculating what the level should be after each addition.

Chicken with Three-Tomato Salsa

This dish is the epitome of summer eating, when you can find tomatoes right from the field.

Serves: 4

Active time: 15 minutes

Start to finish: 40 minutes*

Each serving contains:

342 calories

144 calories from fat

16 g fat

2.5 g saturated fat

41 g protein

8 g carbohydrates

4 (6-oz.) boneless, skinless chicken breasts

¼ cup olive oil

4 garlic cloves, peeled and minced

Salt and freshly ground black pepper to taste

1 red tomato, rinsed, cored, seeded, and finely chopped

1 orange tomato, rinsed, cored, seeded, and finely chopped

1 yellow tomato, rinsed, cored, seeded, and finely chopped

½ red onion, peeled and finely chopped

½ red bell pepper, seeds and ribs removed, and finely chopped

1 jalapeño chili, rinsed, seeds and ribs removed, and finely chopped

3 TB. chopped fresh cilantro

1 TB. chopped fresh oregano or 1 tsp. dried

1 TB. chopped fresh basil or 1 tsp. dried

¼ cup red wine vinegar

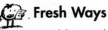 **Fresh Ways**

Food has to be at least ¾-inch thick for an instant-read thermometer to be effective. For thinner food, you can judge by eye or poke it with the tip of a paring knife.

1. Light a charcoal or gas grill according to the manufacturer's instructions. Begin cooking when the fire is medium-hot.

2. Rinse chicken, pat dry with paper towels, and trim of all visible fat. Place chicken between 2 sheets of plastic wrap, and pound to an even ½-inch thickness.

3. Combine 2 tablespoons olive oil and 2 garlic cloves in a small bowl. Spread mixture on chicken, and sprinkle chicken with salt and pepper to taste.

4. Combine red tomato, orange tomato, yellow tomato, red onion, red bell pepper, jalapeño, cilantro, oregano, basil, vinegar, remaining 2 tablespoons olive oil, and remaining 2 garlic cloves in a large bowl. Season to taste with salt and pepper, and stir well. Set aside.

5. Grill chicken for 3 to 4 minutes per side, uncovered, or until cooked through and no longer pink. To serve, place chicken on plates and top with salsa. Serve immediately.

Variation: Veal scallops can be used instead of the chicken.

Caribbean Pork Chops

The paste that's rubbed on these pork chops have all the hallmark flavors of Jamaican "jerk" seasonings.

4 (8-oz.) pork loin chops

1 large onion, peeled and diced

4 garlic cloves, peeled

1 TB. dried thyme

1 TB. granulated sugar

1½ tsp. cayenne

1 tsp. freshly ground black pepper

1 tsp. ground *allspice*

½ tsp. ground cinnamon

Salt to taste

Serves: 4
Active time: 15 minutes
Start to finish: 40 minutes*
Each serving contains:
392 calories
171 calories from fat
19 g fat
6.5 g saturated fat
44 g protein
9 g carbohydrates

1. Light a charcoal or gas grill according to the manufacturer's instructions. Begin cooking when the fire is hot.

2. Rinse pork chops, and pat dry with paper towels. Trim chops of excess fat, and set aside.

3. Combine onion, garlic, thyme, sugar, cayenne, black pepper, allspice, cinnamon, and salt in a blender, and purée.

4. Rub pork chops on both sides with the spice paste and grill for 5 to 6 minutes per side or until an instant-read thermometer registers 150°F. Serve immediately.

Variation: Try boneless, skinless chicken breasts instead of the pork chops. Cook them over a medium-hot fire for 4 to 6 minutes on a side or until an instant-read thermometer registers 160°F.

Fast Talk

Allspice comes from small berries of a pimiento tree native to the West Indies. The spice got its English name because its flavor is like a combination of cinnamon, nutmeg, and cloves.

Steak with Shiitake Cognac Sauce

Steak takes on new elegance when topped with a creamy sauce laced with potent cognac.

Serves: 4

Active time: 15 minutes

Start to finish: 45 minutes*

Each serving contains:

994 calories

570 calories from fat

63 g fat

29 g saturated fat

62 g protein

11 g carbohydrates

Speedy Solutions

Many classic French recipes include a step for igniting liquor such as cognac, but it's not really necessary. The alcohol cooks off as the sauce cooks, although there is a minute trace left.

1 lb. fresh shiitake mushrooms

4 (10-oz.) boneless rib-eye, New York strip, or filet mignon steaks

Salt and freshly ground black pepper to taste

5 TB. unsalted butter

½ cup cognac

1½ cups dry red wine

1 TB. fresh thyme or 1 tsp. dried

18 scallions, rinsed, trimmed, with all but 2 inches of green tops discarded

4 TB. water

1. Light a charcoal or gas grill according to the manufacturer's instructions. Begin cooking when the fire is hot.

2. Wipe shiitake mushrooms with a damp paper towel. Discard stems, slice mushrooms, and set aside.

3. Season both sides of steaks with salt and pepper to taste.

4. Heat 3 tablespoons butter in a heavy 12-inch skillet over medium-high heat. Add mushrooms, and cook, stirring frequently, for 3 minutes or until mushrooms begin to brown. Season to taste with salt and pepper, and continue to cook, stirring frequently, until liquid has evaporated. Remove mushrooms from the pan with a slotted spoon, and set aside.

5. Add cognac to the skillet, and cook over high heat until only 2 tablespoons remain. Add wine and thyme, and cook until liquid is ¾ cup. Return mushrooms to the skillet, season to taste with salt and pepper, and keep warm.

6. While sauce is reducing, heat remaining 2 tablespoons butter in a medium skillet and add scallions and water. Cook over high heat until mixture comes to a boil, shaking the pan to distribute butter. Lower heat to medium, and continue to cook until water has evaporated and scallions are glazed. Set aside.

7. Grill steaks to desired doneness. To serve, place steaks on plates and top with sauce and scallions. Serve immediately.

Variation: Rib lamb chops can be substituted for the steak.

Steak with Southwest Corn Sauce

The sweet flavor of fresh corn in this creamy sauce is balanced by chili and vegetables.

4 (10-oz.) boneless rib-eye or New York strip steaks	1 small onion, peeled and diced
1 TB. Herbes de Provence	1 red bell pepper, seeds and ribs removed, and finely chopped
1 TB. dry mustard	
4 garlic cloves, peeled and minced	3 TB. chili powder
Salt and freshly ground black pepper to taste	½ cup dry red wine
	2 cups beef stock
4 ears fresh corn, shucked	½ cup heavy cream
2 TB. olive oil	

> Serves: 4
>
> **Active time:** 25 minutes
>
> **Start to finish:** 45 minutes*
>
> **Each serving contains:**
>
> 714 calories
>
> 299 calories from fat
>
> 33 g fat
>
> 15 g saturated fat
>
> 70 g protein
>
> 30 g carbohydrates

1. Light a charcoal or gas grill according to the manufacturer's instructions. Begin cooking when the fire is hot.

2. Rinse steak, pat dry with paper towels, and trim of excess fat.

3. Combine Herbes de Provence, mustard, garlic, salt, and pepper in a small bowl. Rub mixture on both sides of steaks, and set aside.

4. Cut kernels from corn using a sharp serrated knife. Place ¼ kernels in a food processor fitted with a steel blade or in a blender, and purée until smooth.

5. Heat oil in a saucepan over low heat. Add onion and red bell pepper, and cook, stirring frequently, for 3 minutes or until onion is translucent. Add chili powder, and cook over low heat, stirring constantly, for 1 minute.

6. Add wine, stock, and puréed corn, and bring to a boil over medium-high heat, stirring occasionally. Cook, stirring occasionally, for 15 minutes or until sauce is reduced by ½.

7. Add cream and remaining corn kernels to sauce, and cook over medium heat, stirring occasionally, for 5 minutes. Season to taste with salt and pepper, and keep sauce hot. (Sauce can be prepared up to 2 days in advance and refrigerated, tightly covered. Reheat over low heat, stirring occasionally.)

 Fresh Ways

The carbohydrates in corn create a natural thickening agent for the sauce, so no roux or cornstarch is necessary. If you want the sauce thicker, add a few tablespoons cornmeal.

8. Grill steaks to desired doneness. Top steaks with sauce, and serve immediately.

Variation: Chicken breasts can be substituted for the steaks. If cooking chicken, use chicken stock rather than beef stock in the sauce.

Butterflied Leg of Lamb with Garlic, Rosemary, and Lemon

Garlic and rosemary are the classic Aegean way to flavor lamb, and I find that lemon zest is a good addition to cut some of the meat's richness.

Serves: 6

Active time: 10 minutes

Start to finish: 50 minutes*

Each serving contains:

319 calories

116 calories from fat

13 g fat

5 g saturated fat

47 g protein

1 g carbohydrates

1 (3-lb.) boneless and butterflied leg of lamb

5 garlic cloves, peeled and minced

Zest of 1 lemon

3 TB. fresh chopped rosemary or 1 TB. dried

Salt and freshly ground black pepper to taste

1. Light a charcoal or gas grill according to the manufacturer's instructions. Begin cooking when the fire is hot.

2. Rinse lamb and pat dry with paper towels.

3. Combine garlic, lemon zest, rosemary, salt, and pepper in a small bowl. Rub mixture on lamb, and allow it to sit at room temperature until the grill is ready.

4. Sear lamb over a hot fire, uncovered, for 5 minutes per side or until exterior is browned. Move lamb to medium heat, and grill for an additional 5 to 8 minutes per side or until an instant-read thermometer registers 125°F for medium-rare or until desired doneness. Remove lamb from the grill, and allow lamb to *rest* for 5 minutes before carving. Carve against the grain, and serve immediately.

Fast Talk

To **rest** is to allow thick pieces of meat to sit for anywhere from 5 to 15 minutes during which time the juices are reabsorbed into the fiber of the meat, making the food juicier when carved.

Chapter 18

Burger Bonanza

In This Chapter

- ◆ Lean fish burgers
- ◆ Flavorful poultry burgers
- ◆ Marvelous meaty burgers

Burger is synonymous with *grilling*. And as you'll discover when cooking the recipes in this chapter, the definition of *burger* goes far beyond beef. The only common denominator to these yummy burgers is that the basic food is ground and they're served between two pieces of some type of bread. But that's where the similarity stops.

In these pages, you'll find burgers made with succulent shrimp and rich tuna as well as burgers with lean ground turkey. And of course, I've included beef burgers, too. But they're not your run-of-the-mill burgers. Mine are flavored with international spice.

Between the Bread

The bread that transforms your burger from a patty to a sandwich is an important part of the finished dish and can harmonize with other flavors. Choose a sturdy bread or bun that will stand up to the burgers' juice or wet condiments. Use crusty buns, and be sure to grill your buns, too, to create additional crust. I've given some suggestions for buns in the recipes, but don't feel you're limited to those. Look around your bakery and use whatever bun appeals to you.

Classy Condiments

The condiments that top your burger should always be of top quality. Ketchup, mustard, and mayonnaise are the classics, but you can add additional options by shopping the supermarket's other aisles. Here are some ideas to vary the fare:

- Any dip you'd use with a potato chip or tortilla chip is perfect for burger topping, such as ranch dip, blue cheese dip, or our old friend onion dip. Or try some of the dip recipes you'll find in Chapter 3!

- Hummus, the Middle Eastern dip made from garbanzo beans, is now a refrigerated standard. It comes with many flavor additions, from roasted garlic to lemon.

- Thick salad dressings such as creamy Italian or Thousand Island work well.

- Use barbecue sauces and chutneys straight from the bottle.

Note: In most recipes in this chapter, the "Start to finish time" includes 30 minutes for the grill to heat.

Middle Eastern Lentil Burgers

Seasonings like aromatic cumin and coriander flavor these healthful meatless burgers.

2 cups *lentils*, picked over, washed, and drained

1 qt. water

1 tsp. salt

¾ cup pine nuts

2 TB. vegetable oil

1 medium onion, peeled and chopped

2 garlic cloves, peeled and minced

2 tsp. ground coriander

1 tsp. ground cumin

Salt and freshly ground black pepper to taste

6 sesame buns, sliced in half

Lettuce, tomato, and mayonnaise for serving

> Serves: 6
>
> **Active time:** 30 minutes
>
> **Start to finish:** 40 minutes*
>
> **Each serving contains:**
>
> 513 calories
>
> 171 calories from fat
>
> 19 g fat
>
> 2 g saturated fat
>
> 23 g protein
>
> 64 g carbohydrates

1. Light a charcoal or gas grill according to the manufacturer's instructions. Begin cooking when the fire is hot.

2. Place lentils in a 2-quart saucepan, and cover with 1 quart water and at least 1 teaspoon salt. Bring to a boil over medium-high heat, reduce heat to low, and simmer, covered, for 20 to 25 minutes or until cooked. Drain lentils, and place in a mixing bowl.

3. While lentils are simmering, place pine nuts in a small dry skillet over medium-high heat. Toast nuts, shaking pan frequently, for 2 to 3 minutes or until browned. Set aside.

4. While lentils are cooking, heat oil in a small skillet over medium-high heat. Add onion and garlic, and cook, stirring frequently, for 3 minutes or until onion is translucent. Add coriander and cumin, and cook, stirring constantly, for 1 minute. Add onion mixture to lentils, and stir well.

5. Purée ½ cup pine nuts and 1 cup lentil mixture in a food processor fitted with a metal blade. Scrape mixture back into the mixing bowl, and add remaining pine nuts. Season to taste with salt and pepper. Form mixture into 6 (¾-inch-thick) burgers.

6. Grill buns cut side down until toasted. Grill burgers for 3 minutes per side, turning gently with a spatula. Serve immediately on buns with lettuce, tomato, and mayonnaise.

 Fast Talk

Lentils are tiny lens-shape pulses and one of the oldest foods in the world. We commonly find brownish-gray lentils, but they also come in bright red, green, and yellow.

Creole Shrimp Burgers

This is a burger version of the New Orleans po' boy sandwich, with vegetables included in the patties.

Serves: 4

Active time: 20 minutes

Start to finish: 45 minutes*

Each serving contains:

665 calories

163 calories from fat

18 g fat

3 g saturated fat

46 g protein

79 g carbohydrates

2 TB. vegetable oil

1½ lb. large (21 to 30 per lb.) raw shrimp

1 small onion, peeled and chopped

2 garlic cloves, peeled and minced

1 celery rib, rinsed, trimmed, and chopped

1 red bell pepper, seeds and ribs removed, and finely chopped

3 TB. chopped fresh chives

3 TB. chopped fresh parsley

½ tsp. hot red pepper sauce or to taste

Cajun seasoning to taste

4 long submarine rolls, split in half

Lettuce, tomato, and tartar sauce for serving

Speedy Solutions

While they're a bit more expensive, you can save a lot of time by buying prepeeled shrimp. Or try Easy Peel shrimp. These have already been deveined, and the peels slip right off.

1. Light a charcoal or gas grill according to the manufacturer's instructions. Begin cooking when the fire is hot.

2. Peel and devein shrimp. Rinse shrimp, and set aside.

3. Heat oil in a large skillet over medium-high heat. Add onion, garlic, celery, and red bell pepper. Cook, stirring frequently, for 5 to 7 minutes or until vegetables are soft. Scrape mixture into a mixing bowl.

4. Finely chop ½ pound shrimp, and add to the mixing bowl. Purée remaining 1 pound shrimp in a food processor fitted with a steel blade. Add to the bowl, along with chives, parsley, hot red pepper sauce, and Cajun seasoning. Form mixture into 8 (¾-inch-thick) burgers.

5. Grill rolls cut side down until toasted. Sear shrimp burgers for 2 minutes per side over hot heat and then cook for an additional 3 or 4 minutes per side over medium heat or until cooked through. Serve immediately placing 2 patties on each roll, with lettuce, tomato, and tartar sauce.

Variation: You can use scallops or a firm-fleshed whitefish such as cod or tilapia instead of shrimp.

Dilled Salmon Burgers

Dill and salmon are a timeless combination, and those foods are sparked by some Dijon mustard for these moist burgers.

1 (1¼-lb.) salmon fillet

¼ cup Dijon mustard

¼ cup chopped fresh dill

Salt and freshly ground black pepper to taste

¼ cup mayonnaise

¼ cup sour cream

2 TB. vegetable oil

4 rolls (your choice), split in half

Lettuce, tomato, and thinly sliced red onion for serving

Serves: 4

Active time: 20 minutes

Start to finish: 2 hours, including 1½ hours for chilling

Each serving contains:

615 calories

334 calories from fat

37 g fat

7 g saturated fat

37 g protein

33 g carbohydrates

1. Rinse salmon, pat dry with paper towels, and cut into 1-inch pieces. Chop salmon in a food processor fitted with a steel blade using on-and-off pulsing. Place salmon in a mixing bowl and add 2 tablespoons Dijon mustard and 2 tablespoons dill. Season to taste with salt and pepper.

2. Form salmon mixture into 4 (1-inch-thick) burgers. Cover burgers with plastic wrap, and refrigerate for at least 1½ hours. (Mixture can be made up to 1 day in advance and refrigerated, tightly covered.)

3. After 1 hour, light a charcoal or gas grill according to the manufacturer's instructions. Begin cooking when the fire is hot.

4. While burgers are chilling, combine mayonnaise and sour cream with remaining Dijon mustard and dill. Stir well, and refrigerate until ready to use.

5. Grill rolls cut side down until toasted. Rub burgers with oil, and grill on a hot grill for 3 minutes per side for medium-rare or to desired doneness. Serve immediately on rolls with sauce, lettuce, tomato, and onion slices.

Variation: Instead of salmon, try this with tuna or a firm-fleshed whitefish like cod or halibut.

Stale Stuff

Don't skip refrigerating the burgers. The chilling time gives the burgers time to solidify so there's no fear they'll fall apart on the grill.

Italian Turkey Burgers

These lean turkey burgers are seasoned with herbs and spices and then topped with mozzarella cheese and marinara sauce.

Serves: 4

Active time: 20 minutes

Start to finish: 40 minutes*

Each serving contains:

841 calories

318 calories from fat

35 g fat

10 g saturated fat

55 g protein

79 g carbohydrates

 Fresh Ways

The dark meat of poultry should be cooked to an internal temperature of 165°F to ensure it's cooked properly at the bone, and burgers should be cooked to the same temperature.

2 TB. olive oil

½ small red onion, peeled and chopped

3 garlic cloves, peeled and minced

1½ lb. ground turkey

¼ cup freshly grated Parmesan cheese

3 TB. chopped fresh parsley

2 TB. chopped fresh basil or 2 tsp. dried

1 TB. chopped fresh oregano or 1 tsp. dried

Salt and freshly ground black pepper to taste

4 Italian rolls, split in half

¼ lb. whole milk mozzarella cheese, sliced

½ cup marinara sauce

Lettuce and thinly sliced red onion for serving

1. Light a charcoal or gas grill according to the manufacturer's instructions. Begin cooking when the fire is hot.

2. Heat olive oil in a small skillet over medium-high heat. Add onion and garlic, and cook, stirring frequently, for 5 minutes or until onion is soft. Scrape mixture into a mixing bowl.

3. Add turkey, Parmesan cheese, parsley, basil, and oregano. Season to taste with salt and pepper. Mix thoroughly, and form mixture into 4 (¾-inch-thick) burgers.

4. Grill rolls cut side down until toasted. Sear burgers over high heat for 2 minutes per side and then place burgers over medium heat. Continue to cook for 3 to 5 minutes per side or until burgers register 165°F on an instant-read thermometer and are cooked through.

5. Top burgers with mozzarella slices, cover grill, and cook for 2 minutes or until cheese is melted. Place burgers on rolls, top with marinara sauce, and serve immediately with lettuce and onion slices.

Variation: No turkey? Try ground pork or ground veal.

New England Turkey Burgers

Dried cranberries and maple are two of the flavors topping these burgers made moister with grated apple.

1¼ lb. ground turkey

1 Golden Delicious apple, peeled, cored, and grated

2 tsp. dry mustard

½ tsp. dried thyme

Salt and freshly ground black pepper to taste

½ cup barbecue sauce

½ cup pure maple syrup

½ cup cider vinegar

¼ cup dried cranberries

1 tsp. lemon zest

½ tsp. ground cinnamon

½ tsp. ground ginger

4 rolls (your choice), sliced in half

Lettuce, tomato, and thinly sliced red onion for serving

Serves: 4
Active time: 15 minutes
Start to finish: 40 minutes*
Each serving contains:
507 calories
119 calories from fat
13 g fat
3 g saturated fat
34 g protein
65 g carbohydrates

1. Light a charcoal or gas grill according to the manufacturer's instructions. Begin cooking when the fire is hot.

2. Combine turkey, apple, 1 teaspoon dry mustard, and thyme in a mixing bowl. Season to taste with salt and pepper. Form mixture into 4 (1-inch thick) burgers.

3. Combine barbecue sauce, maple syrup, cider vinegar, dried cranberries, lemon zest, cinnamon, ginger, and remaining 1 teaspoon dry mustard in a small saucepan. Bring to a boil over medium-high heat, stirring occasionally. Reduce heat to low and simmer sauce for 3 minutes. Divide sauce into 2 small bowls.

4. Grill rolls cut side down until toasted. Sear burgers over high heat for 2 minutes per side and then place burgers over medium heat. Continue to cook, basting with sauce every 2 minutes, for 3 to 5 minutes per side or until burgers register 165°F. Do not baste for the last 2 minutes, and discard basting sauce. Serve immediately on rolls with lettuce, tomato, and red onion slices. Pass second bowl of sauce separately.

Variation: Instead of turkey, try ground pork or ground veal.

 Fresh Ways

Apple adds moisture as well as a sweet flavor to foods. These burgers cook so quickly that the apple retains its texture and makes the burgers juicier.

Mexican Burgers

Spicy chorizo sausage enlivens the taste of the beef in these cheese-filled burgers.

Serves: 4

Active time: 15 minutes

Start to finish: 40 minutes*

Each serving contains:

983 calories

670 calories from fat

74 g fat

23 g saturated fat

48 g protein

28 g carbohydrates

½ lb. *chorizo*

1 lb. ground chuck

2 shallots, peeled and finely chopped

4 garlic cloves, peeled and minced

3 TB. chopped fresh cilantro

2 TB. chili powder

2 tsp. ground cumin

1 tsp. dried oregano

Salt and cayenne to taste

1 cup grated jalapeño Jack cheese

¾ cup mayonnaise

2 TB. diced canned green chilies, drained

1 TB. freshly squeezed lime juice

4 rolls (your choice), sliced in half

Lettuce, tomato slices, and thinly sliced red onion for serving

Fast Talk

Chorizo
(*chore-EAT-zoh*) is a highly seasoned pork sausage flavored with garlic, chili powder, and other spices and used in Mexican and Spanish cooking. The best substitute is linguiça.

1. Light a charcoal or gas grill according to the manufacturer's instructions. Begin cooking when the fire is hot.

2. Remove casings from chorizo, if necessary, and chop chorizo finely in a food processor fitted with a steel blade using on-and-off pulsing. Combine chorizo, ground chuck, shallots, 3 garlic cloves, cilantro, chili powder, cumin, and oregano in a mixing bowl. Season to taste with salt and cayenne. Mix well, and form mixture into 8 (½-inch-thick) patties. Place ¼ cup grated cheese on 4 burgers, and top with remaining 4 patties. Press together gently to enclose cheese.

3. Combine mayonnaise, remaining garlic, green chilies, and lime juice in a small bowl. Season with salt and cayenne, and stir well. Set aside.

4. Grill rolls cut side down until toasted. Grill burgers for a total time of 4 to 6 minutes per side or to an internal temperature of 125°F for medium-rare or to desired doneness. To serve, place burgers on bottom half of rolls and top each with mayonnaise. Serve immediately with lettuce, tomato, and red onion slices.

Variation: Try ground turkey instead of beef. Cook burgers to an internal temperature of 160°F on an instant-read thermometer or until cooked through and no longer pink.

Caribbean Burgers

Curry and aromatic spices flavor these beef burgers.

1½ lb. ground chuck

3 TB. chopped fresh cilantro

4 garlic cloves, peeled and minced

1 TB. freshly squeezed lime juice

2 tsp. curry powder

2 tsp. ground cumin

1 tsp. ground allspice

3 to 5 dashes hot red pepper sauce

Salt to taste

4 rolls (your choice), split in half

½ cup jarred mango chutney

Lettuce, tomato, and thinly sliced red onion for serving

> Serves: 4
>
> **Active time:** 15 minutes
>
> **Start to finish:** 40 minutes*
>
> **Each serving contains:**
>
> 486 calories
>
> 175 calories from fat
>
> 19 g fat
>
> 7 g saturated fat
>
> 39 g protein
>
> 37 g carbohydrates

1. Light a charcoal or gas grill according to the manufacturer's instructions. Begin cooking when the fire is hot.

2. Combine ground chuck, cilantro, garlic, lime juice, curry powder, cumin, allspice, and red pepper sauce in a mixing bowl. Season to taste with salt. Form mixture into 4 (1-inch-thick) burgers.

3. Grill rolls cut side down until toasted. Grill burgers for a total time of 4 to 6 minutes per side or to an internal temperature of 125°F for medium-rare or to desired doneness. To serve, place burgers on bottom half of rolls and top each with chutney. Serve immediately with lettuce, tomato, and red onion slices.

Variation: Ground pork or turkey can be substituted for the beef. Cook pork to an internal temperature of 150°F or to desired doneness. Cook turkey to an internal temperature of 165°F on an instant read thermometer or until cooked through and no longer pink.

 Fresh Ways

> Small quantities of lemon and lime juice are added to many recipes not for their flavor, but to boost the other flavors in the dish. In the same way, they're drizzled on sweet fresh fruit to enliven the taste.

Chinese Pork Burgers

Crunchy water chestnuts, scallions, and ginger give a decidedly Asian accent to these delicate pork burgers.

Serves: 4

Active time: 20 minutes

Start to finish: 45 minutes*

Each serving contains:

660 calories

348 calories from fat

39 g fat

14 g saturated fat

36 g protein

39 g carbohydrates

🖐 Stale Stuff

When a sauce contains a high percentage of sugar, like this one made with hoisin sauce, you should only baste food for the last few minutes of cooking, especially when cooking over anything but low heat. Otherwise, you'll burn the sugar in the sauce.

1½ lb. ground pork

12 scallions, rinsed, trimmed, and thinly sliced

4 TB. grated fresh ginger

¼ cup chopped fresh cilantro

4 garlic cloves, peeled and minced

3 TB. soy sauce

2 TB. dry sherry

½ cup chopped water chestnuts

Freshly ground black pepper to taste

½ cup Dijon mustard

¼ cup hoisin sauce

4 sesame rolls, split in half

Lettuce and tomato slices for serving

1. Light a gas or charcoal grill according to the manufacturer's instructions. Begin cooking when the fire is medium-hot.

2. Combine ground pork, 6 scallions, ginger, cilantro, garlic, soy sauce, sherry, water chestnuts, and pepper in a mixing bowl. Mix well and form into 4 (¾-inch-thick) burgers.

3. Combine Dijon mustard and hoisin sauce in a bowl, whisk well, and set aside.

4. Grill rolls cut side down until toasted. Grill burgers for a total of 4 or 5 minutes per side or until burgers are cooked to 150°F on an instant-read thermometer. Baste burgers with sauce for last 4 minutes of grilling.

5. Add remaining scallions to remaining sauce. Serve immediately on rolls with lettuce and tomato slices. Pass sauce separately.

Variation: Ground turkey or ground veal can be used instead of the pork.

Bombay Lamb Burgers

Succulent dried apricots and curry flavor these yogurt-topped lamb patties.

½ **pt. plain** *yogurt*

2 **TB. vegetable oil**

1 **medium onion, peeled and finely chopped**

2 **garlic cloves, peeled and minced**

1½ **lb. ground lamb**

½ **cup finely chopped dried apricots**

¼ **cup chopped fresh cilantro**

1 **TB. curry powder**

Salt and freshly ground black pepper to taste

2 **tsp. ground cumin**

4 **pita bread**

Cucumber and tomato slices for serving

Serves: 4

Active time: 30 minutes

Start to finish: 40 minutes*

Each serving contains:

800 calories

433 calories from fat

48 g fat

18.5 g saturated fat

38 g protein

52 g carbohydrates

1. Light a charcoal or gas grill according to the manufacturer's instructions. Begin cooking when the fire is hot.

2. Place yogurt in a strainer set over a mixing bowl. Shake strainer gently a few times, and allow yogurt to drain for at least 30 minutes at room temperature or up to 6 hours refrigerated. Discard whey from mixing bowl, and place yogurt in the bowl. Set aside.

3. Heat oil in a small skillet over medium-high heat. Add onion and garlic, and cook, stirring frequently, for 5 minutes or until onion is soft. Scrape mixture into a mixing bowl, and add ground lamb, dried apricots, cilantro, and curry powder. Season to taste with salt and pepper. Mix well, and form mixture into 4 (1-inch-thick) burgers.

4. Grill burgers for a total time of 4 to 6 minutes per side or to an internal temperature of 130°F for medium-rare or to desired doneness.

5. While burgers are grilling, combine drained yogurt and cumin in a small bowl.

6. To serve, split pita bread and place burgers inside. Top each with yogurt and cucumber and tomato slices. Serve immediately.

Variation: Ground beef can be substituted for the ground lamb.

Fast Talk

Yogurt is a dairy product usually made from cow's milk, but it can be made from either goat's milk or sheep's milk. It coagulates into a soft custard texture from being invaded by friendly bacteria that give it a slightly tart taste. When drained, it becomes firmer as the watery whey drips off.

Flavor Without Fuss:
Marinated Grilled Dishes

In This Chapter

- ◆ Exciting Asian approaches
- ◆ Lusty Latin flavors
- ◆ Subtle European seasoning

There are many times that you anticipate hours—or even days—in advance using the grill to cook a delicious dinner, and those are the times when you'll be leafing through the recipes in this chapter. These are all for foods that need a leisurely few hours to marinate before their trip to the grill.

While the length of time from start to finish is measured in hours instead of minutes, your actual time in preparing the food is never more than 25 minutes. Marinades are quick to make and easy to use, and their flavors are drawn from cuisines around the world.

The Soaking Solutions

The secret to all the recipes in this chapter is that they're soaked for a time period in a marinade to give them flavor, and in some cases to tenderize the food as well. This process of soaking foods in the marinade is called marinating.

Most marinades contain some sort of acid. It can be citrus juice or juices, any sort of vinegar, liquor, or any type of wine. Generally the rule holds true that you'll use white wine for white foods like chicken and fish and red wine for red meats. The liquid is the key to a marinade, but other ingredients run the gamut from garlic and onions to puréed olives and herbs.

 Stale Stuff

While the resealable plastic bag is the perfect choice for marinating foods, marinating can also be done in a mixing bowl or roasting pan. Just be sure the pan is glass, ceramic, or stainless steel and *not* aluminum. Aluminum makes the food taste metallic.

The length of time you marinate food depends on the food. Delicate fish should not be marinated for more than a few hours, while dense beef or lamb could be marinated overnight. Check individual recipes for the correct amount of time, and don't exceed that time.

Combination Cooking

Certain cuts of meat, such as a butterflied leg of lamb or a thick steak, can be started on a grill and then finished in the oven. Using this method enables you get the perfect heating throughout. The center is rare while the exterior is done but not overly done and dry. How does this work? The heat transferred by the high heat of the grill starts to heat through to the center and then the oven's more gentle heat finishes the process.

Begin by grilling the meat over a hot grill for 4 minutes on a side and then place the meat in a 375°F oven for the time shown in the following table.

Times for Combination Grilling and Roasting

Thickness	Time
2 inches	10 to 15 minutes
3 inches	18 to 22 minutes
4 inches	25 to 30 minutes

This method of cooking is ideal if you're grilling for a large group. You can sear thick steaks or chops early in the day and then arrange them on a number of baking sheets for completion right before dinner is served.

Salmon Provençale

Heady balsamic vinegar is joined with wine and herbs to give this fish the sunny flavors of Southwestern France.

4 (6-oz.) salmon fillets

¼ cup balsamic vinegar

1 cup dry white wine

3 TB. Dijon mustard

4 garlic cloves, peeled and minced

2 TB. chopped fresh parsley

1 TB. Herbes de Provence

Salt and freshly ground black pepper to taste

¼ cup olive oil

1 cup mesquite or applewood chips

1. Rinse salmon and pat dry with paper towels. Skin salmon by running the blade of a boning knife between the meat and skin.

2. Combine vinegar, wine, Dijon mustard, garlic, parsley, Herbes de Provence, salt, and pepper in a heavy resealable plastic bag, and mix well. Add olive oil and mix well again. Add salmon and marinate, refrigerated, for 3 to 8 hours, turning the bag occasionally.

3. Light a charcoal or gas grill according to the manufacturer's instructions. If you're using a charcoal grill, soak mesquite chips in water to cover for 30 minutes. When the fire is hot, drain wood chips and scatter them on the fire. If you're using a gas grill, create a tinfoil packet for the chips and poke holes in the top. Place packet on grill.

4. Drain salmon, and discard marinade. Cook salmon on a medium grill, covered, for 6 to 8 minutes, turning gently with a wide spatula, or until fish it is opaque at the edges and slightly translucent in the center. Serve immediately.

Variation: Cod, halibut, or sea bass can be used instead of salmon.

Serves: 4

Active time: 15 minutes

Start to finish: 3½ hours, including 3 hours for marinating

Each serving contains:

549 calories

302 calories from fat

33.5 g fat

6 g saturated fat

36.5 g protein

15 g carbohydrates

⏱ Speedy Solutions

Although it's against traditional wisdom, I find it easier to fillet fish starting at the head rather than the tail end. Cut around the gills, and use the backbone of the fish as guide. Slice along the backbone, and you'll get the fillet off in one piece.

Aegean Swordfish

Lemon and oregano are hallmarks of grilled fish in Greece, and they're part of this marinade, too.

Serves: 4

Active time: 10 minutes

Start to finish: 2¼ hours, including 2 hours for marinating

Each serving contains:

521 calories

326 calories from fat

36 g fat

6 g saturated fat

45 g protein

2 g carbohydrates

4 (8-oz.) swordfish steaks

¼ cup freshly squeezed lemon juice

Zest of 1 lemon

6 garlic cloves, peeled and minced

¼ cup chopped fresh parsley

2 TB. dried oregano

1 TB. fresh thyme or 1 tsp. dried

Salt and freshly ground black pepper to taste

½ cup olive oil

1. Rinse swordfish steaks and set aside.

2. Combine lemon juice, lemon zest, garlic, parsley, oregano, thyme, salt, and pepper in a heavy resealable plastic bag, and mix well. Add olive oil, and mix well again. Add swordfish and marinate, refrigerated, for 2 to 3 hours, turning the bag occasionally.

3. Light a charcoal or gas grill according to the manufacturer's instructions.

4. When the fire is hot, remove fish from marinade and discard marinade. Grill fish for 3 or 4 minutes on each side or until slightly translucent in the center. Serve immediately.

Variation: Other firm-fleshed fish such as sea bass, halibut, or scrod can be substituted for the swordfish.

 **Stale Stuff**

When marinating in a strong acid such as lemon juice, it's important to marinate food for only the amount of time specified. Otherwise the acid will "cook" the food and you end up with food that has an unappealing color or texture.

Caribbean Shrimp

A combination of citrus juices, rum, and herbs give these shrimp an island accent.

2 lb. jumbo (11 to 15 per lb.) raw shrimp

2 shallots, peeled and chopped

2 garlic cloves, peeled and minced

Juice of 1 lime

½ cup freshly squeezed orange juice

½ cup white wine

2 TB. dark rum

2 TB. soy sauce

2 TB. chopped fresh parsley

1 TB. chopped fresh rosemary or 1 tsp. dried

Salt and freshly ground black pepper to taste

Serves: 6
Active time: 10 minutes
Start to finish: 2½ hours, including 2 hours for marinating
Each serving contains:
205 calories
24 calories from fat
3 g fat
0.5 g saturated fat
31 g protein
6 g carbohydrates

1. Peel and devein shrimp. Place shrimp in a heavy resealable plastic bag. Add shallots, garlic, lime juice, orange juice, wine, rum, soy sauce, parsley, and rosemary. Season to taste with salt and pepper. Mix well, and add shrimp. Marinate shrimp, refrigerated, for a minimum of 1 or up to 4 hours, turning the bag occasionally.

2. Light a charcoal or gas grill according to the manufacturer's instructions. Begin cooking when the fire is hot.

3. Remove shrimp from marinade, reserving marinade. Grill shrimp uncovered, for 3 minutes per side or until cooked through.

4. White shrimp are grilling, boil down marinade until it is reduced by ½. Spoon a few tablespoons over each portion of shrimp. Serve immediately or at room temperature.

Variation: Any firm-fleshed whitefish fillet, such as halibut, whitefish, or snapper can be used in place of the shrimp. The cooking time is the same.

 **Fresh Ways**

When grilling small foods like shrimp it's easier to turn them if they've been skewered with two skewers. Insert the skewers as parallel lines, and you can use tongs to turn the food evenly.

Middle Eastern Chicken

Aromatic spices like cumin and coriander give this grilled chicken its regional flavor.

Serves: 4

Active time: 10 minutes

Start to finish: 4¾ hours, including 4 hours for marinating

Each serving contains:

932 calories

615 calories from fat

68 g fat

13 g saturated fat

62 g protein

14 g carbohydrates

4 to 8 chicken pieces (breasts, thighs, legs), with bones and skin

¼ cup balsamic vinegar

1 small onion, peeled and chopped

3 garlic cloves, peeled and minced

¼ cup chopped fresh parsley

3 TB. ground cumin

2 TB. ground coriander

1 TB. granulated sugar

1 tsp. ground cinnamon

½ tsp. cayenne or to taste

Salt to taste

¾ cup olive oil

1. Rinse chicken and pat dry with paper towels.

2. Combine vinegar, onion, garlic, parsley, cumin, coriander, sugar, cinnamon, cayenne, and salt in a heavy resealable plastic bag. Mix well, add olive oil, and mix well again. Add chicken and marinate for a minimum of 4 hours, refrigerated, turning the bag occasionally.

3. Light a charcoal or gas grill according to the manufacturer's instructions. Begin cooking when the fire is medium-hot.

4. Remove chicken from marinade and discard marinade. Grill chicken for 12 minutes per side or until white meat registers 160°F and dark meat registers 180°F on an instant-read thermometer. Serve immediately.

Variation: You could also use pork chops instead of chicken pieces.

Speedy Solutions

I like to mince the marinade ingredients because the pieces then cling to the food when it's grilled, but if you want to save time, combine all the marinade ingredients in a food processor fitted with a steel blade or in a blender and purée. It'll taste the same.

Chicken Satay with Spicy Peanut Sauce

This easy peanut sauce can also be used as a dressing for chicken salad or cold noodles.

4 (6-oz.) boneless, skinless chicken breasts

¾ cup soy sauce

1 cup firmly packed dark brown sugar

⅔ cup freshly squeezed lime juice

4 TB. Chinese chili paste with garlic

10 garlic cloves, peeled and minced

3 TB. Asian sesame oil

8 to 12 (8-in.) bamboo skewers

1 cup chunky peanut butter

½ cup very hot tap water

3 scallions, rinsed, trimmed, and chopped

¼ cup chopped fresh cilantro

Serves: 4

Active time: 15 minutes

Start to finish: 3½ hours, including 3 hours for marinating

Each serving contains:

916 calories

400 calories from fat

44 g fat

7 g saturated fat

59 g protein

78 g carbohydrates

1. Rinse chicken and pat dry with paper towels. Trim chicken of all visible fat, and cut into 1-inch cubes.

2. Combine ½ cup soy sauce, ½ cup brown sugar, ⅓ cup lime juice, 2 tablespoons Chinese chili paste, 4 cloves garlic, and 1 tablespoon sesame oil in a heavy resealable plastic bag. Mix well and add chicken. Marinate chicken for a minimum of 3 hours, refrigerated, turning the bag occasionally.

3. Light a charcoal or gas grill according to the manufacturer's instructions. Cover bamboo skewers in water to soak. Begin cooking when the fire is hot.

4. Combine peanut butter, water, scallions, cilantro, remaining ¼ cup soy sauce, remaining ½ cup brown sugar, remaining ⅓ cup lime juice, remaining 2 tablespoons chili paste, remaining 6 garlic cloves, and remaining 2 tablespoons sesame oil in a mixing bowl. Whisk well, and set aside.

5. Drain chicken from marinade and discard marinade. Thread chicken on soaked skewers. Grill chicken for 3 minutes per side, turning it in quarter turns to grill all 4 sides, until chicken registers 160°F on an instant-read thermometer. Serve immediately accompanied by peanut sauce.

Variation: Try this recipe with pork or beef cubes or extra-large shrimp instead of chicken.

Stale Stuff

When skewering food for grilling, don't just jam the pieces together on the sticks. Food cooks at a slower rate if it's pressed together. You want the pieces to be just touching.

Cranberry-Maple Spareribs

Here, cranberry and orange flavor the ribs and then maple syrup adds to the succulent glaze.

Serves: 6

Active time: 10 minutes

Start to finish: 6½ hours, including 6 hours for marinating

Each serving contains:

936 calories

643 calories from fat

71 g fat

26 g saturated fat

49 g protein

21 g carbohydrates

1 cup cranberry juice

2 TB. orange juice concentrate

4 garlic cloves, peeled and minced

1 shallot, peeled and minced

1 TB. fresh thyme or 1 tsp. dried

½ tsp. ground allspice

Salt and freshly ground black pepper to taste

2 (2-lb.) racks baby back ribs, cut into 6 servings

⅓ cup pure maple syrup

1. Combine cranberry juice, orange juice concentrate, garlic, shallot, thyme, allspice, salt, and pepper in a heavy resealable plastic bag. Mix well, and add ribs. Marinate ribs, refrigerated, for a minimum of 6 hours and up to 18 hours, turning the bag occasionally.

2. Light a charcoal or gas grill according to the manufacturer's instructions. Begin cooking when the fire is medium-hot.

3. Remove ribs from marinade, and reserve marinade. Grill ribs over medium-hot fire, covered, turning occasionally, for 20 minutes or until almost cooked through.

4. While ribs are grilling, combine reserved marinade and maple syrup in a small saucepan, and boil over medium heat until mixture is reduced to ⅓ cup.

5. Brush underside of ribs with the glaze, and grill for 2 minutes. Turn ribs, brush the top side, and grill for 2 minutes more. (Ribs can be grilled 1 day in advance and reheated, uncovered, in a 375°F oven for 10 to 12 minutes or until hot.)

Variation: You could also use pork chops or pieces of chicken with bones in place of the ribs. Cook chicken to an internal temperature of 165°F on an instant-read thermometer and pork chops to an internal temperature of 155°F.

Stale Stuff

While it was a luxury even a few decades ago, it's now easy to find authentic maple syrup in most supermarkets. So there's no reason to ever use anything else—and certainly not "pancake syrup" or any artificially flavored product.

Stuffed Flank Steak

This dish looks stunning when it's brought to the table, with a colorful filling of sautéed vegetables in the center of each slice.

1 (1½-lb.) *flank steak*, cut from the thick end

1 cup dry red wine

1 shallot, peeled and chopped

4 garlic cloves, peeled and minced

1 TB. Herbes de Provence

Salt and freshly ground black pepper to taste

¼ cup olive oil

2 TB. unsalted butter

1 green bell pepper, seeds and ribs removed, and chopped

1 red bell pepper, seeds and ribs removed, and chopped

1 large onion, peeled and chopped

2 TB. beef stock

¼ cup freshly grated Parmesan cheese

½ cup Italian breadcrumbs

2 TB. chopped fresh parsley

1 TB. chopped fresh oregano or 1 tsp. dried

1 TB. fresh thyme or 1 tsp. dried

Serves: 4
Active time: 25 minutes
Start to finish: 3¾ hours, including 3 hours for marinating
Each serving contains:
631 calories
334 calories from fat
37 g fat
13 g saturated fat
42 g protein
21 g carbohydrates

1. Rinse flank steak and pat dry with paper towels. *Score* steak lightly in a diamond pattern on both sides. Cut a deep pocket in the center of flank steak from the side of steak that extends to within ½ inch of sides of meat.

2. Combine wine, shallot, 2 garlic cloves, and Herbes de Provence in a heavy resealable plastic bag. Season to taste with salt and pepper. Mix well, add olive oil, and mix well again. Add steak, and marinate, refrigerated, for a minimum of 3 hours and up to 8 hours.

3. Light a charcoal or gas grill according to the manufacturer's instructions. Begin cooking when the fire is hot.

4. Melt butter in a 12-inch skillet over medium heat. Add green bell pepper, red bell pepper, onion, and remaining garlic. Cook, stirring frequently, for 10 minutes or until vegetables are soft. Remove the pan from the heat and stir in stock, Parmesan cheese, breadcrumbs, parsley, oregano, and thyme. Season to taste with salt and pepper, and mix well.

 Fast Talk

To **score** is to make shallow cuts in food, frequently in a diamond pattern. In the case of flank steak, it keeps the meat from curling as it grills, but it can also be used as a way to speed absorption of the flavors in a marinade.

5. Gently stuff vegetable mixture into steak pocket and skewer the opening closed with turkey-trussing skewers or wooden toothpicks soaked in water. Sprinkle meat with salt and pepper.

6. Grill steak uncovered for 3 to 4 minutes per side for medium-rare or to desired doneness. Allow steak to rest for 5 minutes and then carve into slices. Serve immediately.

Mexican Steaks with Chipotle Mayonnaise

The smoky flavor of chipotle chilies underscores the grilled taste of these spicy steaks.

Serves: 4

Active time: 20 minutes

Start to finish: 3½ hours, including 3 hours for marinating

Each serving contains:

956 calories

597 calories from fat

66 g fat

14 g saturated fat

66 g protein

9 g carbohydrates

4 (10-oz.) New York strip or boneless rib-eye steaks

1 cup dry red wine

¼ cup red wine vinegar

1 small onion, peeled and chopped

4 garlic cloves, peeled and minced

1 large jalapeño chili, rinsed, seeds and ribs removed, and finely chopped

2 TB. ground cumin

1 TB. dried oregano, preferably Mexican

Salt to taste

½ cup olive oil

½ cup mayonnaise

1 *chipotle chili in adobo sauce,* finely chopped

2 tsp. adobo sauce

1. Rinse steaks and pat dry with paper towels.

2. Combine wine, vinegar, onion, 3 garlic cloves, jalapeño, cumin, and 2½ teaspoon oregano in a heavy resealable plastic bag. Add salt to taste, and mix well. Add olive oil, and mix well again. Add steaks and marinate, refrigerated, for 3 to 5 hours, turning the bag occasionally.

3. Light a charcoal or gas grill according to the manufacturer's instructions. Begin cooking when the fire is hot.

4. Combine mayonnaise, chipotle chili, adobo sauce, remaining garlic, and remaining oregano in a mixing bowl. Whisk well.

5. Remove steaks from marinade and discard marinade. Grill steaks uncovered for 3 to 4 minutes per side for medium rare or to desired doneness. To serve, slice steaks into ¾-inch slices and top with sauce. Serve immediately.

Variation: Lamb chops can be substituted for the steak.

Fast Talk

Chipotle chilies are dried jalapeño chilies that have been smoked. They're canned in a spicy sauce similar to a hot red pepper sauce made from chilies, vinegar, and salt.

Korean Steak

In this authentic Korean dish, the grilled steak is topped with a spicy sauce flavored with cilantro and garlic.

4 (10-oz.) New York strip or boneless rib-eye steaks

1 cup soy sauce

¼ cup sweet sherry

3 TB. granulated sugar

7 garlic cloves, peeled and minced

2 TB. Asian sesame oil

1 tsp. red pepper flakes or to taste

½ cup firmly packed cilantro leaves

⅓ cup vegetable oil

2 TB. freshly squeezed lime juice

½ jalapeño or serrano chili, rinsed, seeds and ribs removed, and diced

Serves: 4

Active time: 10 minutes

Start to finish: 3½ hours, including 3 hours for marinating

Each serving contains:

590 calories

207 calories from fat

23 g fat

7 g saturated fat

70 g protein

19 g carbohydrates

1. Rinse steaks and pat dry with paper towels.

2. Combine ¾ cup soy sauce, sherry, sugar, 4 garlic cloves, 1 tablespoon Asian sesame oil, and red pepper flakes in a heavy resealable plastic bag. Mix well, and add steaks. Marinate steaks, refrigerated, for a minimum of 3 hours, turning the bag occasionally.

3. Light a charcoal or gas grill according to the manufacturer's instructions.

Fresh Ways

You can increase the number of servings from 4 to 6 for any recipe without increasing the amount of marinade. When you get to 8 servings, though, you should double the marinade.

4. Combine remaining ¼ cup soy sauce, remaining 3 garlic cloves, remaining 1 tablespoon sesame oil, cilantro, vegetable oil, lime juice, and jalapeño in a food processor fitted with a steel blade or in a blender. Purée until smooth, and set aside.

5. Remove steaks from marinade and discard marinade. Grill steaks uncovered for 3 to 4 minutes per side for medium-rare or to desired doneness. To serve, slice steaks into ¾-inch slices and top with sauce. Serve immediately.

Variation: Thick pork chops can be substituted for the beef steaks. Cook them to an internal temperature of 150°F.

Rosemary Lamb Chops

While there's not a lot of liquid in this marinade, it still enters the meat well via slits cut in the chops.

Serves: 4

Active time: 15 minutes

Start to finish: 2 hours, including 1½ hours for marinating

Each serving contains:

721 calories

299 calories from fat

33 g fat

10.5 g saturated fat

96 g protein

2 g carbohydrates

8 (1½-in.) loin lamb chops

3 garlic cloves, peeled

3 anchovy fillets

¼ cup fresh rosemary leaves

¼ cup fresh parsley leaves

½ tsp. dried thyme

Freshly ground black pepper to taste

3 TB. olive oil

2 TB. dry red wine

1. Rinse lamb chops and pat dry with paper towels.

2. Combine garlic, anchovies, rosemary, parsley, thyme, pepper, oil, and wine in a food processor fitted with the steel blade. Purée until smooth.

3. Using a small sharp knife, make several shallow incisions in both sides of each lamb chop. Rub marinade generously over both sides of chops, and press it into incisions. Place chops on a platter, and marinate chops at room temperature for 1½ to 2 hours or refrigerated for up to 8 hours.

4. Light a charcoal or gas grill according to the manufacturer's instructions. Grill chops over a hot fire for 5 or 6 minutes per side for medium-rare or to desired doneness.

Variation: No lamb chops? Try boneless rib-eye or strip sirloin steaks instead, each about 10 ounces.

Fresh Ways

If you have an aversion to anchovies, feel free to pass them over in this recipe. But then do add salt to taste to the marinade to compensate.

Part 7

Desserts on a Deadline

Ahhh … dessert. That delicious ending to a meal. Those are the recipes in this part.

The first chapter features fresh fruits from all seasons. You'll find ways to quickly glorify summer's ripest berries and ways to use apples for dessert quesadillas. The next chapter also contains a lot of fruit. These become the stars of baked goods, joined by a number of rich cookies.

The last chapter contains everything chocolate—from rich and gooey fondues to frozen delights. For those of us who consider *chocolate* and *dessert* to be synonymous, it doesn't get any better than that.

Chapter 20

Fruity Favorites

In This Chapter

- ◆ Yummy cooked fruit combinations
- ◆ Dressed-up berries
- ◆ Fruity tropical treats

Come summer, there's nothing better than ripe fresh fruit straight from a farmers' market, and in this chapter, you'll find recipes that put those fantastic fruits to work! These simple dishes glorify the vivid color and luscious flavor of ripe fruits.

Berries are good sources of vitamins and are on the list of foods high in disease-fighting antioxidants—not to mention there's nothing better than berries for a fast dessert. But berries aren't the only fruit. Also in this chapter you'll find recipes for some stalwarts like bananas and pineapples, ripe at any time of the year.

The Fruit Family

The common factor that unites fruit botanically as a group is a seed (or many seeds). That seed is more obvious in some fruits than in others, but it's always present in fruit. Here's some tips on choosing some of the fruits featured in this chapter:

Blueberries   Look for plump (not shriveled) berries with a slight grayish patina.

Peaches   Peaches, high in beta-carotene, are ripe if they're soft when gently pressed. The easiest way to peel peaches is to drop them into boiling water for 30 seconds. Remove them from the water with a slotted spoon, and the skins will slip right off when you rub the fruit.

Raspberries   When choosing fresh raspberries, look at the bottom of the container, and choose a package that has the least amount of juice pooled in the bottom—a sign that the berries are not damaged or moldy.

Fresh Ways _____

There are two basic types of peaches: clingstone and freestone. They taste similar, and the only difference is whether or not the flesh clings to the pit. Regardless of which you pick, choose the ripest peach you can find.

Strawberries   Strawberries do not ripen once they've been picked, so what you buy is what you get. Because most companies "top dress" the packages with the "hero berries" on the top, check out the bottom of the package.

Regardless of the species of bright berry, they're treated the same way. Do not rinse berries prior to storing them, but always rinse them prior to eating them. Cut the green caps off of strawberries right before they're rinsed.

Fig and Raspberry Gratin

The vivid fruits in this dessert are enhanced by a flavorful topping.

2 (½-pt.) containers fresh raspberries

1 (1-pt.) container fresh figs

¾ cup sour cream

3 TB. whole milk

5 TB. firmly packed dark brown sugar

Serves: 4
Active time: 10 minutes
Start to finish: 12 minutes
Each serving contains:
317 calories
78 calories from fat
9 g fat
5 g saturated fat
4 g protein
62 g carbohydrates

1. Preheat an oven broiler.

2. Gently rinse raspberries and pat dry. Place berries in an oven-proof 7×12-inch gratin dish or 9×9-inch baking dish.

3. Rinse and stem figs, and cut into ⅓-inch slices.

4. Mix sour cream with milk, and spread mixture over raspberries. Top with sliced figs, and sprinkle with brown sugar.

5. Broil for 2 to 3 minutes or until sugar is melted and fruit is warm. Serve immediately.

Variation: You can use blueberries instead of raspberries and thinly sliced peeled peaches instead of figs.

Fresh Ways

Fruits are always more flavorful if they're warm or at room temperature and not chilled. You can take the chill off any fruit quickly using the microwave set at medium (50 percent). The amount of time depends on the size of the fruit and how many you're warming at once.

Blueberry Shortbread Gratin

Crumbled cookies create a crunchy topping for this easy and fast dessert.

Serves: 6
Active time: 10 minutes
Start to finish: 25 minutes
Each serving contains:
432 calories
121 calories from fat
13 g fat
5 g saturated fat
4 g protein
83 g carbohydrates

2 qt. fresh blueberries, rinsed and picked over

¼ cup fruit-only blueberry preserves

2 TB. instant *tapioca*

1 tsp. grated lemon zest

2 cups crumbled shortbread cookies

¼ cup granulated sugar

½ tsp. ground cinnamon

3 TB. unsalted butter, diced into 12 pieces

1½ cups vanilla ice cream (optional)

1. Preheat the oven to 400°F.

2. Place blueberries in a greased 9×13-inch baking pan. Mix with preserves, tapioca, and lemon zest.

3. Combine cookie crumbs, sugar, and cinnamon in a mixing bowl. Sprinkle mixture evenly over berries, and dot with butter. Bake for 20 to 25 minutes or until top is browned and berries are bubbling. Serve immediately or at room temperature, topped with ice cream (if using).

Variation: Don't care for blueberries? Try raspberries or blackberries instead with the appropriate fruit jam.

 Fast Talk

Tapioca (*tap-ee-OH-kah*) is a starch that comes from the roots of the cassava plant. It's used like cornstarch as a thickening agent.

Mixed Berry Compote

Various fresh berries create a flavorful hot syrup to top ice cream.

1 cup fresh strawberries

1 cup fresh blueberries

1 cup fresh raspberries

½ cup granulated sugar

½ cup water

2 TB. crème de cassis

3 TB. unsalted butter, cut into small pieces

2 cups vanilla ice cream

Serves: 4

Active time: 10 minutes

Start to finish: 25 minutes

Each serving contains:

437 calories

194 calories from fat

22 g fat

13 g saturated fat

4 g protein

56 g carbohydrates

1. Rinse strawberries, blueberries, and raspberries, keeping them in separate dishes. Discard green tops from strawberries, and slice strawberries, if large.

2. Combine sugar, water, and crème de cassis in a heavy 2-quart saucepan. Bring to a boil over high heat, reduce the heat to medium, and simmer mixture for 10 minutes. Add strawberries and blueberries, and cook for 2 minutes, stirring gently a few times. Add raspberries and butter, heating just until butter melts.

3. To serve, divide ice cream into serving dishes and top each with berries.

Stale Stuff

It's important to take the time to reduce the sugar syrup in this recipe; otherwise, it won't be as intensely flavored if the water has not evaporated. You don't have to worry about it being dry, though. The fruit adds its own moisture back to the dish.

Dumpling-Topped Berry Grunt

Grunts (or slumps) are steamed dumplings on top of fruits, dating from the Colonial era.

Serves: 6

Active time: 15 minutes

Start to finish: 27 minutes

Each serving contains:

229 calories

60 calories from fat

7 g fat

4 g saturated fat

3 g protein

41 g carbohydrates

⅔ **cup freshly squeezed orange juice**

1 **cup fresh blackberries, rinsed**

1 **cup fresh blueberries, rinsed**

1 **cup fresh strawberries, rinsed, capped, and halved**

2 **tsp. grated orange zest**

½ **cup granulated sugar**

1 **TB. cornstarch**

2 **TB. cold water**

¾ **cup all-purpose flour**

1 **tsp. baking powder**

¼ **tsp. ground cinnamon**

Pinch salt

3 **TB. unsalted butter, cut into small pieces**

⅓ **cup whole milk**

Vanilla ice cream (optional)

1. Combine orange juice, blackberries, blueberries, strawberries, orange zest, and ¼ cup sugar in a large skillet with a lid. Bring to a boil over medium-high heat, stirring occasionally. Cover, reduce heat to medium, and simmer for 5 minutes. Mix cornstarch into water, and stir to dissolve. Uncover the skillet, stir cornstarch mixture into fruit, and simmer for 2 minutes or until lightly thickened.

2. Combine flour, remaining ¼ cup sugar, baking powder, cinnamon, and salt. Cut in butter with a pastry blender, two knives, or your fingertips until mixture resembles coarse meal. Add milk to flour mixture, and mix just until moist dough forms. Spoon 6 mounds of dough on top of fruit in skillet.

3. Cover and simmer for 15 minutes or until a toothpick inserted in topping comes out clean. Serve hot with vanilla ice cream (if using).

Fresh Ways

Pastry blenders have three or four wire half-moon-shaped blades attached to a handle. Rocking it back and forth through a bowl with flour and butter breaks up the butter into tiny pieces similar to a coarse meal. Pastry blenders were once a part of every cook's kitchen, but today, more people make pie crust with the aid of a food processor instead.

Fresh Berries with Lemon Mousse

The tangy flavor of lemon in this light mousse enhances the fruit it tops.

6 large egg yolks

¾ cup granulated sugar

½ cup freshly squeezed lemon juice

2 tsp. grated lemon zest

2 TB. Grand Marnier

1½ cups heavy cream

4 cups assorted fresh berries (blueberries, raspberries, blackberries, or sliced strawberries)

Serves: 6

Active time: 20 minutes

Start to finish: 45 minutes, including 20 minutes for chilling

Each serving contains:

417 calories

244 calories from fat

27 g fat

15 g saturated fat

5 g protein

40 g carbohydrates

1. Beat egg yolks with sugar in a saucepan with an electric mixer at medium speed until thick and light colored. Beat in lemon juice and lemon zest, and place the pan over low heat. Heat, stirring constantly, until mixture is thick enough to coat the back of the spoon. Remove the pan from the heat, and beat in Grand Marnier. Scrape mixture into a pie plate, and chill for at least 20 minutes or until cold. While mixture is chilling, chill a mixing bowl and electric beaters in the freezer.

2. Beat cream in the chilled bowl until stiff peaks form. Fold custard mixture into whipped cream.

3. To serve, divide berries into dishes and spoon mousse on top.

Variation: For a twist, try lime juice and lime zest instead of lemon juice and lemon zest.

Fresh Ways

Don't waste all the egg whites from a recipe like this one that requires just the yolks. Use them along with whole eggs for omelets or scrambled eggs that will be lower in cholesterol. Or make them into meringue cookies.

Peach Skillet Cake

The creamy topping on this cake is browned under the broiler for a dramatic presentation.

Serves: 6

Active time: 10 minutes

Start to finish: 30 minutes

Each serving contains:

277 calories

128 calories from fat

14 g fat

8 g saturated fat

11 g protein

26 g carbohydrates

3 TB. unsalted butter

3 ripe peaches, peeled, seeded, and cut into 8 wedges each

3 TB. granulated sugar

1 cup cottage cheese

¾ cup sour cream

1 tsp. pure vanilla extract

¾ cup all-purpose flour

3 large eggs

1 TB. confectioners' sugar

Sweetened whipped cream for serving (optional)

1. Preheat the oven broiler.

2. Melt butter in a 12-inch ovenproof skillet. Arrange peach wedges in one layer in the skillet and sprinkle with 1 tablespoon sugar. Cook over medium heat for 5 minutes, turn wedges over with a slotted spatula, and cook for 3 more minutes.

3. While peaches are cooking, combine cottage cheese, sour cream, vanilla extract, flour, eggs, and remaining 2 tablespoons sugar in a food processor fitted with a steel blade or in a blender. Purée until smooth.

4. Pour batter over peaches in the skillet. Cover and cook over low heat on top of the stove for 6 minutes. Uncover the skillet and broil 6 inches from the broiler element for 6 to 8 minutes or until browned.

5. Invert cake onto a serving plate, sprinkle with confectioners' sugar, cut into wedges, and serve immediately, passing whipped cream separately (if using).

Variation: No peaches? Try Golden Delicious apples instead.

Speedy Solutions

Traditionally peaches are peeled by dropping them into boiling water for 30 seconds and then using a paring knife to slip off the skin. This method works, but I find it's faster to peel them with a paring knife or vegetable peeler.

Easy Berry Trifle

A trifle is a traditional English dessert combining berries and some sort of creamy custard, and this one is so easy because the custard doesn't need cooking.

1 cup *mascarpone* cheese

1 cup sour cream

⅓ cup granulated sugar

1 tsp. pure vanilla extract

1 cup puréed raspberries

2 TB. framboise or any raspberry flavored liqueur

12 or 24 ladyfingers (depending on size)

2 (½-pt.) containers fresh raspberries, rinsed

Serves: 6

Active time: 15 minutes

Start to finish: 1 hour, including 45 minutes for chilling

Each serving contains:

482 calories

298 calories from fat

33 g fat

20 g saturated fat

7 g protein

41 g carbohydrates

1. Combine mascarpone, sour cream, ¼ cup sugar, and vanilla extract in a mixing bowl, and whisk until smooth.

2. In another bowl, combine remaining sugar, puréed raspberries, and Framboise. Arrange ⅓ ladyfingers in one layer in a baking dish, and pour syrup evenly over them.

3. Spoon ¼ cream filling into a 4-cup glass bowl, and add ⅓ raspberries. Add ⅓ ladyfingers, pushing them into filling. Repeat with remaining cream, fruit, and ladyfingers, ending with a layer of cream. Cover the bowl with plastic wrap, and refrigerate for at least 45 minutes.

4. To serve, spoon onto serving plates, digging the spoon in vertically to give each diner many layers.

Variation: This trifle is also great with strawberries or blackberries if you don't have raspberries.

Fast Talk

Mascarpone is a rich double or triple cream cheese made from milk and famous in the Lombardy region of Italy. It resembles cream cheese but has a far higher butter content. If you can't find any, use half cream cheese and half unsalted butter instead.

Lemon Curd Mascarpone Fondue

This creamy dessert is not too sweet, and the warm temperature makes it special.

Serves: 6

Active time: 15 minutes

Start to finish: 20 minutes

Each serving contains:

324 calories

235 calories from fat

26 g fat

16 g saturated fat

4 g protein

20 g carbohydrates

3 large eggs

½ cup granulated sugar

⅔ cup freshly squeezed lemon juice

1 TB. grated lemon zest

6 TB. unsalted butter, cut into ¼-inch dice

1 TB. cornstarch

½ cup mascarpone

1. Combine eggs and sugar in a heavy 1-quart saucepan, and whisk until thick and lemon colored. Add ½ cup lemon juice, lemon zest, and butter. Place the pan over medium-low heat, and cook, whisking frequently, for 5 to 6 minutes or until *curd* is thick and small bubbles begin to appear on the surface.

2. Combine remaining lemon juice and cornstarch in a small bowl, and stir to dissolve cornstarch. Add to fondue, and bring to a simmer, stirring constantly. Cook over low heat for 1 to 2 minutes or until fondue has thickened. Remove the pan from the heat, and whisk in mascarpone.

3. Transfer fondue to a fondue pot or other pot with a heat source, and serve with hulled strawberries (halved if large), clementine segments, donut holes, waffle squares, angel food cake cubes, pound cake cubes, coconut macaroons, or sugar cookies.

Variation: Try this with lime juice and lime zest in place of lemon juice and zest.

Fast Talk

Curd is most often refers to cheese (e.g., separating the curd from the liquid whey), but it's also the name of a family of thick fruit spreads, especially popular in England, made from sugar, butter, fruit juice, and eggs. When the curd is cool, it's spread on breakfast pastries.

Bananas Foster Fondue

Bananas Foster is the signature dessert from famed Brennan's in New Orleans, and this fondue is a liquid version.

2 very ripe bananas
½ cup heavy cream
4 TB. unsalted butter

½ cup firmly packed dark brown sugar
¼ cup crème de banana
2 tsp. cornstarch

> Serves: 6
> **Active time:** 10 minutes
> **Start to finish:** 15 minutes
> **Each serving contains:**
> 290 calories
> 141 calories from fat
> 16 g fat
> 10 g saturated fat
> 1 g protein
> 33 g carbohydrates

1. Place bananas and cream in a food processor fitted with a steel blade or in a blender. Purée until smooth, and set aside.

2. Melt butter in a heavy 1-quart saucepan over medium heat, and add brown sugar. Cook for 3 minutes, stirring occasionally. Add banana purée, and bring to a boil over medium heat, stirring occasionally. Reduce the heat to low, and simmer for 3 minutes, stirring occasionally.

3. Combine crème de banana and cornstarch in a small bowl, and stir to dissolve cornstarch. Add to fondue, and bring to a simmer, stirring constantly. Cook over low heat for 1 to 2 minutes or until fondue has thickened.

4. Transfer fondue to a fondue pot or other pot with a heat source, and serve with hulled strawberries (halved if large), donut holes, waffle squares, butter cookies, angel food cake cubes, pound cake cubes, brownie cubes, coconut macaroons, or sugar cookies.

Speedy Solutions

If you have bananas that are getting overly ripe, freeze them right in the peels. Once thawed, the bananas are ready to peel and all set to go in any dish that requires mashed banana such as this fondue or banana bread.

Piña Colada Fondue

Pineapple and coconut are the dominant flavors in this rum-laced fondue.

Serves: 6

Active time: 15 minutes

Start to finish: 15 minutes

Each serving contains:

205 calories

125 calories from fat

14 g fat

12 g saturated fat

2 g protein

10 g carbohydrates

2 cups diced fresh pineapple or 2 cups crushed pineapple packed in pineapple juice, drained

1 cup sweetened cream of coconut (such as Coco López)

½ cup rum

1 TB. freshly squeezed lime juice

1 TB. cornstarch

1. Place 1 cup pineapple in a food processor fitted with a steel blade or in a blender. Purée until smooth. Finely chop remaining 1 cup pineapple.

2. Combine all pineapple, cream of coconut, and rum in a heavy 1-quart saucepan. Bring to a boil over medium heat, stirring occasionally. Reduce the heat to low, and simmer mixture for 5 minutes, stirring occasionally.

3. Combine lime juice and cornstarch in a small bowl, and stir to dissolve cornstarch. Add to fondue, and bring to a simmer, stirring constantly. Cook over low heat for 1 to 2 minutes or until fondue has thickened.

4. Transfer fondue to a fondue pot or other pot with a heat source, and serve with hulled strawberries (halved if large), banana chunks, clementine segments, dried coconut slices, crystallized ginger, donut holes, angel food cake cubes, pound cake cubes, coconut macaroons, or sugar cookies.

Fresh Ways

Any dessert fondue can instantly become a dessert sauce to top berries or a slice of pound cake. You don't have to limit these fondue recipes to occasions on which you'll be dipping.

21

The Best Baked Goods

In This Chapter

- ◆ Homey fruit desserts
- ◆ Quick cakes
- ◆ Creative cookies

If you think baking is too time-consuming, wait until you try the recipes in this chapter! These recipes for homey cakes, cobblers, and cookies are on the table in a matter of minutes.

Most of these baked goods contain luscious fresh fruit, which makes them healthful as well as delicious. And there's a lot of room to improvise and substitute whatever fruits are the prettiest and freshest at your market.

Procedural Matters

While cooking is a form of art, when it comes to baking, science class enters the equation as well. Before you put on your apron, you should know some general pointers on procedures to be used for all genre of baked goods.

Fresh Ways

> Planning ahead also applies to preheating the oven. Some ovens can take up to 25 minutes to reach a high temperature, such as 400°F. The minimum heating time should be 15 minutes, and most cookie doughs and batters do not take that long to prepare. If you turn your oven on and then start preparing your dough or batter, you should be in good shape.

Be sure to use the correct measuring cups for the ingredient: measure dry ingredients in dry measure cups; measure liquids in liquid measure cups. Spoon dry ingredients from the container or canister into the measuring cup and then sweep the top with a straight edge such as the back of a knife or a spatula to measure it properly. *Do not* dip the cup into the canister or tap it on the counter to produce a level surface.

Level tablespoons and teaspoons, too; a rounded ½ teaspoon can really measure almost 1 teaspoon. If the box or can doesn't have a straight edge built in, level the excess in the spoon back into the container with the back of a knife.

Careful Creaming

Perhaps the most vital step in the creation of a cookie dough or cake batter is the "creaming" of the butter and sugar. During this process, air is beaten in and trapped in the butter's crystalline structure. It's the number and size of the air bubbles (which then become enlarged by the carbon dioxide produced by baking soda or baking powder) that leavens a dough or batter to produce a high, finely textured product.

Speedy Solutions

> If you're in a hurry to begin a batter, you can grate the butter through the large holes of a box grater. *Do not* soften butter in a microwave oven. It will become too soft.

For successful creaming, start with butter at the correct temperature: approximately 70°F. Remove butter from the refrigerator and cut each stick into approximately 30 slices. Allow them to sit at room temperature for 15 to 20 minutes to soften.

Begin creaming by beating the butter alone with a mixer on medium speed until it has broken into small pieces. Then add the sugar a few tablespoons at a time, scraping the bowl frequently. When properly creamed, the texture of the butter and sugar mixture will be light and fluffy.

Caramel Apple Quesadillas

This dessert has all the flavors and textures of a great apple pie, but it's ready in minutes!

8 (6-in.) flour tortillas

24 caramel candies, unwrapped

¼ cup whole milk

½ tsp. ground cinnamon

2 Golden Delicious apples, peeled, cored, and thinly sliced

3 TB. unsalted butter, melted

⅓ cup granulated sugar

1. Preheat the oven to 400°F, and cover 2 baking sheets with heavy-duty aluminum foil.

2. Soften tortillas by wrapping them in plastic wrap and heating them in a microwave oven on high (100 percent) for 10 to 15 seconds or until pliable.

3. Place caramel candies and milk in a small microwave-safe bowl, and microwave for 45 seconds on medium (50 percent). Stir, and repeat as necessary until caramel is smooth. Stir in cinnamon.

4. Spread caramel mixture on tortillas to about ½ inch from the edge. Arrange apple slices over half of each tortilla, and fold over the other half. Press down with the palm of your hand.

5. Place quesadillas on the baking sheet, brush each with 1 tablespoon butter and sprinkle with 2 tablespoons sugar. Bake for 10 minutes, turn with a spatula, brush with remaining butter, and sprinkle with remaining sugar. Bake for an additional 10 minutes or until quesadillas are browned. Allow to sit for 3 minutes, cut in half, and serve immediately.

> Serves: 4
>
> **Active time:** 10 minutes
>
> **Start to finish:** 30 minutes
>
> **Each serving contains:**
>
> 619 calories
>
> 177 calories from fat
>
> 20 g fat
>
> 9 g saturated fat
>
> 9 g protein
>
> 106 g carbohydrates

Stale Stuff

Dessert quesadillas aren't the norm, so it's really important to buy plain flour tortillas rather than flavored ones.

Cherry Clafouti

This French dessert is like a popover studded with bits of luscious fresh fruit.

Serves: 6

Active time: 9 minutes

Start to finish: 30 minutes

Each serving contains:

361 calories

107 calories from fat

12 g fat

6 g saturated fat

10.5 g protein

54 g carbohydrates

1 cup granulated sugar

6 TB. all-purpose flour

6 large eggs

2 cups whole milk

2 tsp. pure vanilla extract

2 tsp. grated orange zest

½ tsp. salt

3 cups dark sweet cherries, halved and pitted

2 TB. unsalted butter, cut into bits

Vanilla ice cream (optional)

1. Preheat the oven to 400°F. Grease a 9×13-inch baking pan.

2. Reserve 3 tablespoons sugar, and combine remaining sugar, flour, eggs, whole milk, vanilla extract, orange zest, and salt in a food processor fitted with a steel blade or in a blender. Purée until smooth.

3. Arrange cherries in a single layer in the prepared baking pan, and pour custard over them. Bake for 20 to 25 minutes or until top is puffed and springy to the touch. Remove from the oven and increase the oven temperature to broil.

4. Sprinkle *clafouti* with remaining 3 tablespoons sugar, dot with butter, and broil under the broiler about 3 inches from the heat for 1 minute or until it is browned. Serve immediately with ice cream (if using).

Variation: No cherries? Try raspberries, blueberries, or chopped peaches or apricots instead.

Fast Talk

Clafouti originated in the Limousin region of France. It's basically a dessert that combines fruit and a batter. Any fruit that holds its shape while baking, such as cherries, plums, or peaches, can be used.

Blueberry Crème Fraîche Tart

The tangy taste of crème fraîche, similar to that of sour cream, is the perfect foil for vividly flavored berries.

1 (9-in.) pie shell (homemade or purchased)

3 large eggs

½ cup granulated sugar

1 tsp. pure vanilla extract

1¼ cups *crème fraîche*

1 pt. fresh blueberries, rinsed

Serves: 8

Active time: 15 minutes

Start to finish: 2½ hours, including 2 hours for chilling

Each serving contains:

282 calories

165 calories from fat

18 g fat

8 g saturated fat

4 g protein

26 g carbohydrates

1. Preheat the oven to 375°F.

2. Prick bottom and sides of piecrust with a fork, press in a sheet of parchment paper, and fill pie plate with dried beans, rice, or metal pie stones. Bake for 10 to 15 minutes. Remove weights and parchment, and bake an additional 15 minutes or until golden brown. Set aside, and reduce the oven temperature to 350°F.

3. While crust is baking, whisk eggs and sugar in the top of a double boiler for 2 minutes or until thick and lemon colored. Add vanilla extract and crème fraîche, and stir well. Place mixture over water that's simmering in the bottom of the double boiler. Heat, stirring constantly, until mixture is hot and starting to thicken.

4. Place blueberries in the bottom of piecrust and pour warm custard over. Bake for 10 minutes or until custard is set. Chill for at least 2 hours before serving. (The pie can be baked 1 day in advance and refrigerated, tightly covered.)

Variation: You could also use raspberries or blackberries instead of blueberries.

Fast Talk

Crème fraîche is a thickened cream with the texture and flavor of sour cream; however, it does not curdle when boiled. You can make it at home by adding 2 tablespoons buttermilk to 1 cup heavy cream and allowing the mixture to sit at room temperature for 8 to 12 hours or until thickened.

Gingered Pear Crisp

Pears are one of the glories of fall, and they are enhanced in this easy recipe by a crunchy topping flavored with aromatic ginger.

Serves: 6

Active time: 15 minutes

Start to finish: 40 minutes

Each serving contains:

475 calories

161 calories from fat

18 g fat

8 g saturated fat

6 g protein

76 g carbohydrates

6 medium ripe pears, peeled, cored, and sliced

¾ cup firmly packed dark brown sugar

⅓ cup all-purpose flour

2 TB. finely chopped *crystallized ginger*

¾ tsp. ground cinnamon

½ tsp. ground ginger

1 tsp. pure vanilla extract

1½ cups granola cereal

5 TB. unsalted butter, melted

Vanilla ice cream or sweetened whipped cream (optional)

1. Preheat the oven to 375°F. Grease a 9×13-inch baking pan.

2. Combine pears, ⅓ cup brown sugar, ¼ cup flour, crystallized ginger, ¼ teaspoon cinnamon, ginger, and vanilla extract. Spread mixture into the prepared baking pan.

3. Combine remaining brown sugar, remaining flour, remaining cinnamon, granola cereal, and melted butter. Mix well, and sprinkle mixture over pears. Bake for 25 minutes or until pear mixture is bubbly and topping is golden brown. Serve hot or warm with sweetened whipped cream or vanilla ice cream (if using).

Variation: You can personalize this recipe in myriad ways with the topping. Visit the bulk food section of your market and select the granola flavor combination that appeals to you. You can also add nuts, more spices, or dried fruits.

Fast Talk

Crystallized ginger is fresh ginger that's preserved by being candied in sugar syrup. It's then tossed with coarse sugar. It's very expensive in little bottles in the spice aisle, but most whole foods markets sell it in bulk.

Strawberry-Rhubarb Cobbler

Cobblers are as at home on the breakfast or brunch table as a treat as they are after dinner.

1 cup granulated sugar

2 TB. Grand Marnier or Cointreau

1½ lb. (3 cups) rhubarb, rinsed and thinly sliced

1 TB. cornstarch

2 TB. cold water

1 cup all-purpose flour

1½ tsp. baking powder

4 TB. unsalted butter, cut into ½-inch pieces

1 large egg, lightly beaten

2 TB. whole milk

1 pt. fresh strawberries, rinsed, capped, and halved

Serves: 6
Active time: 25 minutes
Start to finish: 45 minutes
Each serving contains:
352 calories
86 calories from fat
10 g fat
5.5 g saturated fat
5 g protein
61 g carbohydrates

1. Preheat the oven to 400°F. Grease a 9×13-inch baking pan.

2. Reserve 2 tablespoons sugar, and set aside. Combine remaining sugar, Grand Marnier, and rhubarb in a saucepan. Bring to a boil over medium heat, stirring occasionally. Cook, stirring occasionally, for 12 minutes or until rhubarb is soft. Stir cornstarch into water, and stir cornstarch mixture into rhubarb. Simmer for 2 minutes or until thick and bubbly. Remove from heat, and keep warm.

3. While rhubarb is cooking, stir together flour, remaining 2 tablespoons sugar, and baking powder in a medium bowl. Cut in butter using a pastry blender, two knives, or your fingertips until mixture resembles coarse meal. Stir together egg and milk, and add to flour mixture, stirring just to moisten until a moist dough forms.

4. Turn out dough onto lightly floured surface, and knead five or six times. Roll dough to a rectangle 14 inches long. Cut lengthwise into ½-inch-wide strips.

5. Stir strawberries into rhubarb mixture. Transfer mixture to the prepared baking pan. Weave dough strips over fruit mixture to make a lattice top by placing alternate strips horizontally and vertically across the pan. Trim the strips to fit the baking pan. Place the baking pan on a foil-lined baking sheet. Bake for 20 to 25 minutes or until fruit is tender and lattice top is golden. Serve hot or at room temperature.

Speedy Solutions

There's a fine line between a cobbler that's full enough to support the crust and one that's spilling hot juices into the oven. That's why it's important to always use a baking sheet under it; it saves a lot of oven-cleaning time.

Strawberry Shortcake

Rich biscuits, luscious berries, and whipped cream are a time-honored combination for good reason—it's delicious!

Serves: 6

Active time: 15 minutes

Start to finish: 40 minutes, including 10 minutes for cooling

Each serving contains:

985 calories

551 calories from fat

61 g fat

38 g saturated fat

9 g protein

95 g carbohydrates

 **Fast Talk**

Cream of **tartar** comes from the acid deposited inside wine barrels. It's used in conjunction with baking soda to produce the same chemical reaction as that caused by baking powder.

3 cups all-purpose flour	**2 cups heavy cream**
¾ cup granulated sugar	**1 qt. strawberries**
1 TB. *cream of tartar*	**⅓ cup crème de cassis or Chambord**
2¼ tsp. baking soda	**⅓ cup confectioners' sugar**
¼ tsp. salt	
½ lb. (1 cup) unsalted butter	

1. Preheat the oven to 375°F and grease 2 baking sheets.

2. Combine flour, ⅓ cup sugar, cream of tartar, baking soda, and salt in a medium mixing bowl.

3. Melt 3 tablespoons butter in a small saucepan over low heat or in a microwave-safe dish on medium (50 percent) for 45 seconds or until melted, and set aside.

4. Cut remaining butter into ¼-inch cubes. Cut butter into flour mixture using a pastry blender, two knives, or your fingertips until mixture resembles coarse meal. Add 1 cup cream, and blend until just blended.

5. Scrape dough onto a floured surface and knead lightly. Roll dough ¾ inch thick, cut out 6 (4-inch) rounds, and place them on the baking sheet. Brush rounds with melted butter. Cut out 6 (2½-inch) rounds, and place them on top of larger rounds. Brush tops with butter. Bake for 15 to 17 minutes or until shortcakes are golden brown. Cool for at least 10 minutes on a wire rack.

6. While shortcakes are baking, rinse strawberries, discard green caps, and slice. Toss strawberries with crème de cassis. Set aside.

7. Just prior to serving, whip remaining cream with confectioners' sugar until stiff peaks form. To serve, separate the top and bottom rounds. Mound strawberries on larger round, and top with whipped cream and smaller round. Serve immediately.

Variation: You can substitute any berry for the strawberries. Peeled peach slices work nicely, too.

Oatmeal Cranberry Cookies

These homey cookies are scented with cinnamon and have crunchy nuts for texture and vivid dried cranberries for flavor.

1 cup chopped walnuts

1 cup all-purpose flour

1 tsp. ground cinnamon

½ tsp. baking soda

Pinch salt

6 TB. unsalted butter, softened

½ cup granulated sugar

½ cup firmly packed dark brown sugar

2 large eggs, at room temperature

1 tsp. pure vanilla extract

1¼ cups quick-cooking or old-fashioned oats (not instant)

1 cup dried cranberries

> Yield: 24 cookies
>
> **Active time:** 15 minutes
>
> **Start to finish:** 40 minutes, including 12 minutes for cooling
>
> **Each serving contains:**
>
> 165 calories
>
> 65 calories from fat
>
> 7 g fat
>
> 2 g saturated fat
>
> 4 g protein
>
> 23 g carbohydrates

1. Preheat the oven to 350°F, and grease 2 baking sheets.

2. Toast walnuts in a single layer on an ungreased baking sheet for 5 to 7 minutes or until browned, and set aside. Increase the oven temperature to 375°F.

3. While the oven is preheating, sift together flour, cinnamon, baking soda, and salt.

4. Place butter, granulated sugar, and brown sugar in a large mixing bowl. Beat with an electric mixer on low speed to combine, raise the speed to high, and beat for 2 minutes or until light and fluffy. Add eggs and vanilla extract, and beat for 2 minutes more. Reduce the speed to low and add flour mixture until just blended in. Stir in oats, cranberries, and toasted walnuts.

5. Drop batter by rounded tablespoon measures onto the baking sheets, spacing them 2 inches apart. Bake for 12 minutes for chewy cookies and 15 minutes for crisp cookies. Move cookies with a spatula to a cooling rack and cool completely.

Variation: Instead of cranberries, try raisins, dried blueberries, or dried currants. Out of cinnamon? Substitute with ground ginger.

Speedy Solutions

An easy way to warm eggs to room temperature is to place them in a cup of hot tap water for 5 minutes while you gather the rest of the ingredients.

Chocolate Malted Cookies

If you're a fan of chocolate malts, you'll love these homey cookies with the same flavor.

Yield: 24

Active time: 15 minutes

Start to finish: 35 minutes, including 15 minutes for cooling

Each serving contains:

196 calories

76 calories from fat

8.5 g fat

5 g saturated fat

2 g protein

28.5 g carbohydrates

2 cups all-purpose flour

1 tsp. baking soda

½ tsp. salt

1¾ sticks (¾ cup) unsalted butter, cut into small pieces

1 cup firmly packed light brown sugar

½ cup granulated sugar

2 large eggs, at room temperature

1 tsp. pure vanilla extract

½ cup malt powder

2 cups semisweet chocolate chips

1. Preheat the oven to 350°F, and grease 2 baking sheets.

2. While the oven is preheating, sift together flour, baking soda, and salt.

3. Place butter, brown sugar, and granulated sugar in a large mixing bowl. Beat with an electric mixer on low speed to combine, raise the speed to high, and beat for 2 minutes or until light and fluffy. Add eggs and vanilla extract, and beat for 2 minutes more. Reduce the speed to low and add flour mixture and malt powder until just blended in. Stir in chocolate chips.

4. Drop batter by rounded tablespoon measures onto the baking sheets, spacing them 2 inches apart. Bake for 10 minutes for chewy cookies and 12 minutes for crisp cookies. Move cookies with a spatula to a cooling rack and cool completely.

Variation: Any sort of chips—from white chocolate to butterscotch or peanut butter—work in place of the semisweet chips.

Fresh Ways

If you don't have enough cooling racks for cookies, start them on the rack and then transfer them to sheets of plastic wrap onto which granulated sugar has been sprinkled. The sugar keeps the bottoms from sticking.

Carrot Cookie Sandwiches

These cookies are a hand-holdable version of classic carrot cake, complete with the creamy icing.

1 cup chopped walnuts

1¼ cups all-purpose flour

½ tsp. ground cinnamon

½ tsp. ground ginger

½ tsp. baking soda

¼ tsp. salt

10 TB. unsalted butter

½ cup firmly packed light brown sugar

½ cup granulated sugar

1 large egg, at room temperature

¾ tsp. pure vanilla extract

1 cup firmly packed grated carrot

¼ cup sweetened coconut

¼ cup finely chopped fresh pineapple

¼ cup raisins

1 (3-oz.) pkg. cream cheese, softened

1 cup confectioners' sugar

Yield: 12 cookies

Active time: 15 minutes

Start to finish: 45 minutes, including 20 minutes for cooling

Each serving contains:

260 calories

87 calories from fat

10 g fat

2.5 g saturated fat

5 g protein

40 g carbohydrates

1. Preheat the oven to 350°F, and grease 2 baking sheets.

2. Toast walnuts in a single layer on an ungreased baking sheet for 5 to 7 minutes or until browned, and set aside. Increase the oven temperature to 375°F.

3. While the oven is preheating, sift together flour, cinnamon, ginger, baking soda, and salt.

4. Place 8 tablespoons butter, brown sugar, and granulated sugar in a large mixing bowl. Beat with an electric mixer on low speed to combine, raise the speed to high, and beat for 2 minutes or until light and fluffy. Add egg and ½ teaspoon vanilla extract, and beat for 2 minutes more. Reduce the speed to low and add flour mixture until just blended in. Stir in carrot, coconut, pineapple, raisins, and toasted walnuts.

5. Drop batter by rounded tablespoon measures onto the baking sheets, spacing them 2 inches apart (you should have 24 cookies). Bake for 12 to 14 minutes or until lightly browned. Cool cookies for 1 minute and then transfer cookies with a spatula to a cooling rack and cool completely.

Speedy Solutions

When you need just a small amount of a fruit, like the pineapple in this recipe, it makes sense to pay more per pound and buy a precut slice at the supermarket. That way there's no waste and it's easier to chop.

6. While cookies are cooling, combine cream cheese, confectioners' sugar, remaining 2 tablespoons butter, and remaining ¼ teaspoon vanilla extract in a food processor fitted with a steel blade. Blend until smooth, and scrape mixture into a mixing bowl.

7. Create cookie sandwiches by spreading frosting on the flat side of 1 cookie and topping it with the flat side of a second cookie. Store at room temperature.

Fudgy Brownies

These brownies are incredibly moist and chewy and deliver an intense chocolate flavor.

Yield: 16 brownies

Active time: 15 minutes

Start to finish: 1½ hours, including 30 minutes for cooling

Each serving contains:

217 calories

133 calories from fat

15 g fat

6 g saturated fat

4 g protein

21 g carbohydrates

4 oz. (4 squares) unsweetened chocolate

1 stick (½ cup) unsalted butter

1 cup chopped walnuts

½ tsp. pure vanilla extract

2 large eggs, at room temperature

1¼ cups granulated sugar

Pinch salt

½ cup all-purpose flour

1. Preheat the oven to 350°F, and grease and flour an 8×8-inch baking pan.

2. Melt chocolate and butter in a heavy saucepan over low heat, stirring frequently until mixture is melted and smooth. Remove the pan from the heat, and set aside for 5 to 7 minutes to cool.

3. Toast walnuts in a single layer on an ungreased baking sheet for 5 to 7 minutes or until browned, and set aside.

4. Combine vanilla extract, eggs, sugar, and salt in a bowl, and whisk well. Stir in cooled chocolate mixture, and beat well. Add flour, mix well, and stir in toasted walnuts. Scrape batter into the prepared pan, and smooth the top. Bake for 45 minutes or until top is dry and a toothpick inserted in the center comes out almost clean. Remove brownies from the oven and cool on a rack. Cut into squares when cool. (Brownies can be baked up to 2 days in advance and kept at room temperature, tightly covered.)

 Fresh Ways

Store soft cookies and crisp cookies in different containers to keep the crisp ones crisp, and always store cookies at room temperature.

Chocolate Cravings

In This Chapter

- ◆ Gooey chocolaty fondues
- ◆ Frozen chocolaty treats
- ◆ Baked chocolaty treasures

Chocolate might be the Americas' most delicious contribution to the cuisines of the world. Some folks—me included—can justly call ourselves "chocoholics" and think *all* desserts should be chocolate. You folks are in luck, because chocolate dessert recipes are all you'll find in this chapter.

Chocolate can take a wide range of dessert forms, from luscious fondues that can be on the table in a matter of minutes to some sophisticated options like individual cakes or an elegant soufflé that takes just a little longer. Now on to the sweet stuff!

Chocolate 101

The key to the success for all chocolate desserts is to use a high-quality product. Here's a quick guide to the various types of chocolate used for the desserts in this chapter:

Unsweetened   Also referred to as *baking* or *bitter* chocolate, this is the purest of all cooking chocolate and it contains no sugar.

Bittersweet   This chocolate is slightly sweetened with sugar, and the amount varies depending on the manufacturer. You can use it interchangeably with semisweet chocolate.

Stale Stuff _____

It's important (with noted exceptions) to use the type of chocolate specified in the recipe because the amount of additional sugar and other ingredients are calculated according to the sweetness level of the chocolate.

Semisweet   This chocolate is sweetened with sugar, but unlike bittersweet, it also can have added flavorings such as vanilla. It's available in bar form as well as chips and pieces.

Unsweetened cocoa powder   This is powdered chocolate that has had a portion of the cocoa butter removed. Cocoa keeps indefinitely in a cool place.

White   Actually ivory in color, white chocolate is technically not chocolate at all; it's made from cocoa butter, sugar, and flavoring.

Handle with Care

Except when you're eating chocolate out of your hand or folding chips into cookie dough, chocolate needs a bit of special handling. Use these tips when handling the sweet stuff:

Chopping chocolate into fine pieces makes melting easier. You can do this in a food processor fitted with a steel blade. Begin by breaking it with a heavy knife rather than breaking it with your hands. Body heat is sufficiently high enough to soften the chocolate so it won't chop evenly.

Most chocolate needs careful melting because it scorches easily. You can melt it in a number of ways:

- Melt chunks in the top of a double boiler placed over barely simmering water.

- Melt chopped chocolate in a microwave-safe bowl on high (100 percent) for 20 seconds. Stir and repeat as necessary.

- Preheat the oven to 250°F. Place chopped chocolate in the oven and immediately turn off the heat. Stir after 3 minutes, and return to the warm oven if necessary.

Classic Chocolate Fondue

Desserts don't get any easier or more luscious than dipping food into a vat of liquid chocolate!

½ **cup heavy cream**

10 oz. bittersweet chocolate, chopped

2 or 3 TB. liquor or liqueur (rum, bourbon, tequila, Cognac, brandy, triple sec, Grand Marnier, Chambord, kirsch, *amaretto*, Frangelico, crème de cacao, crème de banana, Irish cream liqueur, or Kahlúa)

Serves: 6
Active time: 15 minutes
Start to finish: 15 minutes
Each serving contains:
331 calories
215 calories from fat
24 g fat
14.5 g saturated fat
3 g protein
30.5 g carbohydrates

1. Combine cream and chocolate in a heavy 1-quart saucepan. Stir over very low heat to melt chocolate. When mixture is smooth and chocolate is melted, stir in liquor. (This can be done up to 4 hours ahead. Reheat over very low heat or in a microwave.)

2. Transfer fondue to a fondue pot or other pot with a heat source, and serve with hulled strawberries (halved if large), banana chunks, clementine segments, apple slices, donut holes, waffle squares, butter cookies, angel food cake cubes, cake cubes, brownie cubes, biscotti, or sugar cookies.

Variation: If you're serving the fondue to children or adults who cannot tolerate alcohol, you can substitute ¼ to ½ teaspoon pure almond, coconut, or peppermint extract for the liquor or liqueur.

Fast Talk

Amaretto is a liqueur that has the flavor of almonds but is frequently distilled from the kernels of apricot pits as well. It was invented in Saronno, Italy, but now many varieties are made in the United States.

Bittersweet Chocolate Coconut Cream Fondue

This is like a molten version of an Almond Joy candy bar with both chocolate and coconut sharing star billing.

Serves: 6

Active time: 15 minutes

Start to finish: 15 minutes

Each serving contains:

417 calories

300 calories from fat

33 g fat

23 g saturated fat

5 g protein

30 g carbohydrates

9 oz. bittersweet chocolate, chopped

1 oz. unsweetened chocolate, chopped

1 cup sweetened cream of coconut (such as Coco López)

½ cup heavy cream

¼ cup dark rum

¼ tsp. pure coconut extract

1. Combine bittersweet chocolate, unsweetened chocolate, cream of coconut, and cream in a heavy 1-quart saucepan. Stir over very low heat to melt chocolate. When mixture is smooth and chocolate is melted, stir in rum and coconut extract. (This can be done up to 4 hours ahead. Reheat over very low heat or in a microwave.)

2. Transfer fondue to a fondue pot or other pot with a heat source, and serve with hulled strawberries (halved if large), banana chunks, *clementine* segments, apple slices, dried coconut slices, dried apricots, crystallized ginger, donut holes, waffle squares, butter cookies, angel food cake cubes, cake cubes, brownie cubes, coconut macaroons, or sugar cookies.

Fast Talk

Clementines are a member of the Mandarin orange family and are identified by their loose skin that peels right off. Clementines are about the size of a golf ball, and they are usually seedless with tangy orange flavor.

White Chocolate Cranberry Orange Fondue

Hints of orange flavor this pale mixture dotted with vivid dried cranberries.

1 cup freshly squeezed orange juice

½ cup heavy cream

10 oz. white chocolate, chopped

1 TB. grated orange zest

½ cup dried cranberries, coarsely chopped

2 TB. triple sec or other orange-flavored liqueur

Serves: 6
Active time: 15 minutes
Start to finish: 25 minutes
Each serving contains:
406 calories
205 calories from fat
23 g fat
15 g saturated fat
4 g protein
42 g carbohydrates

1. Place orange juice in a heavy 1-quart saucepan. Bring to a boil over high heat and cook, stirring occasionally, 10 minutes or until liquid is reduced by ¾. Add cream, chocolate, and orange zest, and reduce heat to very low. Stir over very low heat to melt chocolate. When mixture is smooth and chocolate is melted, stir in dried cranberries and liqueur. (This can be done up to 4 hours ahead. Reheat over very low heat or in a microwave.)

2. Transfer fondue to a fondue pot or other pot with a heat source, and serve with hulled strawberries (halved if large), banana chunks, clementine segments, apple slices, donut holes, waffle squares, butter cookies, angel food cake cubes, cake cubes, brownie cubes, biscotti, or sugar cookies.

Variation: Substitute dried blueberries or dried cherries for the dried cranberries in this if you like.

Speedy Solutions

If you need to grate a lot of citrus zest, save time by using a vegetable peeler to separate the colored zest from the bitter white pith beneath it. Then place the strips in a mini-food processor. Chop the strips finely into zest at high speed.

Candy Bar Quesadillas

This crispy dessert is like a fast version of a turnover; personalize it with your choice of candy.

Serves: 4

Active time: 7 minutes

Start to finish: 20 minutes

Each serving contains:

819 calories

441 calories from fat

49 g fat

28 g saturated fat

12.5 g protein

84 g carbohydrates

Stale Stuff

Be careful when buying unsalted butter. Many packages are labeled "sweet butter" because all butter is made from sweet cream and not sour cream. But the term "sweet butter" is not an indication that salt has not been added.

8 (6-in.) flour tortillas

1 (8-oz.) pkg. cream cheese, softened

4 (1.5- to 2-oz.) candy bars (plain or flavored chocolate bars with or without additional ingredients: Snickers, Three Musketeers, or Almond Joy), each cut into thin slices

4 TB. unsalted butter, melted

⅓ cup granulated sugar

1. Preheat the oven to 450°F, and cover a baking sheet with heavy-duty aluminum foil.

2. Soften tortillas by wrapping them in plastic wrap and heating them in a microwave oven on high (100 percent) for 10 to 15 seconds or until pliable.

3. Spread tortillas out on a counter, and divide cream cheese amongst them. Spread cream cheese over ½ of each tortilla, and top with equal amounts of candy bar slices. Press quesadillas together gently into half circles, and place them on the baking sheet. Brush tops with melted butter, and sprinkle with ½ sugar.

4. Bake quesadillas for 5 minutes. Turn with a spatula, brush other side with butter, and sprinkle with remaining sugar. Bake an additional 3 or 4 minutes, or until quesadillas are browned. Remove from the oven, and serve immediately.

Mini-Molten Chocolate Tortes

These easy tortes have a center that remains soft so they create their own sauce.

10 TB. unsalted butter

⅓ cup granulated sugar

¼ lb. semisweet chocolate, chopped

2 large eggs

2 large egg yolks

⅓ cup confectioners' sugar

¾ tsp. pure vanilla extract

4 TB. all-purpose flour

2 TB. unsweetened cocoa powder

Sweetened whipped cream (optional)

Fresh raspberries (optional)

Serves: 4
Active time: 15 minutes
Start to finish: 30 minutes
Each serving contains:
602 calories
372 calories from fat
41 g fat
24 g saturated fat
7 g protein
52 g carbohydrates

1. Preheat the oven to 400°F. Grease 4 (6-ounce) custard cups with 2 tablespoons butter, and sprinkle with 2 tablespoons granulated sugar. Place in a shallow baking pan, and set aside.

2. Combine remaining 8 tablespoons butter and chopped semisweet chocolate in a small saucepan, and melt over low heat, stirring constantly. Remove the pan from the heat and cool.

3. Beat eggs, egg yolks, confectioners' sugar, and vanilla extract with a mixer on high for 5 minutes or until mixture is thick and pale yellow. Reduce speed to medium and beat in chocolate mixture. Sift flour and cocoa powder over chocolate mixture, and beat on low speed just until blended. Spoon batter into the prepared custard cups. (You can do this up to 2 hours in advance. Keep at room temperature.)

4. Bake for 12 to 14 minutes or until cakes rise slightly and feel firm at the edges and softer in the center when pressed gently. Cool in custard cups for 5 minutes. Invert with pot holders onto dessert plates, and serve with sweetened whipped cream and top with fresh raspberries (if using).

Variation: If you want to make this a sinfully rich dessert, place a chocolate truffle in the center of each cup before baking. The short bake time will just melt the center.

Stale Stuff

Always use pure extracts in cooking. They may cost a bit more, but you only use them in minute quantities, and they last for up to 2 years after they're opened. The flavor of extracts is intense, and the chemical taste from artificial extracts is unpleasant.

White Chocolate Strawberry Sundaes

This frozen treat uses purchased ice cream as the base and can be personalized in myriad ways.

1 pt. strawberry ice cream	**½ cup Chambord or other berry-flavored liqueur**
6 oz. white chocolate, chopped	**⅔ cup heavy cream**
1⅓ cup sliced strawberries	**4 TB. confectioners' sugar**

> **Serves:** 4
>
> **Active time:** 10 minutes
>
> **Start to finish:** 1 hour, including 50 minutes for freezing
>
> **Each serving contains:**
>
> 536 calories
>
> 254 calories from fat
>
> 28 g fat
>
> 17 g saturated fat
>
> 5 g protein
>
> 52 g carbohydrates

1. Place ice cream in a microwave oven, and microwave for 15 seconds on high (100 percent). Repeat, if necessary, until ice cream softens.

2. Scoop ice cream into a mixing bowl, and stir in white chocolate, strawberries, and ¼ cup Chambord. Refreeze ice cream mixture for at least 50 minutes.

3. While mixture is freezing, combine cream and confectioners' sugar in a chilled mixing bowl. Beat with an electric mixer until soft peaks form.

4. To serve, divide ice cream into 4 bowls and drizzle with remaining Chambord. Top with whipped cream, and serve immediately.

Variation: This recipe is open to endless variations; the only constant is the proportion of ice cream to chocolate. You can use any ice cream flavor, any type of chocolate, and any additions from fruits to nuts.

Fresh Ways

In addition to providing flavor, the inclusion of liquor or a liqueur in a recipe means the mixture won't freeze rock-solid. (Alcohol doesn't freeze.)

Quick Mocha Soufflé

You might think soufflés are difficult to make, but this one is really easy, and it rises every time!

1 TB. unsalted butter, softened

4 TB. granulated sugar

4 oz. bittersweet chocolate, chopped

¼ cup strong coffee

¼ cup heavy cream

4 large eggs, separated

2 large egg whites

Serves: 4

Active time: 15 minutes

Start to finish: 45 minutes

Each serving contains:

346 calories

211 calories from fat

23.5 g fat

13 g saturated fat

10 g protein

29 g carbohydrates

1. Preheat the oven to 400°F. Prepare a 6-cup soufflé dish by rubbing it with butter and dusting it well with 2 tablespoons granulated sugar. Knock out any excess sugar.

2. Combine chocolate, coffee, and cream in a small saucepan, and place it over low heat, stirring occasionally, until melted. Remove pan from the heat, and beat mixture until thick and glossy. Add egg yolks, one at a time, beating well after each addition.

3. Beat egg whites at medium speed with an electric mixer until frothy, increase the speed to high, and whip until stiff peaks form, gradually adding remaining 2 tablespoons sugar. Fold in chocolate mixture, and scrape mixture into the soufflé dish.

4. Place the dish in the center of the oven, and immediately turn the oven down to 375°F. Bake for 30 minutes or until puffed, and serve immediately.

Variation: You can substitute 2 tablespoons Grand Marnier or amaretto and 2 tablespoons water for the coffee.

 **Stale Stuff**

Always be sure a bowl in which you're beating egg whites is totally free from grease. Even a speck will keep the egg whites from beating properly.

Chocolate Pudding

This homey pudding is thick and rich; it's the quintessential chocolate comfort food.

Serves: 4

Active time: 9 minutes

Start to finish: 10 minutes

Each serving contains:

765 calories

354 calories from fat

39 g fat

23 g saturated fat

11.5 g protein

103 g carbohydrates

1 cup granulated sugar	2 large egg yolks, lightly beaten
4 TB. cornstarch	
½ lb. bittersweet chocolate, chopped	2 TB. unsalted butter
	½ tsp. pure vanilla extract
Pinch salt	1 cup vanilla ice cream
2⅔ cups whole milk	

1. Combine sugar, cornstarch, chocolate, and salt in a heavy 2-quart saucepan. Add milk and egg yolks, and whisk well. Place the saucepan over medium heat and bring to a boil, whisking constantly. Simmer 1 minute, whisking constantly. Remove the pan from the heat, and whisk in butter and vanilla extract.

2. Serve immediately, topped with ice cream, or chill and serve cold.

Variation: For mocha pudding, add 1 tablespoon instant coffee powder to the pudding. You can also use any flavor of ice cream instead of vanilla.

Fresh Ways

Cornstarch prevents eggs from scrambling when they come to a boil. That's why this pudding can simmer while a custard cannot.

Chocolate Peanut Butter Turnovers

These pastries join crispy puff pastry with sensuous chocolate and crunchy peanut butter.

4 oz. bittersweet chocolate, chopped

¼ cup chunky peanut butter

¼ tsp. pure vanilla extract

1 large egg

2 tsp. water

1 (17.25-oz.) pkg. frozen puff pastry sheets, thawed

2 TB. granulated sugar

Serves: 4
Active time: 10 minutes
Start to finish: 25 minutes
Each serving contains:
948 calories
591 calories from fat
66 g fat
19 g saturated fat
16 g protein
81 g carbohydrates

1. Preheat the oven to 425°F, and lightly grease a baking sheet.

2. Combine chocolate, peanut butter, and vanilla extract in a small bowl. Stir well.

3. Combine egg and water in another small bowl, and whisk well.

4. Trim uneven edges from pastry sheets, and cut each into 4 squares. Place ⅛ chocolate mixture in the center of each square, and fold squares on the diagonal into triangles. Seal edges by *crimping* with the tines of a fork.

5. Brush tops of turnovers with egg wash and sprinkle with sugar. Cut 3 small steam vents into each turnover with a sharp paring knife. Bake turnovers for 12 minutes or until golden brown. Remove turnovers from the oven and cool for 3 minutes. Serve immediately or at room temperature.

Fast Talk

Crimping, also called *fluting,* means pinching or pressing two pastry edges together with your fingers or a fork, sealing the dough while forming a decorative edge.

Chocolate Bread Pudding with Easy Bourbon Caramel Sauce

Hot bread pudding topped with a bourbon-laced sauce elevates this New Orleans' classic to new levels.

Serves: 6

Active time: 15 minutes

Start to finish: 50 minutes

Each serving contains:

926 calories

441 calories from fat

49 g fat

20 g saturated fat

19 g protein

102 g carbohydrates

Stale Stuff

The thinner the pieces of bread, the faster they absorb custard for a bread pudding. But you can't slice the bread too thinly or it will fall apart.

1 cup chopped pecans

1¼ cups whole milk

1¼ cups light cream

½ cup granulated sugar

½ lb. semisweet chocolate, chopped

8 large eggs

¾ tsp. pure vanilla extract

Pinch salt

½ lb. (about an 8-inch loaf) egg bread, such as challah, thinly sliced

1 cup jarred caramel sauce

¼ cup bourbon

¼ tsp. ground cinnamon

1. Preheat the oven to 375°F. Grease a 10×14-inch baking pan.

2. Place pecans on a baking sheet, and toast in the oven for 4 to 6 minutes or until browned. Remove nuts from the oven and set aside.

3. Combine milk, cream, and sugar in a large, heavy saucepan over medium-high heat. Stir until sugar dissolves and mixture comes to boil. Remove the pan from the heat. Add chocolate, and stir until smooth.

4. Beat eggs, vanilla extract, and salt in a large bowl to blend. Gradually whisk in chocolate mixture. Add bread slices. Let stand, stirring occasionally, for about 10 minutes or until bread absorbs some of custard and breaks into pieces.

5. Transfer mixture to the prepared baking pan, and cover with aluminum foil. Bake for 20 minutes, remove foil, and bake for an additional 10 minutes or until a knife inserted in the center comes out clean. Cool for 5 minutes before serving. (You can bake pudding 1 day in advance and refrigerate, tightly covered. Heat in a 350°F oven, covered with aluminum foil, for 30 minutes or until hot.)

6. While pudding is baking, combine caramel sauce, toasted pecans, bourbon, and cinnamon in a small saucepan. Heat, stirring occasionally, until hot. To serve, spoon sauce on top of warm bread pudding.

Appendix A

Glossary

al dente   Italian for "against the teeth." Refers to pasta or rice that's neither soft nor hard, but just slightly firm against the teeth.

all-purpose flour   Flour that contains only the inner part of the wheat grain. Usable for all purposes from cakes to gravies.

allspice   Named for its flavor echoes of several spices (cinnamon, cloves, nutmeg), allspice is used in many desserts and in rich marinades and stews.

amaretto   A popular almond liqueur.

anchovies (also **sardines**)   Tiny, flavorful preserved fish that typically come in cans. Anchovies are a traditional garnish for Caesar salad, the dressing of which contains anchovy paste.

arugula   A spicy-peppery garden plant with leaves that resemble a dandelion and have a distinctive—and very sharp—flavor.

bain marie   A water bath that cooks food gently by surrounding it with simmering water.

bake   To cook in a dry oven. Dry-heat cooking often results in a crisping of the exterior of the food being cooked.

balsamic vinegar   Vinegar produced primarily in Italy from a specific type of grape and aged in wood barrels.

basil   A flavorful, almost sweet, resinous herb delicious with tomatoes and used in all kinds of Italian or Mediterranean-style dishes.

baste   To keep foods moist during cooking by spooning, brushing, or drizzling with a liquid.

bean thread noodles   Thin translucent strands made from the starch of green mung beans.

beat   To quickly mix substances.

Belgian endive   A plant that resembles a small, elongated, tightly packed head of romaine lettuce.

bisque   A creamed seafood soup that's puréed.

black pepper   A biting and pungent seasoning made from crushing whole peppercorns.

blanch   To place a food in boiling water for about 1 minute (or less) to partially cook the exterior.

blend   To completely mix something, usually with a blender or food processor, more slowly than beating.

blue cheese   A blue-veined cheese that crumbles easily and has a somewhat soft texture, usually sold in a block.

boil   To heat a liquid to a point where water is forced to turn into steam, causing the liquid to bubble.

bok choy (also **Chinese cabbage**)   A member of the cabbage family with thick stems, crisp texture, and fresh flavor. It's perfect for stir-frying.

braise   To cook with the introduction of some liquid, usually over an extended period of time.

breadcrumbs   Tiny pieces of crumbled dry bread, often used for topping or coating.

Brie   A creamy cow's milk cheese from France with a soft, edible rind and a mild flavor.

broil   To cook in a dry oven under the overhead high-heat element.

broth   *See* stock.

brown   To cook in a skillet, turning, until the food's surface is seared and brown in color, to lock in the juices.

brown rice   Whole-grain rice including the germ with a characteristic pale brown or tan color.

bruschetta (or **crostini**)   Slices of toasted or grilled bread with garlic and olive oil, often with other toppings.

bulgur   A wheat kernel that's been steamed, dried, and crushed and is sold in fine and coarse textures.

canapés   Bite-size hors d'oeuvres usually served on a small piece of bread or toast.

capers   Flavorful buds of a Mediterranean plant, ranging in size from *nonpareil* (about the size of a small pea) to larger, grape-size caper berries produced in Spain.

caramelize   To cook sugar over low heat until it develops a sweet caramel flavor or to cook vegetables develop a caramel color.

caviar   Salted and sieved fish roe (eggs) from any species of fish. The best known is from sturgeon from the Caspian Sea.

cayenne   A fiery spice made from (hot) chili peppers, especially the cayenne chili, a slender, red, and very hot pepper.

challah   An egg-rich ceremonial Jewish bread served on the Sabbath and holidays.

cheddar   The ubiquitous hard cow's milk cheese with a rich, buttery flavor that ranges from mellow to sharp.

chevre   French for "goat milk cheese," chevre is a typically creamy-salty soft cheese.

chili powder   A seasoning blend that includes chili pepper, cumin, garlic, and oregano. Proportions vary among different versions, but they all offer a warm, rich flavor.

chili sauce   A chunky sweet condiment similar to ketchup in flavor.

chilis (or **chiles**)   Any one of many different "hot" peppers, ranging in intensity from the relatively mild ancho pepper to the blisteringly hot habañero.

Chinese chili paste with garlic   A fiery thick paste made from fermented fava beans, red chilies, and garlic.

Chinese five-spice powder   A seasoning blend of cinnamon, anise, ginger, fennel, and pepper.

chipotle chilies in adobo sauce   Smoked jalapeño chilies packed in a thick spicy sauce similar to hot red pepper sauce.

chives   A member of the onion family, chives grow in bunches of long leaves that resemble tall grass.

chop   To cut into pieces, usually qualified by an adverb such as *"coarsely* chopped," or by a size measurement such as "chopped into ½-inch pieces."

chorizo   A spiced pork sausage eaten alone and as a component in many recipes.

cider vinegar   Vinegar produced from apple cider, popular in North America.

cilantro   A member of the parsley family and used in Mexican cooking (especially salsa) and some Asian dishes.

cinnamon   A sweet, rich, aromatic spice commonly used in baking or desserts.

clafouti   A French dessert that combines fruit and a batter that's baked in the oven and browned under the broiler.

clementine   A member of the Mandarin orange family with a loose skin.

coriander   A rich, warm, spicy seed used in all types of recipes, from African to South American.

crème fraîche   A thickened cream with the texture and flavor of sour cream that does not curdle when it boils.

crimp   To press or pinch pastry edges together to seal a pie or turnover.

crudités   Fresh vegetables served as an appetizer, often all together on one tray.

crystallized ginger   Fresh ginger preserved by being candied in sugar syrup and usually coated with coarse sugar.

cumin   A fiery, smoky-tasting spice popular in Middle Eastern, Latin American, and Indian dishes.

curd   A gelatinous substance resulting from coagulated milk used to make cheese. Curd also refers to dishes of similar texture, such as dishes make with egg (lemon curd).

curry powder   A ground blend of rich and flavorful spices used as a basis for curry and many other Indian-influenced dishes.

custard   A cooked mixture of eggs and milk popular as base for desserts.

dash   A few drops, usually of a liquid, released by a quick shake of, for example, a bottle of hot sauce.

deglaze   To scrape up the bits of meat and seasoning left in a pan or skillet after cooking by adding liquid.

devein   The removal of the dark vein from the back of a large shrimp with a sharp knife.

dice   To cut into small cubes about ¼-inch square.

Dijon mustard   Hearty, spicy mustard made in the style of the Dijon region of France.

dill   A herb perfect for eggs, salmon, cheese dishes, and, of course, vegetables (pickles!).

dollop   A spoonful of something creamy and thick, like sour cream or whipped cream.

dredge   To cover a piece of food with a dry substance such as flour or corn meal.

drizzle   To lightly sprinkle drops of a liquid over food, often as the finishing touch to a dish.

fennel   In seed form, a fragrant, licorice-tasting herb. The bulbs have a much milder flavor and a celerylike crunch and are used as a vegetable in salads or cooked recipes.

fermented black beans   Small black soybeans with a pungent flavor preserved in salt.

feta   A white, crumbly, sharp, and salty cheese popular in Greek cooking and on salads.

fillet   A piece of meat or seafood with the bones removed.

flake   To break into thin sections, as with fish.

floret   The flower or bud end of broccoli or cauliflower.

flour   Grains ground into a meal. Wheat is perhaps the most common flour. Flour is also made from oats, rye, buckwheat, soybeans, etc. *See also* all-purpose flour; cake flour; whole-wheat flour.

fold   To combine a dense and light mixture with a circular action from the middle of the bowl.

fraises du bois   Tiny French strawberries.

frittata   A skillet-cooked mixture of eggs and other ingredients.

fry   *See* sauté.

garbanzo beans (or **chickpeas**)   A yellow-gold, roundish bean used as the base ingredient in hummus.

gardiniera   A combination of pickled vegetables including cauliflower, carrots, and peppers.

garlic   A member of the onion family, a pungent and flavorful element in many savory dishes. A garlic bulb contains multiple cloves.

garnish   An embellishment not vital to the dish but added to enhance visual appeal.

ginger   Available in fresh root or dried, ground form, ginger adds a pungent, sweet, and spicy quality to a dish.

grate   To shave into tiny pieces using a sharp rasp or grater.

grind   To reduce a large, hard substance, often a seasoning such as peppercorns, to the consistency of sand.

Gruyère   A rich, sharp cow milk cheese made in Switzerland that has a nutty flavor.

Herbes de Provence   A seasoning mix including basil, fennel, marjoram, rosemary, sage, and thyme, common in the south of France.

hoisin sauce   A sweet Asian condiment similar to ketchup made with soybeans, sesame, chili peppers, and sugar.

horseradish   A sharp, spicy root that forms the flavor base in many condiments from cocktail sauce to sharp mustards.

infusion   A liquid in which flavorful ingredients such as herbs have been soaked to extract flavor.

Italian seasoning   A blend of dried herbs, including basil, oregano, rosemary, and thyme.

jicama   A juicy, crunchy, sweet, large, round Central American vegetable. **julienne**   A French word meaning "to slice into very thin pieces."

kalamata olives   Traditionally from Greece, these medium-small long black olives have a smoky rich flavor.

kirsch   A clear tart liqueur made from cherries used in cheese fondue and desserts.

knead   To work dough to make it pliable so it holds gas bubbles as it bakes.

lardons   Thin slices of bacon used to flavor foods like quiche and salads.

lentils   Tiny lens-shape pulses used in European, Middle Eastern, and Indian cuisines.

marinate   To soak meat, seafood, or other food in a seasoned sauce, called a marinade, which is high in acid content.

mascarpone   A thick, creamy, spreadable cheese, traditionally from Italy.

medallion   A small round cut, usually of meat or vegetables such as carrots or cucumbers.

meld   To allow flavors to blend and spread over time.

mesclun   Mixed salad greens, usually containing lettuce and assorted greens such as arugula, cress, endive, and others.

mince   To cut into very small pieces smaller than diced pieces, about ⅛ inch or smaller.

molé   A thick spicy Mexican sauce made with unsweetened chocolate and chilies.

nutmeg   A sweet, fragrant, musky spice used primarily in baking.

Old Bay   A seasoning mix containing celery salt, mustard, cayenne, bay leaves, cloves, allspice, ginger, and paprika.

olive oil   A fragrant liquid produced by crushing or pressing olives.

olives   The green or black fruit of the olive tree commonly grown on all sides of the Mediterranean.

oregano   A fragrant, slightly astringent herb used in Greek, Spanish, and Italian dishes.

orzo   A rice-shape pasta used in Greek cooking.

oxidation   The browning of fruit flesh that happens over time and with exposure to air.

paprika   A rich, red, warm, earthy spice that also lends a rich red color to many dishes.

Parmesan   A hard, dry, flavorful cheese primarily used grated or shredded as a seasoning for Italian-style dishes.

parsley   A fresh-tasting green leafy herb, often used as a garnish.

pecans   Rich, buttery nuts, native to North America, that have a high unsaturated fat content.

peppercorns   Large, round, dried berries ground to produce pepper.

pesto A thick spread or sauce made with fresh basil leaves, garlic, olive oil, pine nuts, and Parmesan cheese.

pinch An unscientific measurement term, the amount of an ingredient—typically a dry, granular substance such as an herb or seasoning—you can hold between your finger and thumb.

pine nuts (also **pignoli** or **piñon**) Nuts grown on pine trees, that are rich (read: high fat), flavorful, and a bit pine-y. Pine nuts are a traditional component of pesto and add a wonderful hearty crunch to many other recipes.

pizza stone Preheated with the oven, a pizza stone cooks a crust to a delicious, crispy, pizza-parlor texture.

plump To rehydrate food, especially dried fruits, in hot liquid.

poach To cook a food in simmering liquid, such as water, wine, or broth.

porcini mushrooms Rich and flavorful mushrooms used in rice and Italian-style dishes.

portobello mushrooms A mature and larger form of the smaller crimini mushroom, portobellos are brownish, chewy, and flavorful.

preheat To turn on an oven, broiler, or other cooking appliance in advance of cooking .

prosciutto Dry, salt-cured ham that originated in Italy.

purée To reduce a food to a thick, creamy texture, usually using a blender or food processor.

reduce To boil or simmer a broth or sauce to remove some of the water content, resulting in more concentrated flavor.

reserve To hold a specified ingredient for another use later in the recipe.

rest To allow food to sit for a short period of time before carving so juices will be reabsorbed into the fibers.

rice vinegar Vinegar produced from fermented rice or rice wine, popular in Asian-style dishes. Different from rice wine vinegar.

roast To cook something uncovered in an oven, usually without additional liquid.

rosemary A pungent, sweet herb used with chicken, pork, fish, and especially lamb. A little of it goes a long way.

roux   A mixture of butter or another fat and flour, used to thicken sauces and soups.

sage   An herb with a musty yet fruity, lemon-rind scent and "sunny" flavor.

salsa   A style of mixing fresh vegetables or fresh fruit in a coarse chop.

satay (also **sate**)   A popular Southeast Asian dish of broiled skewers of fish or meat, often served with peanut sauce.

sauté   To pan-cook over lower heat than used for frying.

score   To cut food in a shallow diamond pattern.

sear   To quickly brown the exterior of a food, especially meat, over high heat to preserve interior moisture.

sesame oil   An oil, made from pressing sesame seeds, that's tasteless if clear and aromatic and flavorful if brown.

shallot   A member of the onion family that grows in a bulb somewhat like garlic and has a milder onion flavor.

shellfish   A broad range of seafood, including clams, mussels, oysters, crabs, shrimp, and lobster. Some people are allergic to shellfish, so take care with its inclusion in recipes.

shiitake mushrooms   Large, dark brown mushrooms with a hearty, meaty flavor that are sold both fresh and dried.

shred   To cut into many long, thin slices.

silverskin   The iridescent membrane covering tenderloins that must be scraped off before cooking.

simmer   To boil gently so the liquid barely bubbles.

skewers   Thin wooden or metal sticks, usually about 8 inches long.

skim   To remove fat or other material from the top of liquid.

slice   To cut into thin pieces.

star anise   A spice native to China with a distinct licorice flavor that's part of Chinese five-spice powder.

steep   To let sit in hot water, as in steeping tea in hot water for 10 minutes.

stir-fry   To cook small pieces of food in a wok or skillet over high heat, moving and turning the food quickly to cook all sides.

stock   A flavorful broth made by cooking meats and/or vegetables with seasonings with water.

tamari   A dark sauce made from soybeans with a more mellow and less salty flavor than soy sauce.

tapioca   A starch made from the root of a cassava plant used for thickening in a way similar to cornstarch.

tarragon   A sweet, rich-smelling herb perfect with seafood, vegetables (especially asparagus), chicken, and pork.

thyme   A minty, zesty herb.

toast   To heat something, usually bread, so it's browned and crisp.

tofu   A cheeselike substance made from soybeans and soy milk.

tomatillo   A small, round green fruit in a papery husk with a distinctive spicy flavor.

veal   Meat from a calf, generally characterized by mild flavor and tenderness.

vinegar   An acidic liquid widely used as dressing and seasoning, often made from fermented grapes, apples, or rice. *See also* balsamic vinegar; cider vinegar; rice vinegar; white vinegar; wine vinegar.

walnuts   A rich, slightly woody flavored nut.

wasabi   Japanese horseradish, a fiery, pungent condiment used with many Japanese-style dishes.

water chestnut   A crunchy tuber, popular in many types of Asian-style cooking.

whisk   To rapidly mix, introducing air to the mixture.

white mushrooms   Button mushrooms. When fresh, they have an earthy smell and an appealing "soft crunch."

white vinegar   The most common type of vinegar, produced from grain.

whole-wheat flour   Wheat flour that contains the entire grain.

wine vinegar   Vinegar produced from red or white wine.

wok   A pan with a rounded bottom for quick-cooking.

wood ear mushrooms   A form of Asian dried mushroom with a slightly crunchy texture and very delicate flavor.

Worcestershire sauce   Originally developed in India and containing tamarind, this spicy sauce is used as a seasoning for many meats and other dishes.

yeast   Tiny fungi that, when mixed with water, sugar, flour, and heat, release carbon dioxide bubbles, which, in turn, cause the bread to rise.

yogurt   A dairy product made from cow's milk coagulated into a soft tart custard from being invaded by friendly bacteria.

zest   Small slivers of peel, usually from a citrus fruit such as lemon, lime, or orange.

zester   A kitchen tool used to scrape zest off a fruit. A small grater also works well.

Metric Conversion Tables

The scientifically precise calculations needed for baking are not necessary when cooking conventionally. The tables in this appendix are designed for general cooking. If making conversions for baking, grab your calculator and compute the exact figure.

Converting Ounces to Grams

The numbers in the following table are approximate. To reach the exact amount of grams, multiply the number of ounces by 28.35.

Ounces	Grams
1 oz.	30 g
2 oz.	60 g
3 oz.	85 g
4 oz.	115 g
5 oz.	140 g
6 oz.	180 g
7 oz.	200 g
8 oz.	225 g
9 oz.	250 g

continues

continued

Ounces	Grams
10 oz.	285 g
11 oz.	300 g
12 oz.	340 g
13 oz.	370 g
14 oz.	400 g
15 oz.	425 g
16 oz.	450 g

Converting Quarts to Liters

The numbers in the following table are approximate. To reach the exact amount of liters, multiply the number of quarts by 0.95.

Quarts	Liters
1 cup (¼ qt.)	¼ L
1 pt. (½ qt.)	½ L
1 qt.	1 L
2 qt.	2 L
2½ qt.	2½ L
3 qt.	2¾ L
4 qt.	3¾ L
5 qt.	4¾ L
6 qt.	5½ L
7 qt.	6½ L
8 qt.	7½ L

Converting Pounds to Grams and Kilograms

The numbers in the following table are approximate. To reach the exact amount of grams, multiply the number of pounds by 453.6.

Pounds	Grams; Kilograms
1 lb.	450 g
1½ lb.	675 g
2 lb.	900 g
2½ lb.	1,125 g; 1¼ kg
3 lb.	1,350 g
3½ lb.	1,500 g; 1½ kg
4 lb.	1,800 g
4½ lb.	2 kg
5 lb.	2¼ kg
5½ lb.	2½ kg
6 lb.	2¾ kg
6½ lb.	3 kg
7 lb.	3¼ kg
7½ lb.	3½ kg
8 lb.	3¾ kg

Converting Fahrenheit to Celsius

The numbers in the following table are approximate. To reach the exact temperature, subtract 32 from the Fahrenheit reading, multiply the number by 5, and then divide by 9.

Degrees Fahrenheit	Degrees Celsius
170°F	77°C
180°F	82°C
190°F	88°C
200°F	95°C
225°F	110°C
250°F	120°C
300°F	150°C

continues

continued

Degrees Fahrenheit	Degrees Celsius
325°F	165°C
350°F	180°C
375°F	190°C
400°F	205°C
425°F	220°C
450°F	230°C
475°F	245°C
500°F	260°C

Converting Inches to Centimeters

The numbers in the following table are approximate. To reach the exact number of centimeters, multiply the number of inches by 2.54.

Inches	Centimeters
½ in.	1.5 cm
1 in.	2.5 cm
2 in.	5 cm
3 in.	8 cm
4 in.	10 cm
5 in.	13 cm
6 in.	15 cm
7 in.	18 cm
8 in.	20 cm
9 in.	23 cm
10 in.	25 cm
11 in.	28 cm
12 in.	30 cm

Common Ingredient Yields

Table of Weights and Measures of Common Ingredients

Food	Quantity	Yield
Apples	1 lb.	2½ to 3 cups sliced
Avocado	1 lb.	1 cup mashed fruit
Bananas	1 medium	1 cup, sliced
Bell peppers	1 lb.	3 to 4 cups sliced
Blueberries	1 lb.	3⅓ cups
Butter	¼ lb. (1 stick)	8 TB.
Cabbage	1 lb.	4 cups packed shredded
Carrots	1 lb.	3 cups diced or sliced
Chocolate		
Bulk	1 oz.	3 TB. grated
Morsels	12 oz.	2 cups
Cocoa powder	1 oz.	¼ cup
Coconut, flaked	7 oz.	2½ cups
Cream	½ pt.	1 cup; 2 cups whipped
Cream cheese	8 oz.	1 cup
Flour	1 lb.	4 cups

continues

continued

Food	Quantity	Yield
Lemons	1 medium	3 TB. juice; 2 tsp. zest
Milk	1 qt.	4 cups
Molasses	12 oz.	1½ cups
Mushrooms	1 lb.	5 cups sliced
Onions	1 medium	½ cup chopped
Peaches	1 lb.	2 cups sliced
Peanuts	5 oz.	1 cup
Pecans	6 oz.	1½ cups
Pineapple	1 medium	3 cups diced fruit
Potatoes	1 lb.	3 cups sliced
Raisins	1 lb.	3 cups
Spinach	1 lb.	¾ cup cooked
Squash, summer	1 lb.	3½ cups sliced
Strawberries	1 pt.	1½ cups sliced
Sugar		
Brown	1 lb.	2¼ cups, packed
Confectioner's	l lb.	4 cups
Granulated	1 lb.	2¼ cups
Tomatoes	1 lb.	1½ cups pulp
Walnuts	4 oz.	1 cup

Table of Liquid Measurements

Pinch	=	less than ⅛ tsp.
3 tsp.	=	1 TB.
2 TB.	=	1 oz.
8 TB.	=	½ cup
2 cups	=	1 pt.
1 qt.	=	2 pt.
1 gal.	=	4 qt.

Index

A

Aegean Swordfish, 248
al dente pasta, 90
all-purpose potatoes, 150
allspice, 229
amaretto, 285
appetizers
    Black Bean Cakes, 57
    Chicken in Lettuce Cups, 65
    Deviled Leeks, 58
    dips, 29, 30
        Brie, Stilton, and Wild Mushroom Dip, 37, 38
        Classic Cheese Fondue, 36
        Crab Rangoon Dip, 40
        Guacamole, 33
        Mexican Beef and Chili Dip, 41
        Mexican Black Bean Dip, 34
        Sausage Pizza Dip, 42
        Smoked Trout Dip, 38
        Spinach Dip with Feta and Dill, 35
        Sun-Dried Tomato Dip, 32
        Tuscan White Bean Dip, 31
        Two-Salmon Dip, 39
    finger foods, 44
        Asparagus Wrapped in Herbed Cheese and Prosciutto, 52
        Baked Shrimp Toast Rolls, 51
        Cheddar Crackers, 47
        Fresh Tomato Bruschetta, 45
        Herbed Goat Cheese and Roasted Pepper Spirals, 46
        Salmon Tartare on Cucumber Slices, 49
        Southwest Miniature Crab Cakes, 50
        Southwest Smoked Salmon Pinwheels, 48
        Vietnamese Spring Rolls, 53-54
    seafood appetizers, 56
        Baked Clams Casino, 59
        Bourbon Shrimp, 63
        Crab Cakes with Mustard Sauce, 64
        Creole Marinated Shrimp, 62
        Garlic-Steamed Clams, 60
        Oysters with Green Chili Cilantro Pesto, 61
apples
    Caramel Apple Quesadillas, 273
    safe-handling, 16
appliances, 7-8
arborio rice, 150
Asian Chicken Salad, 169
Asian Eggplant Salad, 138
Asian Shrimp and Stir-Fried Vegetables, 180-181
Asian woks, 194
asparagus, safe-handling, 16
Asparagus Wrapped in Herbed Cheese and Prosciutto, 52
Avgolemono (Greek Lemon Egg Soup with Chicken and Orzo), 77

B

Bacon, Egg, and Arugula Salad, 104
bacon grease, 126
bacteria, food safety, 10-11
Bain marie, 91
Baked Clams Casino, 59
Baked Eggs with Herbed Cheese, 91
baked goods, 271
    Blueberry Crème Fraîche Tart, 275
    Caramel Apple Quesadillas, 273
    Carrot Cookie Sandwiches, 281-282
    Cherry Clafouti, 274
    Chocolate Malted Cookies, 280
    creaming, 272
    Fudgy Brownies, 282
    Gingered Pear Crisp, 276
    Oatmeal Cranberry Cookies, 279
    Strawberry Shortcake, 278
    Strawberry-Rhubarb Cobbler, 277
Baked Macaroni and Cheese with Ham, 100-101
Baked Shrimp Toast Rolls, 51

baked potatoes, 150
baking powder, 84
Balsamic Vinaigrette, 147
Banana Pancakes with Banana Syrup, 86
Bananas Foster Fondue, 269
Basic Pizza Dough, 127
basmati rice, 150
bay leaves, 102
beans
    Black Bean and Papaya Salad, 142
    Black Bean Cakes, 57
    dips
        Mexican Black Bean Dip, 34
        Tuscan White Bean Dip, 31
    green mung beans, 53
    thread noodles, 53
    thread vermicelli, 53
    Tuscan White Bean Soup with Sausage, 78
beef recipes
    Beef Stroganoff, 212
    Cranberry-Maple Spareribs, 252
    Japanese Sautéed Beef with Scallions, 210-211
    Korean Steak, 255-256
    Mexican Beef and Chili Dip, 41
    Mexican Steaks with Chipotle Mayonnaise, 254-255
    Pan-Seared Filet Mignon with Red Wine Sauce, 211
    Stuffed Flank Steak, 253-254
bell peppers
    safe-handling, 17
    Stuffed Peppers, 102-103
bisques, Dilled Corn and Oyster Bisque, 76

bittersweet chocolate, 284
Bittersweet Chocolate Coconut Cream Fondue, 286
bivalves, removing from shell, 56
Black Bean and Papaya Salad, 142
Black Bean Cakes, 57
blanching garlic, 130
blueberries, 260
    Blueberry Crème Fraîche Tart, 275
    Blueberry Shortbread Gratin, 262
boiler potatoes, 150
bolster (part of knife), 14
Bombay Lamb Burgers, 243
Bourbon Shrimp, 63
bowls, mixing, 5
breadcrumbs, Italian, 59
bread pudding, Chocolate Bread Pudding with Easy Bourbon Caramel Sauce, 294
breakfast recipes, 81
    Baked Eggs with Herbed Cheese, 91
    Banana Pancakes with Banana Syrup, 86
    brunch dishes, 93
        Bacon, Egg, and Arugula Salad, 104
        Baked Macaroni and Cheese with Ham, 100-101
        Corned Beef Hash with Baked Eggs, 105
        Grilled Chicken Hash, 98-99
        Sausage and Pepper Hash, 101-102
        Smoked Salmon Hash with Poached Eggs, 97
        Southwest Sweet Potato Pancakes with Salsa Cream, 95

Stuffed Peppers, 102-103
        Summertime Baked Eggs, 96
        Welsh Rarebit with Tomatoes and Bacon, 99-100
    cholesterol reduction, 82
    frittata tips, 82
    Gingerbread Pancakes, 84
    Oven-Baked Apple Pancakes, 83
    pancake tips, 81
    Potato, Onion, and Bacon Frittata, 88
    Raspberry French Toast with Raspberry Sauce, 87
    Vegetable Frittata with Pasta, 90
    Western Frittata, 89
    Whole-Wheat Blueberry Pancakes, 85
Brie, Stilton, and Wild Mushroom Dip, 37-38
brownies, 282
brown rice, 150
brown sugar measurements, 189
brunch recipes, 93
    Bacon, Egg, and Arugula Salad, 104
    Baked Macaroni and Cheese with Ham, 100-101
    Classic Quiche Lorraine, 118
    Corned Beef Hash with Baked Eggs, 105
    Crab Quiche, 116
    Grilled Chicken Hash, 98-99
    Herbed Sausage and Tomato Quiche, 117
quiches, 108

Sausage and Pepper Hash, 101-102

Smoked Salmon Hash with Poached Eggs, 97

Southwest Sweet Potato Pancakes with Salsa Cream, 95

Stuffed Peppers, 102-103

Summertime Baked Eggs, 96

Welsh Rarebit with Tomatoes and Bacon, 99-100

bruschetta, Fresh Tomato Bruschetta, 45

burgers, 233

Bombay Lamb Burgers, 243

breads, 233

Caribbean Burgers, 241

Chinese Pork Burgers, 242

condiments, 234

Creole Shrimp Burgers, 236

Dilled Salmon Burgers, 237

Italian Turkey Burgers, 238

Mexican Burgers, 240

Middle Eastern Lentil Burgers, 235

New England Turkey Burgers, 239

Butterflied Leg of Lamb with Garlic, Rosemary, and Lemon, 232

buttermilk, 85

butter sauces, 64

C

cabbage, safe-handling, 17-18

cakes, Peach Skillet Cake, 266

canapés, 30

Candy Bar Quesadillas, 288

canned stocks, 72

capers, 202

Caramel Apple Quesadillas, 273

carb salads, 149

Coconut Rice and Vegetable Salad, 154

Garlicky Potato Salad, 159

Gemelli with White Beans, Tomatoes, and Sage, 153

Janet's Potato Salad, 158

Rigatoni with Vegetables and Mozzarella, 152

Sesame Noodles with Asian Vegetables, 151

Spicy Asian Brown Rice Salad, 156

Sweet Potato Salad with Mustard Dressing, 160

Tabbouleh with Feta, 157

Thai Rice Salad, 155

Caribbean Burgers, 241

Caribbean Pork Chops, 229

Caribbean Shrimp, 249

Carrot Cookie Sandwiches, 281-282

carrots, safe-handling, 18

caviar, 129

celery, safe-handling, 18

Celery Seed Dressing, 148

cellophane noodles, 53

Cha Gio (Vietnamese Spring Rolls), 53-54

Challah, 87

charcoal grills, 217

Cheddar Crackers, 47

cheese dips

Brie, Stilton, and Wild Mushroom Dip, 37-38

Classic Cheese Fondue, 36

cherries, Cherry Clafouti, 274

chicken recipes, 193

Chicken in Lettuce Cups, 65

Chicken Marsala with Mushrooms and Sage, 201

Chicken Satay with Spicy Peanut Sauce, 251

Chicken with Garlic and Parsley, 198

Chicken with Three-Tomato Salsa, 228

Grilled Chicken Hash, 98-99

Ham and Cheese–Stuffed Chicken, 225

Italian Chicken with Lemon and Capers, 202

Mexican Chicken with Mole Sauce, 226

Middle Eastern Chicken, 250

Poached Chicken with Balsamic Vinegar, 199

stir-frys, 194

Chicken Fajitas, 197

Chicken with Plum Sauce, 196

Mock Mu Shu Chicken, 195

Sweet and Hot Chicken Skewers, 227

Tarragon Chicken with Spring Vegetables, 200

chili

sauce, 204

Turkey Chili, 203

Chili con Queso, 41

chilies, 255

Chinese chili paste with garlic, 151

Chinese five-spice powder, 196

Chinese Pork Burgers, 242

chipotle chilies, 255

chocolate, 283

Bittersweet Chocolate Coconut Cream Fondue, 286

Candy Bar Quesadillas, 288

Chocolate Bread Pudding with Easy Bourbon Caramel Sauce, 294
Chocolate Malted Cookies, 280
Chocolate Peanut Butter Turnovers, 293
Chocolate Pudding, 292
Classic Chocolate Fondue, 285
Mini-Molten Chocolate Tortes, 289
Quick Mocha Soufflé, 291
special handling of chocolate, 284
types of chocolate, 283-284
White Chocolate Cranberry Orange Fondue, 287
White Chocolate Strawberry Sundaes, 290
cholesterol-reducing tips, 82
chorizo, 240
chowders
Dilled Corn and Oyster Bisque, 76
Grilled Corn Chowder, 74
Nantucket Clam Chowder, 75
clafouti (Cherry Clafouti), 274
clams, 56
Baked Clams Casino, 59
Garlic-Steamed Clams, 60
Nantucket Clam Chowder, 75
Classic Cheese Fondue, 36
Classic Chocolate Fondue, 285
Classic Quiche Lorraine, 118
cleaning mussels, 56
clementines, 286
cloud ear mushrooms, 195
cobblers, Strawberry-Rhubarb Cobbler, 277
Coconut Rice and Vegetable Salad, 154

colanders, 5
cole slaws, Gingered Asian Red Cabbage Slaw, 143
colossal shrimp, 179
compote, Mixed Berry Compote, 263
condiments, 234
cookies
Carrot Cookie Sandwiches, 281-282
Chocolate Malted Cookies, 280
Oatmeal Cranberry Cookies, 279
storage, 282
corkscrews, 6
Corned Beef Hash with Baked Eggs, 105
cornstarch, 292
crab
Crab Cakes with Mustard Sauce, 64
Crab Quiche, 116
Crab Rangoon Dip, 40
Southwest Miniature Crab Cakes, 50
crackers, Cheddar Crackers, 47
Cranberry-Maple Spareribs, 252
crème fraîche, 275
creaming, 272
Cream of Celery Soup with Tarragon, 73
cream of tartar, 278
Creole Marinated Shrimp, 62
Creole Shrimp Burgers, 236
Creole Swordfish, 188
crimping, 293
cross-contamination, food safety, 11
crystallized ginger, 276
Cuban Quesadillas, 111

cucumbers
Dilled Cucumbers, 144
safe-handling, 18-19
Thai Cucumber Salad, 145
cumin, 197
curd, 268
cured meats, 105
cuts, knife safety, 14-15

D

desserts, 271
baking tips, 271-272
Bananas Foster Fondue, 269
Blueberry Crème Fraîche Tart, 275
Caramel Apple Quesadillas, 273
Carrot Cookie Sandwiches, 281-282
Cherry Clafouti, 274
chocolate, 283
Bittersweet Chocolate Coconut Cream Fondue, 286
Candy Bar Quesadillas, 288
Chocolate Bread Pudding with Easy Bourbon Caramel Sauce, 294
Chocolate Peanut Butter Turnovers, 293
Chocolate Pudding, 292
Classic Chocolate Fondue, 285
Mini-Molten Chocolate Tortes, 289
Quick Mocha Soufflé, 291
special handling of chocolate, 284
types of chocolate, 283-284

White Chocolate Cranberry Orange Fondue, 287
White Chocolate Strawberry Sundaes, 290
Chocolate Malted Cookies, 280
creaming, 272
Easy Berry Trifle Cake, 267
Fudgy Brownies, 282
Gingered Pear Crisp, 276
Lemon Curd Mascarpone Fondue, 268
Oatmeal Cranberry Cookies, 279
Peach Skillet Cake, 266
Piña Colada Fondue, 270
Strawberry Shortcake, 278
Strawberry-Rhubarb Cobbler, 277
deveining shrimp, 51
Deviled Leeks, 58
dicing foods, 15
Dijon mustard, 111
Dilled Corn and Oyster Bisque, 76
Dilled Cream of Cucumber Soup, 71
Dilled Cucumbers, 144
Dilled Salmon Burgers, 237
dips, 30
Brie, Stilton, and Wild Mushroom Dip, 37-38
Classic Cheese Fondue, 36
Crab Rangoon Dip, 40
Guacamole, 33
Mexican Beef and Chili Dip, 41
Mexican Black Bean Dip, 34
Sausage Pizza Dip, 42
Smoked Trout Dip, 38
Spinach Dip with Feta and Dill, 35

Sun-Dried Tomato Dip, 32
Tuscan White Bean Dip, 31
Two-Salmon Dip, 39
disposables, 8
dough, pizza, 121, 127
dredging foods, 184
dressings
Balsamic Vinaigrette, 147
Celery Seed Dressing, 148
Pear Dressing, 146
Sesame Ginger Dressing, 147-148
Dumpling-Topped Berry Grunt, 264
Dutch ovens, 4

E

Easy Berry Trifle, 267
Easy Peel shrimp, 236
Egg Beaters, 82
Eggplant and Red Pepper Panini, 109
eggplants, safe-handling, 19
eggs
Baked Eggs with Herbed Cheese, 91
cholesterol reduction, 82
Corned Beef Hash with Baked Eggs, 105
freshness, 97
Smoked Salmon Hash with Poached Eggs, 97
Summertime Baked Eggs, 96
electric appliances, 7-8
entrées
beef
Beef Stroganoff, 212
Cranberry-Maple Spareribs, 252
Japanese Sautéed Beef with Scallions, 210-211
Korean Steak, 255-256

Mexican Steaks with Chipotle Mayonnaise, 254-255
Pan-Seared Filet Mignon with Red Wine Sauce, 211
Stuffed Flank Steak, 253-254
burgers, 233
Bombay Lamb Burgers, 243
breads, 233
Caribbean Burgers, 241
Chinese Pork Burgers, 242
condiments, 234
Creole Shrimp Burgers, 236
Dilled Salmon Burgers, 237
Italian Turkey Burgers, 238
Mexican Burgers, 240
Middle Eastern Lentil Burgers, 235
New England Turkey Burgers, 239
chicken, 193
Chicken Fajitas, 197
Chicken in Lettuce Cups, 65
Chicken Marsala with Mushrooms and Sage, 201
Chicken Satay with Spicy Peanut Sauce, 251
Chicken with Garlic and Parsley, 198
Chicken with Plum Sauce, 196
Chicken with Three-Tomato Salsa, 228
Grilled Chicken Hash, 98-99

Ham and Cheese–Stuffed Chicken, 225
Italian Chicken with Lemon and Capers, 202
Mexican Chicken with Mole Sauce, 226
Middle Eastern Chicken, 250
Mock Mu Shu Chicken, 195
Poached Chicken with Balsamic Vinegar, 199
Sweet and Hot Chicken Skewers, 227
Tarragon Chicken with Spring Vegetables, 200
grilled foods, 217
Aegean Swordfish, 248
Butterflied Leg of Lamb with Garlic, Rosemary, and Lemon, 232
Caribbean Pork Chops, 229
Caribbean Shrimp, 249
Chicken Satay with Spicy Peanut Sauce, 251
Chicken with Three-Tomato Salsa, 228
Cranberry-Maple Spareribs, 252
gas versus charcoal, 217
grill safety, 219
grill temperature, 218-219
Ham and Cheese–Stuffed Chicken, 225
Korean Steak, 255-256
marinated grilled dishes, 245-256
Mexican Chicken with Mole Sauce, 226

Mexican Steaks with Chipotle Mayonnaise, 254-255
Middle Eastern Chicken, 250
Rosemary Lamb Chops, 256
Salmon Provençale, 247
Salmon with Tomatillo Sauce, 220
Sea Scallops with Mango Salsa and Chili Vinaigrette, 222-223
Steak with Shiitake Cognac Sauce, 230
Steak with Southwest Corn Sauce, 231-232
Stuffed Flank Steak, 253-254
Sweet and Hot Chicken Skewers, 227
Swordfish with Smoked Cheddar Sauce, 224
Tuna with Ginger Vinaigrette, 221-222
wood chips, 218
lamb
Bombay Lamb Burgers, 243
Butterflied Leg of Lamb with Garlic, Rosemary, and Lemon, 232
Mustard-Crusted Rack of Lamb, 213
Rosemary Lamb Chops, 256
pork
Herb-Crusted Pork Tenderloin, 209
Pork Scaloppine, 207-208
Pork with Prosciutto, Mozzarella, and Sage, 208

salads, 161
Asian Chicken Salad, 169
Gazpacho Chicken Salad, 166-167
Jambalaya Salad, 170-171
Pork, Peach, and Orange Salad, 171-172
Salmon and Cucumber Salad, 165-166
Scallop and Asparagus Salad, 164-165
Smoked Turkey Salad, 168-169
Stir-Fried Chicken and Papaya Salad, 167-168
Thai Shrimp Salad, 163
Vietnamese Beef Salad, 172-173
Warm Lamb Salad, 173-174
turkey
Turkey Chili, 203
Turkey Meatloaf, 204
Veal Scaloppine with Fresh Shiitake Mushrooms, 214
equipment, 3
disposables, 8
knives, 6-7
pots and pans, 4-5
small appliances, 7-8
escarole, 122
extra-virgin olive oil, 134
extracts, 289

F

farmers' markets, 9
Fennel Salad, 140
feta cheese, 35
Fig and Raspberry Gratin, 261

finger foods, 44
Asparagus Wrapped in Herbed Cheese and Prosciutto, 52
Baked Shrimp Toast Rolls, 51
Cheddar Crackers, 47
Fresh Tomato Bruschetta, 45
Herbed Goat Cheese and Roasted Pepper Spirals, 46
Salmon Tartare on Cucumber Slices, 49
Southwest Miniature Crab Cakes, 50
Southwest Smoked Salmon Pinwheels, 48
Vietnamese Spring Rolls, 53-54
fish
Aegean Swordfish, 248
Creole Swordfish, 188
Fish Steamed in Napa Cabbage with Red Pepper Sauce, 186-187
guide, 178
Halibut in White Wine with Pearl Onions and Oranges, 190
Pan-Fried Flounder with Black Walnut Butter, 183-184
Roast Monkfish in Plum Wine Sauce, 185-186
Salmon with Basil Cream Sauce, 189
sauce, 145
Scrod with Red Onion Marmalade, 184-185
seafood dips
Smoked Trout Dip, 38
Two-Salmon Dip, 39
selection, 177-178
skinning, 187

Swordfish with Smoked Cheddar Sauce, 224
Tuna Steaks with Tomato Relish, 191
five-spice powder, 196
fluting, 293
fondues
Bananas Foster Fondue, 269
Bittersweet Chocolate Coconut Cream Fondue, 286
Classic Cheese Fondue, 36
Classic Chocolate Fondue, 285
Lemon Curd Mascarpone Fondue, 268
Piña Colada Fondue, 270
White Chocolate Cranberry Orange Fondue, 287
food-borne illnesses, 11
food processors, 7
food safety, 9-11
Food Safety and Inspection Service (USDA), 10
french toast, Raspberry French Toast with Raspberry Sauce, 87
Fresh Berries with Lemon Mousse, 265
freshness of eggs, 97
Fresh Tomato Bruschetta, 45
frittatas
Potato, Onion, and Bacon Frittata, 88
tips, 82
Vegetable Frittata with Pasta, 90
Western Frittata, 89
fruit recipes, 259
Bananas Foster Fondue, 269
Blueberry Crème Fraîche Tart, 275

Blueberry Shortbread Gratin, 262
Caramel Apple Quesadillas, 273
Cherry Clafouti, 274
Chocolate Malted Cookies, 280
Dumpling-Topped Berry Grunt, 264
Easy Berry Trifle, 267
Fig and Raspberry Gratin, 261
Fresh Berries with Lemon Mousse, 265
Gingered Pear Crisp, 276
Lemon Curd Mascarpone Fondue, 268
Mixed Berry Compote, 263
Oatmeal Cranberry Cookies, 279
Peach Skillet Cake, 266
Piña Colada Fondue, 270
Strawberry Shortcake, 278
Strawberry-Rhubarb Cobbler, 277
Fudgy Brownies, 282
Fusilli with Porcini Puttanesca Sauce, 124

G

gadgets, 5-6
Gardiniera vegetables, 62
garlic
roasting and blanching, 130
safe-handling, 19-20
Garlic-Steamed Clams, 60
Garlicky Potato Salad, 159
gas grills, 217
Gazpacho, 70
Gazpacho Chicken Salad, 166-167
Gemelli with White Beans, Tomatoes, and Sage, 153

ginger
  crystallized, 276
  safe-handling, 20
Gingerbread Pancakes, 84
Gingered Asian Red Cabbage
  Slaw, 143
Gingered Pear Crisp, 276
glass noodles, 53
Greek Lemon Egg Soup
  with Chicken and Orzo
  (Avgolemono), 77
Green Bean and Tomato
  Salad, 137
green mung beans, 53
green shrimp, 179
Grilled Chicken, Sun-Dried
  Tomato, and Mozzarella
  Panini, 110
Grilled Chicken Hash, 98-99
Grilled Corn Chowder, 74
grilled foods, 217
  burgers, 233
    Bombay Lamb Burgers,
      243
    breads, 233
    Caribbean Burgers, 241
    Chinese Pork Burgers,
      242
    condiments, 234
    Creole Shrimp Burgers,
      236
    Dilled Salmon Burgers,
      237
    Italian Turkey Burgers,
      238
    Mexican Burgers, 240
    Middle Eastern Lentil
      Burgers, 235
    New England Turkey
      Burgers, 239
  Butterflied Leg of Lamb
    with Garlic, Rosemary,
    and Lemon, 232
  Caribbean Pork Chops, 229

Chicken with Three-
  Tomato Salsa, 228
gas versus charcoal, 217
grill safety, 219
grill temperature, 218-219
Grilled Reuben Sandwich,
  115
Ham and Cheese–Stuffed
  Chicken, 225
marinated grilled dishes,
  245-256
  Aegean Swordfish, 248
  Caribbean Shrimp, 249
  Chicken Satay with
    Spicy Peanut Sauce,
    251
  combination cooking,
    246
  Cranberry-Maple
    Spareribs, 252
  Korean Steak, 255, 256
  Mexican Steaks with
    Chipotle Mayonnaise,
    254-255
  Middle Eastern Chicken,
    250
  Rosemary Lamb Chops,
    256
  Salmon Provençale, 247
  Stuffed Flank Steak,
    253-254
Mexican Chicken with
  Mole Sauce, 226
Salmon with Tomatillo
  Sauce, 220
Sea Scallops with
  Mango Salsa and Chili
  Vinaigrette, 222-223
Steak with Shiitake Cognac
  Sauce, 230
Steak with Southwest Corn
  Sauce, 231-232
Sweet and Hot Chicken
  Skewers, 227

Swordfish with Smoked
  Cheddar Sauce, 224
Tuna with Ginger
  Vinaigrette, 221-222
wood chips, 218
grills, 8
  panini presses, 107-108
grocery-shopping tips, 8-9
grunt, Dumpling-Topped
  Berry Grunt, 264
Guacamole, 33

H

Halibut in White Wine with
  Pearl Onions and Oranges,
  190
Ham and Cheese–Stuffed
  Chicken, 225
handheld electric mixers, 8
handling produce, 16
  apples, 16
  asparagus, 16
  bell peppers, 17
  cabbage, 17-18
  carrots, 18
  celery, 18
  cucumbers, 18-19
  eggplants, 19
  garlic, 19-20
  ginger, 20
  mangoes, 21
  mushrooms, 21-22
  onions, 22-23
  peaches, 23
  tomatoes, 24
Herb-Crusted Pork
  Tenderloin, 209
Herbed Goat Cheese and
  Roasted Pepper Spirals, 46
Herbed Sausage and Tomato
  Quiche, 117
Herbes de Provence, 32
hinged-grills, 107-108

hinged-top grills, 8
hoisin sauce, 65
hors d'oeuvres
  Black Bean Cakes, 57
  Chicken in Lettuce Cups, 65
  Deviled Leeks, 58
  dips, 29
    Brie, Stilton, and Wild Mushroom Dip, 37-38
    Classic Cheese Fondue, 36
    Crab Rangoon Dip, 40
    Guacamole, 33
    Mexican Beef and Chili Dip, 41
    Mexican Black Bean Dip, 34
    Sausage Pizza Dip, 42
    Smoked Trout Dip, 38
    Spinach Dip with Feta and Dill, 35
    Sun-Dried Tomato Dip, 32
    Tuscan White Bean Dip, 31
    Two-Salmon Dip, 39
  finger foods, 44
    Asparagus Wrapped in Herbed Cheese and Prosciutto, 52
    Baked Shrimp Toast Rolls, 51
    Cheddar Crackers, 47
    Fresh Tomato Bruschetta, 45
    Herbed Goat Cheese and Roasted Pepper Spirals, 46
    Salmon Tartare on Cucumber Slices, 49
    Southwest Miniature Crab Cakes, 50
    Southwest Smoked Salmon Pinwheels, 48
    Vietnamese Spring Rolls, 53-54
  seafood appetizers, 56
    Baked Clams Casino, 59
    Bourbon Shrimp, 63
    Crab Cakes with Mustard Sauce, 64
    Creole Marinated Shrimp, 62
    Garlic-Steamed Clams, 60
    Oysters with Green Chili Cilantro Pesto, 61
hummus, 234

I

immersion blenders, 7
Italian breadcrumbs, 59
Italian Chicken with Lemon and Capers (Pollo Piccata), 202
Italian Turkey Burgers, 238

J

Jambalaya Salad, 170-171
Janet's Potato Salad, 158
Japanese Sautéed Beef with Scallions (Negimaki), 210-211
jasmine rice, 150
jicama, 142
julienned foods, 15, 135
jumbo shrimp, 179

K

Kentucky Hot Brown Sandwich, 114
kirsch, 36
kirschwasser, 36

kitchen equipment, 3
  disposables, 8
  knives, 6-7, 13-15
  pots and pans, 4-5
  small appliances, 7-8
kneading dough, 127
knives, 6-7, 13-15
Korean Steak, 255-256

L

lamb
  Bombay Lamb Burgers, 243
  Butterflied Leg of Lamb with Garlic, Rosemary, and Lemon, 232
  Mustard-Crusted Rack of Lamb, 213
  Rosemary Lamb Chops, 256
Lardons, 118
large shrimp, 179
Leek and Potato Soup (Vichyssoise), 72
leeks, 200
Lemon Curd Mascarpone Fondue, 268
lentils, 235
lettuces, 162
Linguine with White Clam Sauce, 125
liqueur, amaretto, 285
lunch recipes
  brunch recipes, 93
    Bacon, Egg, and Arugula Salad, 104
    Baked Macaroni and Cheese with Ham, 100-101
    Classic Quiche Lorraine, 118
    Corned Beef Hash with Baked Eggs, 105

Crab Quiche, 116
Grilled Chicken Hash,
98-99
Herbed Sausage and
Tomato Quiche, 117
quiches, 108
Sausage and Pepper
Hash, 101-102
Smoked Salmon Hash
with Poached Eggs, 97
Southwest Sweet Potato
Pancakes with Salsa
Cream, 95
Stuffed Peppers,
102-103
Summertime Baked
Eggs, 96
Welsh Rarebit with
Tomatoes and Bacon,
99-100
quesadillas, 111-112
quiches
Classic Quiche Lorraine,
118
Crab Quiche, 116
Herbed Sausage and
Tomato Quiche, 117
sandwiches
Eggplant and Red
Pepper Panini, 109
Grilled Chicken, Sun-
Dried Tomato, and
Mozzarella Panini, 110
Grilled Reuben
Sandwich, 115
Kentucky Hot Brown
Sandwich, 114
Tuna Melt with Olives,
113

M

macaroni and cheese, Baked
Macaroni and Cheese with
Ham, 100-101

mangoes, safe-handling, 21
maple syrup, 252
marinated grilled dishes,
245-256
Aegean Swordfish, 248
Caribbean Shrimp, 249
Chicken Satay with Spicy
Peanut Sauce, 251
combination cooking, 246
Cranberry-Maple
Spareribs, 252
Korean Steak, 255-256
Mexican Steaks with
Chipotle Mayonnaise,
254-255
Middle Eastern Chicken,
250
Rosemary Lamb Chops,
256
Salmon Provençale, 247
Stuffed Flank Steak,
253-254
marjoram, 58
mascarpone, 267
meatloaf, Turkey Meatloaf,
204
metal colanders, 5
Mexican Beef and Chili Dip,
41
Mexican Black Bean Dip, 34
Mexican Burgers, 240
Mexican Chicken with Mole
Sauce, 226
Mexican Steaks with Chipotle
Mayonnaise, 254-255
Middle Eastern Chicken, 250
Middle Eastern Lentil
Burgers, 235
mincing, 15
Mini-Molten Chocolate
Tortes, 289
Mixed Berry Compote, 263
mixing bowls, 5
Mock Mu Shu Chicken, 195
mole, 226

mollusks, 56
mozzarella, 139
mung beans, 53
mushrooms
rehydrating, 180
safe-handling, 21-22
storage, 136
wood ear, 195
mussels, 56
Mustard-Crusted Rack of
Lamb, 213
mustards, Dijon mustard, 111

N

Nantucket Clam Chowder, 75
National Directory of Farmers
Markets, 9
Negimaki (Japanese Sautéed
Beef with Scallions), 210-211
New England Turkey Burgers,
239

O

Oatmeal Cranberry Cookies,
279
Old Bay, 39
olive oil, 134
onions, 22-23
organic stocks, 72
Oven-Baked Apple Pancakes,
83
ovens, Dutch, 4
oysters, 56
Dilled Corn and Oyster
Bisque, 76
Oysters with Green Chili
Cilantro Pesto, 61

P

Pan-Fried Flounder with
Black Walnut Butter,
183-184

Pan-Seared Filet Mignon with Red Wine Sauce, 211
pancakes
  Banana Pancakes with Banana Syrup, 86
  Gingerbread Pancakes, 84
  Oven-Baked Apple Pancakes, 83
  tips, 81
  Whole-Wheat Blueberry Pancakes, 85
panini sandwiches, 108
  Eggplant and Red Pepper Panini, 109
  Grilled Chicken, Sun-Dried Tomato, and Mozzarella Panini, 110
  presses, 107, 108
pans and pots, 4-5
pasta, al dente, 90
Pasta Aglio e Olio (Pasta with Garlic Oil), 123
Pasta Carbonara (Spaghetti with Egg and Bacon), 126
pasta recipes
  contents of pasta, 120
  Fusilli with Porcini Puttanesca Sauce, 124
  Gemelli with White Beans, Tomatoes, and Sage, 153
  Linguine with White Clam Sauce, 125
  Pasta with Garlic and Oil, 123
  Rigatoni with Vegetables and Mozzarella, 152
  shopping tips, 120-121
  Spaghetti with Egg and Bacon, 126
  Spaghetti with Escarole, Pine Nuts, and Raisins, 122
Pasta with Garlic and Oil (Pasta Aglio e Olio), 123
pastry blenders, 264

peaches, 23, 260
Peach Skillet Cake, 266
Pear Dressing, 146
pearl onions, 190
pears, Gingered Pear Crisp, 276
Piña Colada Fondue, 270
piñon, 183
pine nuts, 183
pizza recipes
  Basic Pizza Dough, 127
  pizza dough, 121
  Pizza Margherita, 128
  Prosciutto Pizza, 130
  Smoked Salmon Pizza, 129
plumped foods, 199
Poached Chicken with Balsamic Vinegar, 199
poached foods, 188
Pollo Piccata (Italian Chicken with Lemon and Capers), 202
Porchetta Saltimbocca (Pork with Prosciutto, Mozzarella, and Sage), 208
Pork, Peach, and Orange Salad, 171-172
pork recipes
  Caribbean Pork Chops, 229
  Herb-Crusted Pork Tenderloin, 209
  Pork Scaloppine, 207-208
  Pork with Prosciutto, Mozzarella, and Sage, 208
Potato, Onion, and Bacon Frittata, 88
potatoes, 150
  Garlicky Potato Salad, 159
  Janet's Potato Salad, 158
  Sweet Potato Salad with Mustard Dressing, 160
pots and pans, 4-5
Prawns in Garlic Sauce with Fettuccine, 181-182

produce, 9
  apples, 16
  asparagus, 16
  bell peppers, 17
  cabbage, 17, 18
  carrots, 18
  celery, 18
  cucumbers, 18-19
  eggplants, 19
  garlic, 19-20
  ginger, 20
  mangoes, 21
  mushrooms, 21-22
  onions, 22-23
  peaches, 23
  tomatoes, 24
Prosciutto Pizza, 130
pudding
  Chocolate Bread Pudding with Easy Bourbon Caramel Sauce, 294
  Chocolate Pudding, 292
puréed foods, 34
pure extracts, 289
pure olive oil, 134

Q

quesadillas, 108
  Candy Bar Quesadillas, 288
  Caramel Apple Quesadillas, 273
  Cuban Quesadillas, 111
  Springtime Quesadillas, 112
quiches, 108
  Classic Quiche Lorraine, 118
  Crab Quiche, 116
  Herbed Sausage and Tomato Quiche, 117
Quick Chicken Stock, 69
Quick Mocha Soufflé, 291

R

raspberries, 260
Raspberry French Toast with Raspberry Sauce, 87
raw mussels, 56
recipes, 107
  appetizers, 44
    Asparagus Wrapped in Herbed Cheese and Prosciutto, 52
    Baked Clams Casino, 59
    Baked Shrimp Toast Rolls, 51
    Black Bean Cakes, 57
    Bourbon Shrimp, 63
    Cheddar Crackers, 47
    Chicken in Lettuce Cups, 65
    Crab Cakes with Mustard Sauce, 64
    Creole Marinated Shrimp, 62
    Deviled Leeks, 58
    Fresh Tomato Bruschetta, 45
    Garlic-Steamed Clams, 60
    Herbed Goat Cheese and Roasted Pepper Spirals, 46
    Oysters with Green Chili Cilantro Pesto, 61
    Salmon Tartare on Cucumber Slices, 49
    Southwest Miniature Crab Cakes, 50
    Southwest Smoked Salmon Pinwheels, 48
    Vietnamese Spring Rolls, 53-54
  beef
    Beef Stroganoff, 212
    Cranberry-Maple Spareribs, 252
    Japanese Sautéed Beef with Scallions, 210-211
    Korean Steak, 255-256
    Mexican Steaks with Chipotle Mayonnaise, 254-255
    Pan-Seared Filet Mignon with Red Wine Sauce, 211
    Stuffed Flank Steak, 253-254
  breakfast, 81
    Baked Eggs with Herbed Cheese, 91
    Banana Pancakes with Banana Syrup, 86
    cholesterol reduction, 82
    frittata tips, 82
    Gingerbread Pancakes, 84
    Oven-Baked Apple Pancakes, 83
    pancake tips, 81
    Potato, Onion, and Bacon Frittata, 88
    Raspberry French Toast with Raspberry Sauce, 87
    Vegetable Frittata with Pasta, 90
    Western Frittata, 89
    Whole-Wheat Blueberry Pancakes, 85
  brunch recipes, 93
    Bacon, Egg, and Arugula Salad, 104
    Baked Macaroni and Cheese with Ham, 100-101
    Classic Quiche Lorraine, 118
    Corned Beef Hash with Baked Eggs, 105
    Crab Quiche, 116
    Grilled Chicken Hash, 98-99
    Herbed Sausage and Tomato Quiche, 117
    quiches, 108
    Sausage and Pepper Hash, 101-102
    Smoked Salmon Hash with Poached Eggs, 97
    Southwest Sweet Potato Pancakes with Salsa Cream, 95
    Stuffed Peppers, 102-103
    Summertime Baked Eggs, 96
    Welsh Rarebit with Tomatoes and Bacon, 99-100
  burgers, 233
    Bombay Lamb Burgers, 243
    breads, 233
    Caribbean Burgers, 241
    Chinese Pork Burgers, 242
    condiments, 234
    Creole Shrimp Burgers, 236
    Dilled Salmon Burgers, 237
    Italian Turkey Burgers, 238
    Mexican Burgers, 240
    Middle Eastern Lentil Burgers, 235
    New England Turkey Burgers, 239
  chicken, 193
    Chicken Fajitas, 197
    Chicken Marsala with Mushrooms and Sage, 201

Chicken with Garlic and Parsley, 198
Chicken with Plum Sauce, 196
Italian Chicken with Lemon and Capers, 202
Mock Mu Shu Chicken, 195
Poached Chicken with Balsamic Vinegar, 199
stir-frys, 194
Tarragon Chicken with Spring Vegetables, 200
desserts, 271
Bittersweet Chocolate Coconut Cream Fondue, 286
Blueberry Crème Fraîche Tart, 275
Candy Bar Quesadillas, 288
Caramel Apple Quesadillas, 273
Carrot Cookie Sandwiches, 281-282
Cherry Clafouti, 274
Chocolate Bread Pudding with Easy Bourbon Caramel Sauce, 294
Chocolate Malted Cookies, 280
Chocolate Peanut Butter Turnovers, 293
Chocolate Pudding, 292
Classic Chocolate Fondue, 285
Fudgy Brownies, 282
Gingered Pear Crisp, 276
Mini-Molten Chocolate Tortes, 289
Oatmeal Cranberry Cookies, 279

Quick Mocha Soufflé, 291
Strawberry Shortcake, 278
Strawberry-Rhubarb Cobbler, 277
White Chocolate Cranberry Orange Fondue, 287
White Chocolate Strawberry Sundaes, 290
dips, 29
Brie, Stilton, and Wild Mushroom Dip, 37-38
Classic Cheese Fondue, 36
Crab Rangoon Dip, 40
Guacamole, 33
Mexican Beef and Chili Dip, 41
Mexican Black Bean Dip, 34
Sausage Pizza Dip, 42
Smoked Trout Dip, 38
Spinach Dip with Feta and Dill, 35
Sun-Dried Tomato Dip, 32
Tuscan White Bean Dip, 31
Two-Salmon Dip, 39
fruit, 259
Bananas Foster Fondue, 269
Blueberry Crème Fraîche Tart, 275
Blueberry Shortbread Gratin, 262
Caramel Apple Quesadillas, 273
Cherry Clafouti, 274
Chocolate Malted Cookies, 280

Dumpling-Topped Berry Grunt, 264
Easy Berry Trifle, 267
Fig and Raspberry Gratin, 261
Fresh Berries with Lemon Mousse, 265
Gingered Pear Crisp, 276
Lemon Curd Mascarpone Fondue, 268
Mixed Berry Compote, 263
Oatmeal Cranberry Cookies, 279
Peach Skillet Cake, 266
Piña Colada Fondue, 270
Strawberry Shortcake, 278
Strawberry-Rhubarb Cobbler, 277
grilled foods, 217
Aegean Swordfish, 248
Butterflied Leg of Lamb with Garlic, Rosemary, and Lemon, 232
Caribbean Pork Chops, 229
Caribbean Shrimp, 249
Chicken Satay with Spicy Peanut Sauce, 251
Chicken with Three-Tomato Salsa, 228
Cranberry-Maple Spareribs, 252
Ham and Cheese–Stuffed Chicken, 225
Korean Steak, 255-256
marinated grilled dishes, 245-256
Mexican Chicken with Mole Sauce, 226

Mexican Steaks with Chipotle Mayonnaise, 254-255

Middle Eastern Chicken, 250

Rosemary Lamb Chops, 256

Salmon Provençale, 247

Salmon with Tomatillo Sauce, 220

Sea Scallops with Mango Salsa and Chili Vinaigrette, 222-223

Steak with Shiitake Cognac Sauce, 230

Steak with Southwest Corn Sauce, 231-232

Stuffed Flank Steak, 253-254

Sweet and Hot Chicken Skewers, 227

Swordfish with Smoked Cheddar Sauce, 224

Tuna with Ginger Vinaigrette, 221-222

lamb

Bombay Lamb Burgers, 243

Butterflied Leg of Lamb with Garlic, Rosemary, and Lemon, 232

Mustard-Crusted Rack of Lamb, 213

Rosemary Lamb Chops, 256

pasta

Fusilli with Porcini Puttanesca Sauce, 124

Linguine with White Clam Sauce, 125

Pasta with Garlic and Oil, 123

Spaghetti with Egg and Bacon, 126

Spaghetti with Escarole, Pine Nuts, and Raisins, 122

pizza

Basic Pizza Dough, 127

Pizza Margherita, 128

Prosciutto Pizza, 130

Smoked Salmon Pizza, 129

pork

Herb-Crusted Pork Tenderloin, 209

Pork Scaloppine, 207-208

Pork with Prosciutto, Mozzarella, and Sage, 208

quesadillas, 111-112

quiches

Classic Quiche Lorraine, 118

Crab Quiche, 116

Herbed Sausage and Tomato Quiche, 117

salad dressings

Balsamic Vinaigrette, 147

Celery Seed Dressing, 148

Pear Dressing, 146

Sesame Ginger Dressing, 147-148

salads, 133

Asian Chicken Salad, 169

Asian Eggplant Salad, 138

Black Bean and Papaya Salad, 142

Coconut Rice and Vegetable Salad, 154

Dilled Cucumbers, 144

Fennel Salad, 140

Garlicky Potato Salad, 159

Gazpacho Chicken Salad, 166-167

Gemelli with White Beans, Tomatoes, and Sage, 153

Gingered Asian Red Cabbage Slaw, 143

Green Bean and Tomato Salad, 137

Jambalaya Salad, 170-171

Janet's Potato Salad, 158

Pork, Peach, and Orange Salad, 171-172

Rigatoni with Vegetables and Mozzarella, 152

Salmon and Cucumber Salad, 165-166

Scallop and Asparagus Salad, 164-165

Sesame Noodles with Asian Vegetables, 151

Smoked Turkey Salad, 168-169

Spicy Asian Brown Rice Salad, 156

Stir-Fried Chicken and Papaya Salad, 167-168

Stir-Fried Vegetable Salad, 136

Sweet Potato Salad with Mustard Dressing, 160

Tabbouleh with Feta, 157

Thai Cucumber Salad, 145

Thai Rice Salad, 155

Thai Shrimp Salad, 163

Three-Pepper Gazpacho Salad, 141

Tomato and Mozzarella Salad with Oregano, 139

Vietnamese Beef Salad, 172-173

Warm Lamb Salad,
173-174
Warm Vegetable Salad,
135
sandwiches
Eggplant and Red
Pepper Panini, 109
Grilled Chicken, Sun-
Dried Tomato, and
Mozzarella Panini, 110
Grilled Reuben
Sandwich, 115
Kentucky Hot Brown
Sandwich, 114
Tuna Melt with Olives,
113
seafood, 177
Asian Shrimp and Stir-
Fried Vegetables,
180-181
Creole Swordfish, 188
Fish Steamed in Napa
Cabbage with Red
Pepper Sauce, 186-187
Halibut in White Wine
with Pearl Onions and
Oranges, 190
Pan-Fried Flounder with
Black Walnut Butter,
183-184
Prawns in Garlic Sauce
with Fettuccine,
181-182
Roast Monkfish in Plum
Wine Sauce, 185-186
Salmon with Basil
Cream Sauce, 189
Scallops with Pine Nuts,
182-183
Scrod with Red Onion
Marmalade, 184-185
Tuna Steaks with
Tomato Relish, 191

soups, 67
Cream of Celery Soup
with Tarragon, 73
Dilled Corn and Oyster
Bisque, 76
Dilled Cream of
Cucumber Soup, 71
Gazpacho, 70
Greek Lemon Egg Soup
with Chicken and
Orzo, 77
Grilled Corn Chowder,
74
Leek and Potato Soup,
72
Nantucket Clam
Chowder, 75
Quick Chicken Stock, 69
Tuscan White Bean
Soup with Sausage, 78
turkey, 203-204
Veal Scaloppine with Fresh
Shiitake Mushrooms, 214
reductions, 182
rehydration of mushrooms,
180
resting meats, 232
rice dishes, 149
Spicy Asian Brown Rice
Salad, 156
Tabbouleh with Feta, 157
Thai Rice Salad, 155
rice noodles, 163
Rigatoni with Vegetables and
Mozzarella, 152
roasting garlic, 130
roasting pans, 5
Roast Monkfish in Plum Wine
Sauce, 185-186
Rosemary Lamb Chops, 256
roux, 114

S

safety (food safety), 9-11
salad dressings
Balsamic Vinaigrette, 147
Celery Seed Dressing, 148
Pear Dressing, 146
Sesame Ginger Dressing,
147-148
salads, 133
Asian Chicken Salad, 169
Asian Eggplant Salad, 138
Bacon, Egg, and Arugula
Salad, 104
Black Bean and Papaya
Salad, 142
Coconut Rice and
Vegetable Salad, 154
Dilled Cucumbers, 144
Fennel Salad, 140
Garlicky Potato Salad, 159
Gazpacho Chicken Salad,
166-167
Gemelli with White Beans,
Tomatoes, and Sage, 153
Gingered Asian Red
Cabbage Slaw, 143
Green Bean and Tomato
Salad, 137
Jambalaya Salad, 170-171
Janet's Potato Salad, 158
lettuce choices, 162
Pork, Peach, and Orange
Salad, 171-172
Rigatoni with Vegetables
and Mozzarella, 152
Salmon and Cucumber
Salad, 165-166
Scallop and Asparagus
Salad, 164-165
Sesame Noodles with Asian
Vegetables, 151
Smoked Turkey Salad,
168-169

Spicy Asian Brown Rice Salad, 156
Stir-Fried Chicken and Papaya Salad, 167-168
Stir-Fried Vegetable Salad, 136
Sweet Potato Salad with Mustard Dressing, 160
Tabbouleh with Feta, 157
Thai Cucumber Salad, 145
Thai Rice Salad, 155
Thai Shrimp Salad, 163
Three-Pepper Gazpacho Salad, 141
Tomato and Mozzarella Salad with Oregano, 139
Vietnamese Beef Salad, 172-173
Warm Lamb Salad, 173-174
Warm Vegetable Salad, 135
salmon
Dilled Salmon Burgers, 237
Salmon and Cucumber Salad, 165-166
Salmon Provençale, 247
Salmon Tartare on Cucumber Slices, 49
Salmon with Basil Cream Sauce, 189
Salmon with Tomatillo Sauce, 220
Smoked Salmon Hash with Poached Eggs, 97
Smoked Salmon Pizza, 129
Southwest Smoked Salmon Pinwheels, 48
Two-Salmon Dip, 39
sandwiches, 108
Eggplant and Red Pepper Panini, 109
Grilled Chicken, Sun-Dried Tomato, and Mozzarella Panini, 110

Grilled Reuben Sandwich, 115
Kentucky Hot Brown Sandwich, 114
panini presses, 107-108
Tuna Melt with Olives, 113
saucepans, 4
sauces
chili sauce, 204
fish sauce, 145
Hoisin, 65
mole, 226
tamari, 156
sausage
Sausage and Pepper Hash, 101-102
Sausage Pizza Dip, 42
sautéing foods, 205-206
Scallop and Asparagus Salad, 164-165
scallops, 56
Scallop and Asparagus Salad, 164-165
Scallops with Pine Nuts, 182-183
sea scallops, 56
Sea Scallops with Mango Salsa and Chili Vinaigrette, 222-223
scoring foods, 253
Scrod with Red Onion Marmalade, 184-185
seafood, 177
appetizers, 56
Baked Clams Casino, 59
Baked Shrimp Toast Rolls, 51
Bourbon Shrimp, 63
Crab Cakes with Mustard Sauce, 64
Creole Marinated Shrimp, 62
Garlic-Steamed Clams, 60
Oysters with Green Chili Cilantro Pesto, 61

Asian Shrimp and Stir-Fried Vegetables, 180-181
clams, 56
Creole Swordfish, 188
dips
Crab Rangoon Dip, 40
Smoked Trout Dip, 38
Two-Salmon Dip, 39
fish guide, 178
fish selection, 177-178
Fish Steamed in Napa Cabbage with Red Pepper Sauce, 186-187
Halibut in White Wine with Pearl Onions and Oranges, 190
mollusks, 56
mussels, 56
oysters, 56
Pan-Fried Flounder with Black Walnut Butter, 183-184
Prawns in Garlic Sauce with Fettuccine, 181-182
Roast Monkfish in Plum Wine Sauce, 185-186
Salmon with Basil Cream Sauce, 189
scallops, 56
Scallop and Asparagus Salad, 164-165
Scallops with Pine Nuts, 182-183
Sea Scallops with Mango Salsa and Chili Vinaigrette, 222-223
Scrod with Red Onion Marmalade, 184-185
shrimp choices, 179
Tuna Steaks with Tomato Relish, 191
searing foods, 191
sea scallops, 56

Sea Scallops with Mango Salsa and Chili Vinaigrette, 222-223
semisweet chocolate, 284
Sesame Ginger Dressing, 147-148
Sesame Noodles with Asian Vegetables, 151
shrimp
    Asian Shrimp and Stir-Fried Vegetables, 180-181
    Baked Shrimp Toast Rolls, 51
    Bourbon Shrimp, 63
    Caribbean Shrimp, 249
    Creole Marinated Shrimp, 62
    Creole Shrimp Burgers, 236
    deveining, 51
    Prawns in Garlic Sauce with Fettuccine, 181-182
    selection, 179
    Thai Shrimp Salad, 163
shucking bivalves, 56
silverskin, 207
skillets, 4
skinning fish, 187
slaws, Gingered Asian Red Cabbage Slaw, 143
slumps, Dumpling-Topped Berry Grunt, 264
small appliances, 7-8
Smoked Salmon Hash with Poached Eggs, 97
Smoked Salmon Pizza, 129
Smoked Trout Dip, 38
Smoked Turkey Salad, 168-169
solanine, 150
soups, 67
    Cream of Celery Soup with Tarragon, 73
    Dilled Corn and Oyster Bisque, 76

Dilled Cream of Cucumber Soup, 71
Gazpacho, 70
Greek Lemon Egg Soup with Chicken and Orzo, 77
Grilled Corn Chowder, 74
Leek and Potato Soup, 72
Nantucket Clam Chowder, 75
Quick Chicken Stock, 69
roux, 114
Tuscan White Bean Soup with Sausage, 78
Southwest Miniature Crab Cakes, 50
Southwest Smoked Salmon Pinwheels, 48
Southwest Sweet Potato Pancakes with Salsa Cream, 95
Spaghetti with Egg and Bacon (Pasta Carbonara), 126
Spaghetti with Escarole, Pine Nuts, and Raisins, 122
spiced meats, 105
spices
    allspice, 229
    cumin, 197
    Herbes de Provence, 32
    marjoram, 58
    star anise, 210
    tarragon, 73
Spicy Asian Brown Rice Salad, 156
Spinach Dip with Feta and Dill, 35
Springtime Quesadillas, 112
star anise, 210
steaks
    Korean Steak, 255-256
    Mexican Steaks with Chipotle Mayonnaise, 254-255

Pan-Seared Filet Mignon with Red Wine Sauce, 211
Steak with Shiitake Cognac Sauce, 230
Steak with Southwest Corn Sauce, 231-232
Stuffed Flank Steak, 253-254
steeping ingredients, 37
stews, 114
stir-fry recipes, 194
    Chicken Fajitas, 197
    Chicken with Plum Sauce, 196
    Mock Mu Shu Chicken, 195
    Stir-Fried Chicken and Papaya Salad, 167-168
    Stir-Fried Vegetable Salad, 136
stockpots, 4
stocks, 67
    canned, 72
    Quick Chicken Stock, 69
storage
    cookies, 282
    mozzarella, 139
    mushrooms, 136
    olive oil, 134
strawberries, 260
    Strawberry Shortcake, 278
    Strawberry-Rhubarb Cobbler, 277
    White Chocolate Strawberry Sundaes, 290
Stuffed Flank Steak, 253-254
Stuffed Peppers, 102-103
substitutions, meats, 206
Summertime Baked Eggs, 96
Sun-Dried Tomato Dip, 32
sushi vinegar, 144
Sweet and Hot Chicken Skewers, 227

Sweet Potato Salad with Mustard Dressing, 160
Swordfish with Smoked Cheddar Sauce, 224

T

Tabbouleh with Feta, 157
tamari, 156
tapioca, 262
tarragon, 73
Tarragon Chicken with Spring Vegetables, 200
temperature, grills, 218-219
Thai Cucumber Salad, 145
Thai Rice Salad, 155
Thai Shrimp Salad, 163
Three-Pepper Gazpacho Salad, 141
tomatillos, 221
Tomato and Mozzarella Salad with Oregano, 139
tomatoes, safe-handling, 24
trout, Smoked Trout Dip, 38
Tuna Melt with Olives, 113
Tuna Steaks with Tomato Relish, 191
Tuna with Ginger Vinaigrette, 221-222
Turkey Chili, 203
Turkey Meatloaf, 204
turkey recipes
    Italian Turkey Burgers, 238
    New England Turkey Burgers, 239
    Turkey Chili, 203
    Turkey Meatloaf, 204
Tuscan White Bean Dip, 31
Tuscan White Bean Soup with Sausage, 78
Two-Salmon Dip, 39

U

U.S. Department of Agriculture (USDA), 9
unsweetened chocolate, 284
unsweetened cocoa powder, 284
USDA (U.S. Department of Agriculture), 9

V

Veal Scaloppine with Fresh Shiitake Mushrooms, 214
Vegetable Frittata with Pasta, 90
vegetables
    appetizers
        Asparagus Wrapped in Herbed Cheese and Prosciutto, 52
        Deviled Leeks, 58
        Vietnamese Spring Rolls, 53-54
    escarole, 122
    Gardiniera, 62
    salads
        Asian Eggplant Salad, 138
        Black Bean and Papaya Salad, 142
        Dilled Cucumbers, 144
        Fennel Salad, 140
        Gingered Asian Red Cabbage Slaw, 143
        Green Bean and Tomato Salad, 137
        Salmon and Cucumber Salad, 165-166
        Scallop and Asparagus Salad, 164-165
        Stir-Fried Vegetable Salad, 136

Thai Cucumber Salad, 145
Three-Pepper Gazpacho Salad, 141
Tomato and Mozzarella Salad with Oregano, 139
Warm Vegetable Salad, 135
vegetarian recipes
    Asian Eggplant Salad, 138
    Black Bean and Papaya Salad, 142
    Dilled Cucumbers, 144
    Fennel Salad, 140
    Gingered Asian Red Cabbage Slaw, 143
    Green Bean and Tomato Salad, 137
    Middle Eastern Lentil Burgers, 235
    Stir-Fried Vegetable Salad, 136
    Thai Cucumber Salad, 145
    Three-Pepper Gazpacho Salad, 141
    Tomato and Mozzarella Salad with Oregano, 139
    Warm Vegetable Salad, 135
Vichyssoise (Leek and Potato Soup), 72
Vietnamese Beef Salad, 172-173
Vietnamese Spring Rolls, 53-54
vinaigrettes, Balsamic Vinaigrette, 147

W-X-Y-Z

Warm Lamb Salad, 173-174
Warm Vegetable Salad, 135
Welsh Rarebit with Tomatoes and Bacon, 99-100

Western Frittata, 89
white chocolate, 284
    White Chocolate
      Cranberry Orange
      Fondue, 287
    White Chocolate
      Strawberry Sundaes, 290
white long-grain rice, 149
Whole-Wheat Blueberry
  Pancakes, 85
woks, 194
wood chips, 218
wood ear mushrooms, 195

yogurt, 243

zest, 173

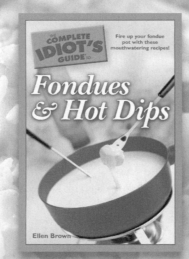
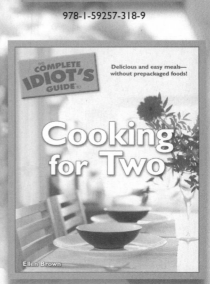